I Saw Two Englands

His last glimpse
of pre-war England
and his first impressions
of England at war

H. V. MORTON

I Saw Two Englands

Revisited and photographed by Tommy Candler

Methuen London

By the same author

A Traveller in Rome · This is Rome · The Waters of Rome · A Traveller in Italy ·
A Traveller in Southern Italy · A Stranger in Spain

In the Steps of the Master · In the Steps of St Paul · In the Steps of Jesus ·
Through Lands of The Bible · This is the Holy Land

In Search of England · The Call of England · H. V. Morton's England · In Search of Wales ·
In Search of Scotland · The Splendour of Scotland · In Scotland Again ·
In Search of Ireland · In Search of South Africa

In Search of London · The Nights of London · H. V. Morton's London · Guide to London ·
Ghosts of London · The Spell of London · The Heart of London · A London Year · London

Blue Days at Sea · Our Fellow Men · Women of The Bible · Middle East · Atlantic Meeting · I James Blunt

First published in Great Britain 1942
by Methuen and Co Ltd
Reprinted ten times
This edition published 1989
by Methuen London
Michelin House, 81 Fulham Road, London sw3 6rb
Copyright in the text is held by the estate of H. V. Morton
Colour illustrations copyright © 1989 Tommy Candler
Design: Christopher Holgate

Printed in Great Britain
by Richard Clay Ltd, Norwich

A CIP catalogue record for this book is available from the British Library

isbn 0-413-62010-7

This book is dedicated
by Tommy Candler to Mary Morton
and to the memory of H. V. Morton,
whose spirit moved her
to follow in his footsteps

I was staying at my friends' country house hotel, Chilston Park in Kent, when *I Saw Two Englands* by H. V. Morton caught my eye on the well-stocked bookshelf in the ladies loo. As I am an avid garden photographer, I thought this might be a wonderful source of new gardens. On reading the first words – 'I set off in May 1939 to enjoy what I think may be a last glimpse of pre-war England. I go to Kent' – suddenly I knew that I had to follow photographically in H. V. Morton's footsteps. This feeling was particularly strong, as not only did he visit all the places I love, but also it was approaching the fiftieth anniversary of the Second World War.

I set off on 17 May as Morton did. It proved to be a most exciting experience with everything uncannily the same: the road sign says 'Oakley Road', as Morton writes 'only eight miles to Westerham'; the swans are still ruffling their feathers on the moat at Ightham, the sunlight still slanting over the old building – and the people still gloat when they have to tell you that you're lost!

Morton's second England, being England at war, I approached with some hesitation, but looking through the photographic archives was fascinating and very moving. I also went on tank manoeuvres on Salisbury Plain, the same today as in 1940, and I found Hush Hush Hall, the wartime home of the BBC, still the same mad architectural fantasy right down to the coronet-topped shower.

Those readers who might like to follow in H. V. Morton's footsteps as I have will find that each chapter is very manageable in a day, since he either recorded a compact area or travelled fast along easy roads. With the aid of his observant eye, you will be guided exactly to the points of interest, where his knowledge of history will bring everything memorably alive. But whether you follow physically or in your imagination as an 'armchair traveller', I hope you will have as much fun as I have.

Tommy Candler

CONTENTS

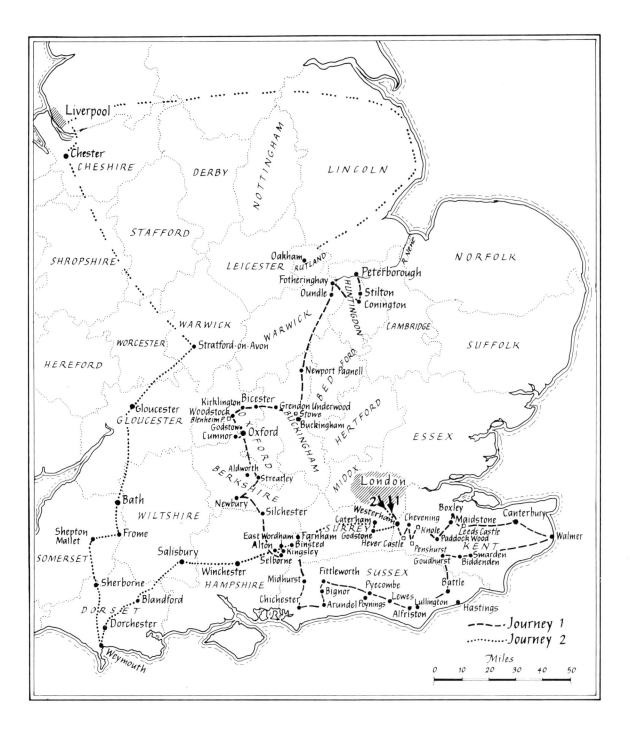

Liverpool

Chester
CHESHIRE
DERBY
NOTTINGHAM
LINCOLN
STAFFORD
SHROPSHIRE
NORFOLK
Oakham
RUTLAND
LEICESTER
Peterborough
Fotheringhay
Oundle
Stilton
Conington
HUNTINGDON
CAMBRIDGE
SUFFOLK
WARWICK
WARWICK
WORCESTER
Stratford-on-Avon
HEREFORD
Newport Pagnell
BEDFORD
Kirklington Bicester
Woodstock
Blenheim P.
Godstow
Cumnor
Oxford
Grendon Underwood
Stowe
Buckingham
BUCKINGHAM
HERTFORD
ESSEX
Gloucester
GLOUCESTER
Aldworth
BERKSHIRE
Streatley
MIDDX.
London
2 1 1
Bath
WILTSHIRE
Newbury
Silchester
Westerham
Caterham
Chevening
Boxley
Maidstone
Canterbury
Knole
Leeds Castle
Shepton
Mallet
Frome
East Wordham
Alton
Farnham
Godstone
Hever Castle
Paddock Wood
Walmer
KENT
SOMERSET
Salisbury
Binsted
Kingsley
Selborne
Penshurst
Smarden
Biddenden
Sherborne
Winchester
HAMPSHIRE
Midhurst
Fittleworth
SUSSEX
Pyecombe
Goudhurst
Battle
Blandford
Chichester
Bignor
Arundel Poynings
Lewes
Lullington
Alfriston
Hastings
DORSET
Dorchester
Weymouth

- - - - Journey 1
· · · · · Journey 2

Miles
0 10 20 30 40 50

CHAPTER ONE

I set off in May 1939 to enjoy what I think may be a last glimpse of pre-war England. I go to Kent. I visit Quebec House at Westerham; Hever Castle, where Anne Boleyn lived; Chevening, the home of Lady Hester Stanhope; Penshurst, the home of Sir Philip Sidney; and Knole, the home of the Sackvilles.

In May 1939 I found myself with some time to spare, and I decided to go away and lose myself in England.

It was the moment when the King and Queen, approaching the coasts of Canada in a fog, had temporarily banished the town of Danzig from the front page, and when the laurel wreath which Mr Chamberlain had worn since Munich was becoming rather shabby. Ministers were busy making apologetic speeches to warn the country that perhaps, after all, Appeasement might not work. The Home Secretary had told the House that it was proposed to darken London at a convenient time in the early hours of the morning so that airmen might go up and see how much of it was visible. Mr Morrison, of the London County Council, had described a voluntary scheme for the removal from London of school children, infants and blind persons, and the Secretary of State for War had announced the date of the first call up of Militiamen, which was to be in June.

The public, aware that an age of spells and incantations had been succeeded by a period of impending doom, held on to its gas-masks, which had been issued during the Munich crisis of the preceding autumn, and hoped for the best. The parks were scarred by lines of trenches; chemist's shops featured window displays of lint and splints, and the words decontaminate and evacuate had passed out of medical language into common speech. Yet the country was technically at peace.

In London, life was heaven for rumour-mongers, gossipers and theorists, all of whom spoke their minds with the dogmatism of ignorance. Whenever I went out, I encountered someone who had just returned from the Continent with certain information that it was all bluff, and there would be no war, or others who were equally certain that before the year was out we should be at war. So what was one to believe?

I thought it would be a good thing to get away from London. No one knew what was going to happen, and it was pointless to go on listening to theories and speculations. If war should come, I said to myself, I should dearly love to have had a last glimpse of pre-war England – the second pre-war England of my generation – and if, after all, it did not come, what could be finer than a journey through England in the Spring?

So upon the seventeenth of May I stood at the window of my house in Chelsea, ready to depart, watching a rainstorm of remarkable violence sweep over the square. It was too fierce to last.

I had no definite plans except that I wanted to go to Kent, a county about which I knew practically nothing. As I threaded my way through the traffic of that morning, and waited vibrating and motionless in traffic jams, my spirits began to rise and I felt more cheerful than I had been for weeks.

I think it was at the Elephant and Castle that I was held up for a long time by a line of lorries loaded with gas-cylinders; as I passed through Lewisham the sun was pitilessly illuminating those tall houses of Georgian brick and Regency stucco which have come down in the world to a shabby, divided life of flats and tenements, and I noticed in front gardens here and there, if I dare call those sooty strips by such a name, uneasy mounds and tumuli roofed with galvanised tin. In those soggy depths the householders proposed to take refuge if war came. The old, black houses gazed down on those dug-outs with an expression of utter amazement. And I too was amazed. I never thought the Ypres Salient could be reborn in a London garden.

I went on, thinking that of all God's creatures Humanity has most skill in adapting itself to changing conditions. Who would have believed that in 1939 suburban rockeries could conceal dug-outs, or that mothers would play

'At Bromley Common a real country thrush was singing in the trees of Holy Trinity churchyard'

games with gas-masks in order that small children might think those sinister gifts amusing additions to the home and no longer show fear at the sight of them?

We have accepted the unthinkable with resignation. That is the distinctive quality of this age, and whether the future were to be bright or grim, this year in England would be like no other we had ever known.

The road to Kent – or at least the one I had taken – is clogged with traffic until you reach Bromley; where there are a few uncertain-looking fields. At Bromley Common a real country thrush was singing in the trees of Holy Trinity churchyard, and I turned right along Oakley Road, where a sign-post said it was only eight miles to Westerham.

I came to a hill and saw a large portion of Kent lying before me. There was an oast-house on the curve of a hill to the left, and a dark wood on the right. Far ahead was spread a chequer-board of fields, lying to the very sky. And soon I was running downhill towards the town of Westerham.

Westerham wears an air of age and quality. On the town green, which slopes gracefully down-hill, I saw the statue of a man waving a sword. He wears a long-waisted coat to his knees, a peruke and a tricorn hat. He is not waving his sword defiantly or dramatically, which is remarkable, because, as you will agree, it is difficult not to wave a sword in either one or other of those ways. And if you have studied the stone and bronze swordsmen who are so lavishly scattered about the world, you will perhaps also agree that defiant and dramatic attitudes, especially in Latin countries, can become monotonous and irritating, so that a mild swordsman is a restful and unusual addition to any town. In Quebec, for instance, which I shall always think of as a city of preposterously active statues, every other street has its lunging, panting swordsman, some at the last gasp on their knees, other with mouths open in an ecstacy of leadership, and all of them lunging and pointing with tremendous verve and enthusiasm at the passers-by. Could Don Quixote have visited Quebec, he would have been fighting a perpetual chain of duels with the great departed, who lean down as if to attack a man who is about to buy a newspaper, or to threaten the existence of a harmless visitor to the post-office. Even politicians in Quebec are charitably depicted in the act of doing something, unlike our own sombre standers and sitters. They are either making speeches or signing treaties, aided by the leaping and flying figures of Faith, Hope and Victory, who gambol in the air round and about them in the best tradition of Gallic baroque. Thinking of those furiously active immortals in Quebec, I approached the tame, but elegant, swordsman of Westerham, and read with a smile that he was none other than General James Wolfe, the hero of Quebec.

It is a good statue and an excellent likeness. Wolfe's sharp, rather peaky features have been admirably portrayed, and although, as I have said, there is nothing dramatic in the way he lifts his sword, as if to smack a reluctant battery mule upon the hindquarters, there is a dramatic appeal in the isolation of his graceful figure against the sky of his native town. He stands there, it seems, not in the centre of a Kentish market town, but high upon the far-off Plains of Abraham.

'General James Wolfe, the hero of Quebec'

Unlike prophets, soldiers are rarely forgotten in thir own country towns, partly perhaps because they offer the sculptor some scope for effect. And certainly Wolfe has not been forgotten in Westerham. His figure is the most prominent object in the town. There is a Wolfe Café and a Wolfe Garage. The wall of the George and Dragon proudly announces that Wolfe once stayed there; and any passer-by can direct you to Wolfe's House.

I discovered, however, that in the bar of the George and Dragon they were less interested in Wolfe than in the demolition of a great mansion which, for some reason or other – probably taxation and death duties – had been pulled down brick by brick and sold in Westerham cattle market.

A little man in a tweed suit put down his glass of beer and informed the company that Mr Winston Churchill, who lives at Chartwell Manor, near Westerham, had bought some of the bricks and tiles.

'Very fond of bricklaying, he is,' explained the little man.

I wandered out into Westerham churchyard, where I had a superb view into the Upper Darenth Valley and over the neighbouring chalk Downs. There were brown and white cows lying on the green pin-cushion hills. I was disappointed by the church, whose interior, much altered and messed about by restorers, does not fulfil the promise of a lovely exterior.

I thought I would go and look at the house, now called Quebec House, where Wolfe lived when he was a boy. It belongs to the National Trust and stands a few yards out of the town, at the bottom of the hilly road leading to Sevenoaks, a dignified mansion of Kent brick, with three gables and three storeys.

Wolfe was not born in this house, but in the vicarage which his father, a colonel in the Army, had rented from the vicar. The family moved into Quebec House when Wolfe was an infant and they remained there for about ten years. As I stood on the step waiting for the bell to be answered, I thought that the building had assumed the benign, motherly air of a genuine birthplace.

OPPOSITE '*I wandered out into Westerham churchyard, where I had a superb view into the Upper Darenth Valley*'

ABOVE '*Quebec House, a dignified mansion of Kent brick*'

The door was opened by a middle-aged lady in a cheerful chintz overall. She wore also the smile of polite resignation which I have noted before upon the faces of those who inhabit National Trust property, and are accordingly obliged at certain times to admit to their dwellings all kinds of people, good, bad and indifferent, wise men and fools.

I was shown into a panelled hall and into a panelled room to the right, which was full of relics. It is difficult to say what degree of fame must be achieved by a hero before such objects as 'eight table knives, eight table forks and one carving fork, formerly in the possession of the Wolfe family' cease to be ridiculous when placed in a glass case. But hero-worship is a profound and deep-seated emotion, and it is undoubtedly true that many people who have no interest in Wolfe, and could give you no clear idea of his life and achievements, have probably gazed with reverence at those knives and forks. While I was reading the labels on these and such-like relics, we were joined by a second lady in middle age, and also in a chintz overall, and before long the three of us were good friends, and I was shown many rooms in the Wolfe mansion which are not usually open to visitors. It must have been an old house even when Mrs Wolfe went to live there in 1727, but, like many such houses, it was brought up to date in the eighteenth century and its original antiquity concealed.

The ladies took me into rooms and up dark stairways where the young Wolfe must have played creepy and exciting games with his brother, Edward. The two little boys and their mother were often alone, for the father was generally away with his regiment. I was glad to have seen those rooms and passages, for I can now picture Wolfe not upon the silent St Lawrence in the darkness of the night, but as a delicate, pale little boy in the silence and the darkness of that old house.

How extraordinarily alike were Wolfe and Nelson, both frail and delicate children and never robust as men, both of them nervous, quick, emotional and talkative, possessing too that rare quality which caused them to be worshipped by the common soldiers and sailors who served under them, and, at the last, meeting the two most dramatic deaths in British history, expiring in the moment of their triumph as if upon a stage.

Perhaps they were both throw-backs to an earlier England, maybe to the emotional Tudor England when men boasted and bragged and were unashamed to shed a tear. Already in their time the upper-class Englishman was, I suspect, altering. He was already on his way to the public school. And it is interesting to remember that upon two notable occasions both Wolfe and Nelson were considered by certain of their contemporaries to have behaved in a manner not befitting the dignity of gentlemen. Before Wolfe sailed for America he dined with Pitt and Temple, and it is said that after dinner, worked up by the thought of the great mission that lay before him, he drew his sword and, to the embarrassment of his hosts, burst 'into a storm of gasconade and bravado' which shocked them profoundly. But I am willing to wager that neither Shakespeare, Drake nor Raleigh would have been shocked or embarrassed by such behaviour. Nelson had precisely the same effect on the Duke of Wellington upon the only occasion those two great men met. It was in the waiting-room of the old Colonial Office in Downing Street. The Duke entered the room and saw a little man with one arm waiting there. He recognised Nelson. As the Duke himself described this meeting, Nelson 'entered at once into conversation with me, if I can call it conversation, for it was almost all on his side and all about himself, and in, really, a style so vain and so silly as to surprise and almost disgust me'. No doubt the Duke would have been equally disgusted with any of the other Elizabethans.

It would indeed be interesting to know the precise period in history when it became ungentlemanly for Englishmen to cry in public, or to boast or brag and indulge in picturesque rhetoric; in other words, the precise moment when the strong, silent, public-school Englishman became the masculine pattern of English conduct.

Such were the thoughts that passed through my mind as I explored Quebec House with the two ladies in chintz overalls. We came in time to the most interesting of all the relics, a pale, elegant Flemish dressing-gown in which Wolfe's body was brought home from Canada to be buried at Greenwich. That garment hangs there like a ghost and really has something painful and tragic about it. As I looked at it, I remembered the line of boats that floated down a dark river in a silence unbroken save for the splash of an oar. Our history books all say that, as the troops were carried down the St Lawrence, the soldier who was soon to die was heard to repeat in a low voice, 'The paths of glory lead but to the grave,' then, turning to his officers, added, 'Gentlemen, I would rather have written that poem than beat the French tomorrow.' There is some reason to doubt the truth of that fine story. There is evidence that Wolfe quoted Gray's *Elegy*, not as the troops were moving out to scale the Heights of Abraham, but on the previous afternoon, when he made a reconnaissance from a boat in order to find a way up the steep cliffs. He had a foreboding that he would not survive the action, and the night before he called a friend to him and confessed his fear, entrusting to him a miniature of Katherine Lowther, the girl whom he hoped to marry.

Wolfe was wounded three times. At first he was shot in the wrist, but, wrapping a handkerchief round the wound, he continued to command the action. He was again shot just as he had given an order to charge; and again he carried on, believing, as he had once said, that 'while a man is able to do his duty, and can stand and hold his arms, it is infamous to retire'. But in the heat of the battle he received a shot in the breast and was unable to stand

any longer. His first anxiety was to conceal his plight from the troops. 'Support me,' he whispered to an officer, 'let not my brave fellows see me fall. The day is ours – keep it.'

It was believed at the time that Wolfe had received his fatal wound from one of his own men, a sergeant whom he had reduced to the ranks for striking a private. This ruffian deserted the the French, and was afterwards known to boast that he had shot Wolfe; but whether this is true or not we shall never know.

When it became known that he lay dead upon the Plains of Abraham the grief of his men was swiftly transformed into fury. They charged the French like madmen. Exactly the opposite occurred to the French when they knew that their leader, Montcalm, was mortally wounded. They lost heart and went to pieces.

Thinking of this battle and of the difference between the French and the English, I remembered that the French Canadians in Quebec preserve the mummified head of Montcalm, and you can see it, as I have seen it, at the Ursuline Convent there. I remember being shown into a visitors' room which is divided from the nunnery by a screen of metal bars. An elderly nun, from whose smooth face all complexity had vanished, approached the bars holding a glass case. Inside was Montcalm's brown and grinning head. It had been varnished and it looked horrible. 'The head of the brave Montcalm,' whispered the nun and then, bowing, disappeared with her ghastly relic.

Having shown me all the Wolfe treasures in Quebec House, the two ladies took me into a room which was probably the old kitchen. It has an immense fireplace in which you could roast an ox. Looking up the chimney, I saw that it had been boarded, and I said that no doubt this had been done to stop the draught.

OVERLEAF '*I was shown into a panelled room to the right, which was full of relics*'

'Oh no,' said one cheerfully. 'That's not the reason why we boarded it up. This is our gas-proof room. You see it has a stone floor and stone walls, and we were told by the ARP that this is the best room in the house for the purpose. We have to make the windows absolutely gas-proof too.'

I came back from the savage age of Wolfe to our own civilised era and looked with interest at the first gas-proof room I had seen. It seemed utterly preposterous that the two charming ladies in chintz overalls should in the year 1939 be preparing to save themselves from poison gas. I wondered what Wolfe, who was always very outspoken on military matters, would have said could he have known the true significance of the boarded chimney in the kitchen at Westerham.

I said goodbye and found my way in a few miles to Edenbridge, which lies to the south.

Here, between two main roads, is a large area of beautiful country some eight miles long by four miles in width. It is watered by the Medway and by the Eden, and it is easy to become lost in the intricacy of its lanes.

I went on to Hever, which I found among quiet lanes bordered by tall trees. Fine-looking cattle grazed in the rich meadows, and the spire of the church is tall and shingled. The village inn is called Henry VIII.

In the twilight of the church I came upon a Knight of the Garter sleeping in full armour. He is Sir Thomas Boleyn, father of Anne Boleyn, and the grandfather of Elizabeth. I reflected that he would not have worn that noble mantle if his dark-haired daughter had not caught the narrow eyes of the King.

'Fine-looking cattle grazed in the rich meadows'

Outside in the sunlight, the cruel and frustrated face of Henry VIII gazes from the inn sign, and a few yards off is a red lodge covered with wisteria, which leads to Hever Castle, once the property of Sir Thomas Boleyn. Henry courted Anne here, and so led her out of musical comedy into Greek tragedy.

Though Hever Castle is not among the show-places of Kent, I had been given permission to see it. The lodge-keeper told me to go on down the path until I came to the castle, when I was to cross the drawbridge and ring a bell.

I entered a park where the birds were singing. Pheasants were running across the grass into the woods. As I walked along I began to think of Henry VIII and Anne Boleyn. It was not the world's most perfect love affair maybe, but is perpetually interesting because of the mighty issues at stake, because of the tragedy in which it ended, and because of the great Queen of England who was the fruit of it.

It is difficult to believe that Anne was ever really in love with Henry, but there can be no doubt that at first he loved her sincerely and devotedly. His tragic search for a wife who would give him a male heir might perhaps never have begun had the infant Elizabeth been a healthy boy. And so certain was the King that Anne's child would be a boy, that he had proclamations all ready and set up in type in which the unborn infant was called 'prince'. Therefore when Elizabeth was born it was necessary for the printer, hastily and clumsily, to add the letters 'ss' to the word. No child could have had a chillier reception than the great Elizabeth . . .

Such thoughts brought me within sight of the castle. I saw, lying on slightly lower ground, at the level of the river, a crenellated grey building and a gate-house rising above the moat. At first I was not sure that Hever was real, for it looked like some castle in a poem. It might have fallen out of a chapter of Froissart. Everything that wealth and good

taste can do to bring a weary old castle back into the world has been done to Hever.

It was smaller than I expected it to be: more of a mediæval manor-house than a castle. It is the modest, embattled home of a country knight who might never have been heard of if his daughter had not become the Queen of England. And this is a part of its charm. If it were twice the size, it would not be so lovely to look at.

Before I crossed the drawbridge, I had a good look at Hever: at the skilfully simple flower-beds round the moat; at the dark maze;

at the formal Elizabethan garden with its fountain, its set of gigantic yew chess-men, the dovecote rising above tall, valeted hedges like little Tudor houses on poles. It is not often that one sees a scene so perfect and so cleverly restrained. It is difficult to believe that art has played so great a part in the creation of this glimpse of Tudor England.

I crossed the moat and rang the bell. I was taken in through the portcullis and across the cobbled courtyard, round which the castle, like many others of its period, is built. In a dining-room hung with dark tapestries I saw the Boleyn arms over the fireplace, and the lock of the door is a peculiar and interesting object. It is a replica of a lock which the Yeomen of the Bedchamber carried round with them when Henry VIII travelled. Every night, before he went to bed, they fixed this special royal lock on the door of the room in which he was to spend the night.

The many lovely rooms at Hever are almost too full of things worth looking at, for William Waldorf Astor, who bought the castle, was a great collector and liked to live with his treasures. A museum curator would have a bad time at Hever, for the desire to place valuable and rare objects behind glass cases is perhaps a natural one. But I think the true charm of collecting is to forget how much things cost and to like them for themselves; and this you can do only if you live with them.

I saw in one room a book of devotion which is believed to be that which Anne Boleyn read while she was waiting for death in the Tower. It is full of marginal notes and on one page, written presumably by her, are the words:

> *Remember me when you do pray,*
> *Hope doth lead from day to day.*

This, though it may not add to her reputation as a poet, no doubt reflects the state of her mind during the horrible days before her death. Almost to the last she thought that the King was only making her suffer in order to try her, and would not take away her life.

Among the bedrooms at Hever is one which for centuries has been pointed out as the room in which Henry VIII stayed when he was courting Anne.

From its window you look into the lovely gardens where he is supposed first to have met her. When he was unable to be with her, he kept touch by letters beginning 'Sweetharte' and 'My own darling', and ending sometimes, like any callow youth, with an outline of a heart inside which he drew her initials.

From the gardens of Hever, which are perhaps even more beautiful than the castle, it is possible to see the most ingenious feature of the restoration. I have never come across anything else like it. Lord Astor was resolved not to spoil the old castle by extending it, and thus altering its proportions, yet he wished to make a lot of additional room for guests and staff. How was he to do it? He decided to build a group of Tudor guest-houses some distance from the castle, but connected with it by a covered passage over the moat. In order to do this, it was necessary to move the river Eden into a new bed. Could any man have paid a greater compliment to an old castle?

I walked back to the village again and had a look at the inn, Henry VIII. There is an interesting story about it. They say that its first name was The Bull and Butcher, but after Anne Boleyn's execution the indignant villagers altered it to The Bullen Butchered.

That, of course, did not please the King, who had the sign taken down and his own name put up in its place. But I have read somewhere that, unwilling to let him have the last word, the villagers obediently altered the name of the inn to Henry VIII, but put up, as a sign, a picture of the King – holding a huge axe!

'I was taken in through the portcullis'

This picture, if indeed it ever existed, has long since vanished, and today a perfectly normal Henry VIII gazes towards the gates of Hever Castle.

How good it is to awaken in England in the month of May, when birds are singing in the early morning and the first sounds of a new day are coming through an open window. On such a morning I left the hotel where I had spent the night and made my way through the lanes to Penshurst, the home of the Sidneys. I looked forward to seeing for the first time one of the finest houses, not only in Kent, but in England. I came to a low stone wall that ran seemingly for miles beside the road encircling a splendid park. About half a mile off, I saw a magnificent palace of old grey stone standing among dark groups of trees.

It was fortunately one of the days when Penshurst, like so many of the great houses in Kent, was open to the public, and a man at the gates told me that I must go down the hill and buy a ticket at the post-office in Leicester Square.

Leicester Square in Penshurst village is a picturesque assembly of houses and cottages.

'How good it is to awaken in England in the month of May'

The post-office sells not only stamps, dog licences and other dull Government matter, but bursts suddenly into a rich and romantic assortment of old glass decanters, fire-backs and Persian rugs. Standing amongst this mixed cargo was an old man who wore a black skullcap. He sold me a ticket for Penshurst Place, and I then asked him, foolishly enough, I admit, whether Leicester Square in Penshurst regards itself as senior or junior to the other Leicester Square. He turned on me a look of blank amazement.

'Sir,' he said with dignity, 'there is no question about it. *This* is the original Leicester Square. The Leicester Square in London was known as Leicester Fields until the time of Charles II, but *this* has been Leicester Square ever since Sir Robert Sidney became Earl of Leicester in 1618. . . . Of *course*, sir, *this* is the original Leicester Square! Why, London's Leicester Square was just a rowdy place where they fought duels when our Leicester Square was the centre of the village . . .'

I backed away from his vehemence. I shall never again walk through Leicester Square (London) without thinking it a bit of an upstart.

Lovely, silver-grey and old, the towers of Penshurst Place lift themselves above four hundred acres of parkland. One glance tells you that this is a great house that has been added to generation by generation. It is not the creation of one age or of one architectural fashion. Some of it is in grey stone, some in red brick; some of the windows are Gothic arches; most are Tudor. It is not a building so much as a growth: an expression of tremendous continuity.

A commissionaire took my ticket and led me through an archway which might have been in the Tower of London; we crossed a paved courtyard towards an old building which looked as though a Gothic church had somehow become wedged in the surrounding masonry. This was the old hall, the very heart of Penshurst Place.

When we entered it – a place like an empty church – I was pleased to think that in a world so full of restlessness a building can remain unchanged for six centuries or more. The Hall of Penshurst is the baronial hall which we have all seen in Christmas Supplements: the hall in which the Baron and his lady sit at the upper table while scullions drag in the Yule Log, and a jester capers behind them. Now the Hall lies silent and deserted, but in no way decayed and, strangest of all, free from any sign of restoration.

Tables and benches, which are said to be over five hundred years old, stand around; the brick hearth is in the centre of the floor and so also are the fire-dogs against which logs are piled. The smoke, which must have filled the hall in clouds, had no way out except through a hole in the roof, now filled in. Beneath the minstrels' gallery is a carved oak screen with two doorways leading to the kitchens.

'And see that narrow glass peephole high up in the wall at the back?' said the commissionaire. 'That's in the withdrawing-room, so that the Baron or his lady, when they had left the hall, could look down and see that the retainers were behaving themselves. It looks straight down on the entrance to the kitchens . . . Now, if you go up that flight of stairs, my wife will meet you and show you the other parts of the house . . .'

I was taken by the housekeeper, for so I imagined her to be, through room after room full of old furniture and pictures. I was shown the first cut-glass chandeliers ever brought to England and given, in a rare mood of generosity, by Queen Elizabeth to faithful old Sir Henry Sidney. I was shown the first folding card-table ever made in England.

As I went through those rooms, so crowded with fine furniture, I was conscious of all the centuries of living which were reflected in them. There were chairs that had been used

by the Sidneys, and a couch on which Queen Elizabeth once reclined; there were chairs and tables of the Stuart period, and furniture of the Georgian age, all happily muddled up together, well used, well sat on by generations of men and women whose portraits gaze from the walls.

Nowhere in those rooms was I for an instant free from sombre or speculative scrutiny. The eyes of men, women and children followed me about; men in doublet and hose, with their hands on their swords; cavaliers; pale, high-bosomed ladies by Lely; groups of solemn, pink-cheeked children.

The stream of English life, flowing steadily and strongly through that great house, has deposited here a portrait, there a staircase, here a new emblazonment, there a set of chairs or a great divan, as it has passed from room to room, century after century. Hever Castle nearby is a labour of one man's love and a tribute to one man's wealth, but in Penshurst Place you will see, not a rich man's treasure trove, but the relics of a family whose members have been born, have lived and have died within the same grey walls.

As the housekeeper walked beside me scattering little scraps of information as one throws corn to a hen, I found myself thinking of great ladies lying in great beds with their heirs, while the genius of English history brooded happily upon the scene. I should think it probably true to say that men have slept in Penshurst Place every night since the Norman Conquest. There has not been a single night for these eight hundred and seventy odd years that some part of that old house has not heard a human footfall.

It was inhabited centuries before the Sidneys came into possession by a series of families, beginning with the de Penchesters and ending with Sir Ralph Fane, a gallant soldier who

'Lovely, silver-grey and old, the towers of Penshurst Place lift themselves above four hundred acres of parkland'

was executed on Tower Hill for conspiracy by order of Edward VI in the year 1552. His manor of Penshurst was immediately bestowed by the young king on his favourite tutor and Chief Steward, Sir William Sidney, a distinguished gentleman who had fought against the Moors in Spain, had commanded the English right wing at Flodden, and had been present with Henry VIII at the Field of the Cloth of Gold. He was succeeded by his son, Sir Henry Sidney, the father of that paragon of all the virtues, Sir Philip Sidney. In early boyhood Sir Henry was brought up at Court in constant companionship with Edward VI, and during the reign of Elizabeth he became, as his father, Sir William, had been in the previous reign, a faithful, honest and devoted servant to his sovereign.

Honesty was one of Sir Henry's outstanding qualities. Indeed, Thomas Fuller might have been thinking of him when he wrote those admirable lines to the 'Faithful Minister', one who refuses to enrich himself in office:

> *My starveling bull,*
> *Ah! Woe is me!*
> *In pasture full*
> *How lean is he!*

Poor Sir Henry learned that serving the Virgin Queen was indeed a lean employment. It was not, for him at any rate, what many a modern lord would call 'good business'. So utterly did he ruin himself in the course of filling a number of high appointments, that he died under a load of debt; and, so far as I know, only one groan escaped him as new honours came his way. When he was asked to become Lord Deputy of Ireland for the fourth time, the faithful minister bowed his head and wrote: 'I am now fifty-four years of age, toothless and trembling, being £5,000 in debt, yea, and £30,000 worse than I was at the time of my most dear King and master, King Edward VI.'

In Ireland and in Wales he served Elizabeth with rare distinction and proved himself a soldier as well as a statesman, but, for all his virtue, it is sad to relate that he received only the frowns of a hard mistress and a mountain of debt. His wife, too, Mary, daughter of John Dudley, Duke of Northumberland, made a terrible sacrifice for the Queen. When Elizabeth caught small-pox in 1562, Lady Mary nursed her so tenderly and continuously that she caught the disease and became so marked that for the rest of her life she feared to show her face in public. Sir Henry wrote of this: 'When I went to Newhaven, I left her a full fair lady, in mine eye, at least, the fairest; and when I returned I found her as foul a lady as a small-pox could make her.' Those two unhappy, faithful servants of the ungrateful Elizabeth died within four months of one another and lie together in Penshurst Church.

I was shown two good portraits of Sir Henry and Lady Sidney. He, as one would imagine, is a grave, bearded man with full and eloquent eyes that have nothing to hide; she is pictured at full length standing beside a chair, her left hand posed gracefully over the back of it, while her right supports a viol almost as tall as herself. She is a beautiful young woman and as grave in expression as her husband. Her large eyes gaze from beneath arched plucked eyebrows. She wears a gown of sprigged brocade whose skirt falls outward in folds over an underskirt, and her waist is pinched into a tight V-shaped bodice of the same brocade. Her sleeves are slashed with transparent muslin that show her arms beneath, and they are caught up with little bows of velvet. A ruff of the thinnest muslin rises like a dropped halo from her shoulders and almost frames her neat head. Such were the father and mother of the great Sir Philip Sidney.

Many a fine portrait of Philip Sidney is to be seen at Penshurst, but there are also other memories of him, some quite improbable. Among these I include his shaving mirror. If the table knives and forks 'formerly in the possession of the Wolfe family' excite visitors to Westerham, what must be the emotion of visitors to Penshurst who can actually look at themselves in the mirror in which Sir Philip Sidney regarded his chin every morning? It is a round piece of magnifying glass set in a rough wooden frame and, said the housekeeper, it was brought home with his effects after his death at the Siege of Zutphen.

I suppose every schoolboy knows the story of the soldier and the drink of water; how, when Sidney was badly wounded at Zutphen and parched with thirst, he saw a wounded soldier gazing longingly at his flask of water, and, with the words, 'Thy necessity is yet greater than mine,' he handed it to the man.

That is a true story, and it carries down the ages the chivalry and the generosity of one of the best-loved Englishmen in history. Although Sidney was only thirty-two when he died, he commanded the affection of his age.

Those who have attempted to walk through his 'Arcadia', stopping now and then to look over a gate at a flowery mead before plodding on again, perhaps find it difficult to understand why they thought so highly of him as a poet. No doubt they had more leisure to read him in those days.

But some part of the secret of his fame was that he had great qualities of heart, mind and character, which, together with his other graceful and manly accomplishments, made him a perfectly balanced and developed human being.

There is a fine portrait at Penshurst of Philip's sister, Mary, who became Countess of Pembroke. Brother and sister were remarkably alike, and their affection for one another added yet another touch of perfection to Sidney's life and character.

Even modern biographers, who have developed to a high degree the lucrative art of dethroning popular idols, have been defeated by Philip and Mary. She outlived him by thirty-five years and is immortalised by perhaps the most beautiful epitaph ever written, lines attributed to Ben Jonson.

Underneath this marble hearse
Lies the subject of all verse;
Sidney's sister, Pembroke's mother,
Death! ere thou hast slain another
Wise and fair and good as she,
Time shall throw a dart at thee.

Philip Sidney's death occurred at the very heyday of his fame. On the morning of the Battle of Zutphen he happened to meet Sir William Pelham, who had omitted to put on his leg armour. Sidney, unwilling to go into battle better armed and protected than his friend, quixotically threw off his own leg armour, and, of course, it was upon the leg, just above the knee, that he was hit by a musket shot. Any modern surgeon might have saved his life, but the wound mortified and he died, having suffered great pain for twenty-six days.

As his father before him, he died in debt. The Low Countries offered to spend half a ton of gold if they might have the honour of burying him, but it was decided to bring his body home. He came in a ship with black sails, on a November day in 1586, and his body lay unburied for three months because no one was willing to advance the large sum necessary for a suitable funeral.

The desire to spend everything on a fine funeral, for which poor people are rebuked so often in these days, is an old and aristocratic English instinct. And the only people now-adays who bury their dead with a lavishness which can compare with that of the lords of the mediæval and Elizabethan times are our poorest citizens.

Sidney's funeral was in the great tradition. Seven hundred mourners followed him to Old St Paul's, and the grief caused by his death has rarely been exceeded in England.

That Philip Sidney should have thrown away his life in the Low Countries is, I think, one of the tragedies of English history. It would be interesting to speculate on the part he might have played had he been spared to live into the Stuart age. Also one wonders in what way history and literature would have been enriched had he been allowed to go off to America and help to colonise that country, as he wanted to do. He received from Elizabeth in 1583 almost the first charter enabling him to go out as a colonist. Two years later he was concerned with Francis Drake and thirty noblemen in secretly planning to fit out a fleet and sail for the Americas, but the plan came to nothing. Elizabeth put her foot down and refused to let Philip go; and so, instead, he went to meet an untimely death at Zutphen.

There was one more picture which interested me greatly at Penshurst. It was a large and rather crude representation of an Elizabethan dance. The central figures are Queen Elizabeth and the Earl of Leicester. It was a surprising picture of the Queen, and the only one I know which shows her in what must have been an unguarded moment. Leicester and the Queen are seen in the act of performing an extraordinary *pas des deux*. He appears to be grasping Her Majesty firmly by the bodice and lifting her into the air rather like a ballet dancer; and there, most comically, the great queen in her jewels and ruff hangs suspended, wearing an expression due to the limitations of the artist.

The housekeeper could tell me nothing about this picture which is simply 'Queen Elizabeth dancing with the Earl of Leicester', but it occurred to me that it must be a representation of a notable incident during Leicester's entertainment of the Queen at Kenilworth in 1575. One evening the Queen was present at a remarkable exhibition of dancing given by an Italian, and well described by Robert Laneham, a servant of the Earl's. 'There was shown before her high-ness,' he wrote, 'by an Italian such feats of agility, in goings, turnings, trumblings, cast-ings, hops, jumps, leaps, skips, springs, gam-baud, somersaults, capretties and flights:

forward, backward, sideways, a downward, an upward and with sundry windings, gyrings and circumflexions as by me is not expressible by pen or speech, I tell you plain.' So here, if I am right, we have what looks like an extremely faithful picture of the great Queen attempting to emulate the agile Italian in his 'capretties and flights'.

When I was travelling in Syria some years ago I became interested in the life of that extraordinary woman, Lady Hester Stanhope, a niece of the great Lord Chatham, who cut herself off from England and went to live in barbaric state in the the hills of the Lebanon, above Beyrout.

Every traveller of note who went to Syria in the nineteenth century sought an audience with her, which was not always granted; and nearly every book of travel or reminiscences written at that time gives an account of her strange receptions, her Eastern dress, her pipe-smoking, her Arab guards, her belief in magic and prophecy, and her exhausting harangues to those who had penetrated her mountain fastness. On one occasion, in the year 1819, a young Englishman, who had been lectured by her for several hours, fainted from fatigue. She summoned her servants to revive him, and quietly remarked that he had been overpowered in listening to the state of disgrace to which his country had been reduced by its Ministers.

She was a woman of great force of character. She possessed a remarkably acute mind and the tongue of a serpent, and she was for several years the most important person in Syria. Her spies covered the country. They told her everything, and she combined the airs of an oriental potentate with open-hearted generosity to the poor. The Arabs and the wild Druses of the Lebanon regarded her with a veneration that bordered on worship.

I have sometimes thought that, had she been a man, she might have done great things in the world, instead of merely taking a place in the attractive, but overcrowded, gallery of English eccentricity.

She was in love with Sir John Moore, and after his death she turned her steps, and her heart, away from England and neither saw, nor wished to see, this country again.

There is a pathetic account of her death in Thomson's *The Land and the Book*. She died on a hot June day, in the year 1839, and the British consul at Beyrout, together with Thomson, who was an American missionary, made a fatiguing journey into the mountains to bury her. They found a scene of frightful and sordid confusion. The place was crowded with her servants, and her body lay on a divan wrapped in waxed cloths dipped in turpentine and spirits. The thirty-five rooms of her rambling 'palace' were mostly full of trash. One was piled with old oil-jars, another with moth-eaten Arab saddles, a third with pipe-stems, and others with books and papers. Anything of value had been stolen the moment life had left her.

'What a death!' commented Thomson. 'Without a European attendant – without a friend, male or female – alone, on the top of this bleak mountain . . . Such was the end of the once gay and brilliant niece of Pitt.'

The burial took place at dead of night in her garden. A vault had been opened for the purpose where years before a French general, who had died during a visit to her, had been interred. Thomson said that they went with torches and lanterns down the winding paths: 'I took a wrong path, and wandered some time in the mazes of these labyrinths,' he wrote. 'When at length I entered the arbour, the first thing I saw were the bones of the general, in a ghastly heap, with the head on top, having a lighted taper stuck in either eye-socket – a hideous, grinning spectacle. It was difficult to proceed with the service under circumstances so novel and bewildering. The consul subsequently remarked that there were curious coincidences between this and the burial of Sir John Moore, her ladyship's early love. In silence, on the lone mountain at midnight, "our lanterns dimly burning", with the flag of her country over her, "she lay like a warrior taking his rest", and we left her "alone in her glory".'

The ancestral home of the Stanhopes is at Chevening Place, in Kent, a few miles north-west of Sevenoaks. At this point the old Pilgrim's Way from Winchester to Canterbury drops down from Surrey into Kent, and until 1792 the road used to run through Chevening Park. The house is not shown to the public, but Lord Stanhope was kind enough to say that, if I would wait until he could spare a day from his duties in London, he would show me the few relics of Lady Hester which remain in the family. Therefore on a Saturday afternoon I went to Chevening.

'Chevening Place . . . stands in a splendid park' – now restored to fine red brick

The house, which stands in a splendid park, is a good example of those formal town houses which Inigo Jones and his contemporaries planted so uncompromisingly amid the green meadows and the woodlands of England. It remains today much as it left the restless hands of the third earl, who, to the dismay of his descendants, covered the fine red brick with cream-coloured tiles, thus ruining the exterior.

It is a tall, disguised Stuart house, with two curving wings on each side, enclosing a wide entrance courtyard separated from the park by iron railings. It is a house that seems still to live in the atmosphere of four-horse coaches; and I felt that a motor-car looked rather ill at ease in the courtyard.

The present Earl is the seventh holder of a title which began with General James Stanhope, who played a great part in helping George I to the throne.

All the Stanhopes have been distinguished servants of the State, one of them, the third Earl and the father of Hester Stanhope, was almost a genius, and the fifth Earl was the author of the standard life of William Pitt, and many other well-known historical works.

Each peer was painted by one of the best artists of his day, so that the dining-room walls at Chevening show a complete record of the family, from the first Earl of Marlborough's time to the father of the present Lord Stanhope. Through the windows of this room you look out to the park rolling away towards woodlands, and in the foreground is a lake on which was launched the first vessel ever propelled by steam.

This was an invention of Charles, the third Earl, who was as entertaining a character as his daughter, Hester, and from him she undoubtedly inherited much of her unusual temperament. He was the 'Red' peer of his day because of his interest in the French Revolution.

He took down the coronets from the front of Chevening and horrified the polite world by appearing at Court with unpowdered hair. He then discarded all signs of rank and wished to be known as Citizen Stanhope, but he modified his opinions in later life and put back the coronets! He had a wild and tempestuous eye and a clever face. There is a full-length portrait of him by Gainsborough at Chevening, which was left unfinished by the artist's death.

Among his inventions were many solid contributions to science, as well as others which, although nothing came of them, strangely anticipated future inventions. In fact he had a queer genius for producing ideas which were just a little too advanced for the time. Lord Stanhope showed me a beautifully made ready-reckoner which his ancestor perfected nearly two hundred years ago. The principle is precisely the same as that employed in the machines used in banks and offices today. Then his printing-press inventions are well known and still bear his name. He perfected a

process of stereotyping which he allowed the Clarendon Press to acquire on the understanding that they gave his foreman £4,000. He gave away many other valuable printing inventions. He also invented the Stanhope lens for testing the skins of fever patients.

Like most inventors, he held some alarming experiments. Convinced that he had hit upon an idea to render houses fire-proof, he constructed a building in the grounds of Chevening and invited a party of friends to inspect it. While they were inside, he piled wood round it and set fire to it. The flames leapt to a height of over eighty feet, but – as an ancient account of the experiment puts it – not one of the imprisoned friends suffered 'the slightest inconvenience'. It is a pity, however, that their comments have not been preserved.

In the light of future events, the most remarkable of his inventions was the steamboat, for which he took out a patent as early as 1790. He spent twenty years, and a great amount of money on it, and once announced in the House of Lords that ships would be propelled by steam. He was received with derision and pronounced to be 'a little madder than usual'. But he was unmoved: 'Some of your Lordships now sitting here will live to see steamships crossing the Atlantic,' he retorted, amid general amusement. He nearly lived to see his prophecy come true, for he died in 1816, three years before the *Savannah* crossed the Atlantic in twenty-three days.

His own steamboat did not perform wonders on Chevening lake; but at least it worked. The interesting point about it was that Stanhope had not used the paddle-box, but a vibrator which worked backwards and forwards through the bottom of the boat, reproducing something like the action of a swan's foot in movement.

With such a man for father and William Pitt's sister for mother, Hester Stanhope could not, perhaps, fail to be a vivid and unusual woman. She was born at Chevening in 1776, and spent much of her girlhood in saving her brothers and sisters from the peril of her father's experiments. She was probably too much like her father to be fond of him, and was rarely happy at home. Her only congenial friend was her uncle, William Pitt, for whom she kept house when she was in her twenties.

As the Prime Minister's hostess she met everybody. She distinguished herself by her wit, her beauty and her high spirits. Pitt, it seems, was a bit afraid of her. On one occasion she managed to blacken the premier's face with a burned cork. 'I let her do as she pleases,' said Pitt helplessly, 'for if she resolved to cheat the devil, she could do it.'

The contrast between her life in the heart of London politics and society, and her masquerade as Queen of the Lebanon, is so strange as almost to be incredible. Lord Stanhope showed me the relics that came home after her death. They are not numerous, but one of them is interesting and pathetic: it is a pendant containing a lock of Sir John Moore's hair. Who would have said she had so much sentiment left in her?

'It was picked up in the bazaars of Beyrout or Aleppo by a traveller who realised its association,' said Lord Stanhope, 'and it was sent back to Chevening.'

Having seen the bleak and terrible fastnesses in which Hester Stanhope spent her life, I was glad to have rounded off the picture with a glimpse of Chevening in Kent, and the quiet English scene from which she, almost ferociously, withdrew.

Knole stands a little way out of Sevenoaks in a fine park full of ancient trees – oak, beech and sycamore. Herds of deer stand beneath the trees, and the more adventurous occasionally advance into the open to accept or reject a biscuit offered by some lover of animals.

I drove in through the gates and saw the house far off, looking as though several colleges in Oxford or Cambridge were taking a walk together in the country. The place, enormous as it looks from a distance, seems to grow larger as you approach it, and I had the uneasy feeling, as I saw the hundreds of windows, that crowds of people, invisible to me, must be watching my solitary advance. But when I reached the noble and austere west front, with its five gables on each side of a grey, embattled gatehouse, there was not a soul to be seen.

There is something uncanny and unnatural in the silence which enfolds these great houses of the past. They were made for a teeming population, not the wage-earners of a capitalistic age, but the dependents, and the families of dependents, of the feudal lord. Now these mansions stand in the loneliness of their old age, silent and almost deserted.

When Richard Sackville, the 3rd Earl of Dorset, inherited Knole in 1609, 126 people sat down to meals in the house every day: steward, chaplain, clerks, cooks, yeomen of the pantry and the buttery, slaughtermen, brewer and under-brewer, footmen, servants, falconer, armourer, grooms, stablemen, and all the other inhabitants of a self-contained community. Today Lord Sackville, the descendant of a family which has inhabited Knole for over three centuries, lives there with a small staff, occupying only a corner of the immense place.

I passed in under the old archway and bought a ticket at the lodge on the left. Before me stretched a great lawn with grey buildings rising round it. Facing me was another tremendous gatehouse, more gables, more leaded windows, and another courtyard paved with stone leading to still another façade.

I went into the house and waited in a huge Renaissance hall until a young woman, whose task it is to convey inquisitive members of the public round Knole, came in and took charge of me.

'Knole . . . before me stretched a great lawn with grey buildings rising round it'

The visitor to Knole finds himself in a maze of corridors and apartments rather like the oldest part of Rome. The long, narrow streets, which are corridors, open out into a piazza, which is a room, and then with haphazard irregularity branch off again to others, smaller or larger.

The main impression is of tall windows full of diamond glass, sunlight burning through stained-glass armorial shields, of hundreds of fine pictures of sad men and women, oak chairs, walnut chairs, and mahogany chairs; and of velvets, brocades and tapestries worn and mellowed by Time.

The possessions of many generations of acquisitive human beings are standing here almost magically preserved from decay. Some of the oldest furniture had been so well treated all its life that if an antique dealer tried to sell it to you you would unhesitatingly declare it to be faked. It looks too good to be true!

The number of rooms in Knole is utterly bewildering. It is difficult to believe that even an Elizabethan or a Stuart nobleman required so many, in days when households were numbered by the hundred.

It is hardly possible that the whole of Knole could ever have been inhabited at one time. There must always have been large uninhabited areas. Even Jacobean Sackvilles must have said to their wives: 'We must make up our minds to go over and live in the east wing next year.'

Miss Victoria Sackville-West, whose charming book, *Knole and the Sackvilles*, should be read by everyone before a visit to Knole, confesses that 'after a life-time of familiarity, I still catch myself pausing to think of the shortest route from one room to another.'

With a memory of the 126 servitors who sat down to meat with my Lord Dorset in 1609, I asked my guide how many servants inhabit this Tudor town today.

'Oh, perhaps a couple of dozen,' she said.

I asked if such great houses get their staff from old families in the neighbourhood, but she said no: they advertise for cooks and parlourmaids like everyone else.

I then asked how many members of such a staff have a sufficient sense of history to appreciate the privilege of living in a house like Knole; but this she was unable to answer.

Unlike Penshurst, Knole has no Sir Philip Sidney to focus the attention of the casual visitor. The Sackvilles, interesting and active as they were, did not produce one great hero, with the result that visitors to Knole come away remembering little about the men and women who lived there.

Perhaps the most interesting Sackville was Thomas, the first Earl of Dorset, who was related to Queen Elizabeth through the Boleyn family. He is remembered now, but probably only by people studying for literary degrees, as the author of a terribly dull play called *Gorbaduc*, the first known English tragedy. It was also our first piece of theatre propaganda, for the privileged author wrote it

with the idea of persuading Elizabeth to marry and provide an heir to the throne.

The theme of the play is Crisis and Uncertainty, which should give it a topical interest. Such lines as the following may appeal to us today:

Bid Kings, bid Cæsars, bid all states beware,
And tell them this from me that tried it true:
Who reckless rules, right soon shall hap to rue.

Other Sackvilles were also in close attendance on Court and State. The fourth Earl fought bravely for Charles I and had the odd distinction of owning all the land on which New York now stands, but there seemed to be no point in such a possession, so it drifted out of the family.

The sixth Earl was sufficiently observant to see Nell Gwynn before his master did, and the seventh Earl, who was also the first Duke of Dorset, was the messenger sent over to Hanover to tell George I that Queen Anne was dead, and that Parliament invited him to occupy the throne.

I have often wondered what monarchs talk about while they are driving through the streets on state progresses, and the Duke has told us what George I talked about on his way to London. He said that thirty-three years previously he had come to England as a suitor for the hand of Queen Anne, but the lady had not favoured him.

He recollected that he rode back to Gravesend on a common post-horse, which stumbled and flung him in the mud; and all the way up to London the King was looking out of the coach in an attempt to identify the place where he had fallen.

In thirteen years' time the Duke was again the bearer of the same tidings. When George I died, the Cabinet appointed him to go to Kew and tell the Prince of Wales that he was George II. HRH was asleep at the time and, upon awakening, refused to believe the news. He said it was only another 'damned trick' of his enemies.

I drove away across the park, thinking, not of earls or dukes, but of dumb-bells. If you have ever wondered why a dumb-bell should have received such an apparently unsuitable name, you can solve the mystery at Knole. In one of the galleries is an object that looks like the windlass which is still in use above wells in country places. Two ropes used to hang down from a roller through holes in the floor into the room below, where Jacobeans would grasp them and pull, causing the roller to revolve and wind up the ropes, which then had to be pulled down again. The exercise was like that of bell-ringing without a bell.

This dumb belfry that gave its name to the gymnastic hand-weights was used as late as the eighteenth century, for Addison says in the *Spectator* that he used this instrument every morning.

I was boasting to a man at Sevenoaks that I had seen most of Kent's finest houses: Chevening, Penshurst, Hever and Knole.

'But you haven't seen Ightham Mote?' he asked. 'You can't be in Kent and fail to see Ightham Mote. If you don't see it, *you'll always regret it*!'

I looked at him with some loathing, for I am one of those people who has been bullied into doing things all his life by the threat that omission to do so will bring life-long regret. Though experience has taught me that I have failed to do many a thing which I have never regretted, still the old blackmail works now and then; and I see myself spending the rest of my life in an agony of helpless remorse.

'I'm afraid I haven't the time,' I told him. 'I must get on to Canterbury.' But this was only a transparent attempt to assert my independence, for, no sooner had I turned my back on him, than I drove straight to Ightham. I was *not* going to regret Ightham all my life. I was *not* going to be pointed out as the man who

had been in Kent and had not seen Ightham Mote!

I came into one of those exquisite triangles of peace and beauty which exist between the hectic main roads of England. About Ightham, the gentle Kentish landscape permits itself a few exotic moments, for I would guarantee that you could take the deep, luxuriant lanes and put them down in Devon, and no one would notice their arrival.

The house I had come to see was well hiden from the steep lane, although only a few yards from it. Every Friday afternoon, the owner, Sir Thomas Colyer-Fergusson, opens it to the public, and, though I had not met a soul in the lanes on the way down, there was quite a small crowd waiting to go in.

I had read somewhere that the word 'mote' has no reference to the 'moat' at Ightham. It is the old word – 'mote' or 'motte' – which means a hill, or mound, on which castles were so often built in the old days.

When I reached the end of the path, I came to an old grey gate-house and a tower, an arched bridge, and a tall yew hedge planted along one side of the moat. The walls of the house rise from still water; some part of the building is of grey stone, some of red brick, and some of Elizabethan timber-work. It is almost text-book of domestic architecture, and the general effect is that of a poem written by Time upon stone and brick, for each century has taken up the pen and written a few lines.

Ightham began its life as an old castle which had to be defended, if necessary, with arrows and boiling oil. Therefore it had to have a moat to repel unwelcome visitors, and it had to have crenellated walls from whose shelter defenders could draw their bows and hurl their javelins. Then times became safer and window-glass was made. The owners turned Ightham from a castle into a house; but they kept the old moat round it. Houses became

'Ightham began its life as an old castle . . . the walls of the house rise from still water'

more comfortable, glass became cheaper, and so each generation brought the old castle up to date; but even the most ambitious of innovators could not alter the original shape and size of the place, because of the water surrounding it.

So Ightham has remained all these years, rather like a city within its walls, subject to every kind of change inside, but unaltered by expansion and growth.

An angry swan was swimming in the moat, ruffling its feathers and making indignant noises. The sunlight slanted over the old building, and the gardens were drowsy with the sound of bees and insects; and the house stood in the sunshine, no longer defiant, but grey and kindly in old age.

The gate was opened by a butler.

In company with the other sightseers, I trooped across the moat and entered a glorious little cobbled courtyard. The house, pierced by tall diamond-paned windows, rose round us on the four sides of the square. I noticed an Elizabethan dog-kennel, empty, and, from the size of the kennel, fortunately empty!

We stood in rooms with Gothic windows and in rooms with Tudor and Jacobean windows, admiring this and that in the hushed, embarrassed tones of uninvited guests. The pressure of other people's lives was strong, and every time I entered a room I half expected to see its occupant beating a hasty retreat. People who are kind enough to open their houses to the public once a week must spend that day being chased from room to room: yet you never catch them at it.

The butler saw us safely across the moat, and we departed, taking with us the memory of a gracious home.

I went up the hill to Ightham Church, which numbers among its memorials a tablet to Dame Dorothy Selby, who lived at Ightham Mote in the time of James I. She is said to be one of the many people who discovered the Gunpowder Plot. It is surely strange that so much fuss was made about discovering the Gunpowder Plot, which, as plots go, seems to have been unusually fair and above-board. One of the plotters even took the trouble to write a letter warning Lord Mounteagle not to attend Parliament, because those who did so would receive a terrible blow, yet 'not see who hurts them'.

The tradition at Ightham is that Lady Selby interpreted this anonymous letter, although what there was that demanded interpretation I cannot imagine. It is a well-known document, and is a clear statement of fact: a warning that something desperate was to be attempted during the sitting of Parliament which made it advisable for Lord Mounteagle, if he valued his safety, not to attend. What could be plainer than that?

The best-known story is that the letter was taken to James I, who had a great love for

'I noticed an Elizabethan dog-kennel, empty, and from the size of the kennel, fortunately empty!'

riddles and mysteries, and that he, having pondered over it for some time, sensibly suggested that they should have a look at the cellars under the House, where, of course, Guy Fawkes was discovered.

If Lady Selby had any part in discovering the plot, I am pretty certain that the document she unravelled was something more subtle than the Mounteagle letter. She is supposed to have solved the mystery with her embroidery needle, which gives an added touch of confusion to the story; and indeed I must confess that, to me, Lady Selby's part in this is more mysterious than the plot itself.

A few miles from Ightham I came to a village on whose wide green stands a white post with a cross-piece. The village is Offham, and the post is the last quintain left in England. In the Middle Ages most villages had a tilting-post, at which youths and young men tested their skill with the lance. There are many kinds of quintains, some of them in the form of human figures, generally with a Saracen's head: and I suppose the dummies used for sword exercise, and familiar to every cavalry soldier, are a survival of the mediæval quintain.

I have ridden at these in my youth, and I remember that the art of it was not to gallop or trot, but to come up at a level canter with your arm and your sword in a line, and then, having thrust your sword into the dummy, to let your arm swing round and the sword withdraw itself as you went past. But you could almost put your arm out if, by bad luck, your sword hit the iron bar inside the dummy.

There were similar penalties for the clumsy tilter at the quintain. The post at Offham illustrates what happened. From one end of the pivoted cross-bar hung a heavy bag of sand. If the horseman was slow in getting away after having hit the target end of the cross-bar, the other end came round and gave him a mighty blow with the sand-bag.

Throughout the Middle Ages young men trained themselves in warlike exercises at the

quintains on the village greens of England, and then, in later times, the sport was seen only at wedding feasts. When Queen Elizabeth was entertained at Kenilworth in 1575, in addition to the 'capretties and flights' pictured at Penshurst, she witnessed a country wedding which was staged for her amusement, in the course of which young men tilted at the quintain, so that it was evidently an old-fashioned sport even in those days.

How and why the quintain of Offham has survived I do not know. I went into the little post-office to ask, but they could tell me only that the occupier of the house called Quintain House, on the side of the village green, is responsible for its repair and maintenance. Offham is evidently proud of its quintain, as it ought to be, for, as the post-master told me, 'there was a terrible to-do' recently when the top-bar was lost.

If Offham revived the old sport of tilting at the quintain, I think half England would go down to Kent to watch it.

CHAPTER TWO

Travelling through the hop gardens of Kent, I come to Maidstone, where I find a clinic in an archbishop's palace and a tithe barn occupied by ARP. I go to Boxley to look for the grave of George Sandys, and on the way to Canterbury pay a visit to Leeds Castle.

The Kentish hops were beginning to climb the poles to the strings above. They were a beautiful fresh green colour, because they had not yet been covered with the vine-spray, called Bordeaux Mixture, which turns them into an iridescent coppery green.

Not far from Maidstone, I found myself in a world of hops. They stretched in straight avenues on each side of the road. Here and there an oast-house lifted its tiled red cone above the trees, and, with the freshness of the hedges and the tender green of the growing hops, formed a picture of Kent which I shall not easily forget.

I think hops are unquestionably the most picturesque crop we grow in this country. Though I prefer to look at a good field of ripe wheat or barley, for there is nothing lovelier than the corn-yellow of those crops and the sight of the wind moving them, there is something fascinating – almost exotic – about hops: they look as a vineyard ought to look.

'There is a joyous, youthful eagerness in the way the green tendrils seem to race each other to the tops of the poles'

At this time of the year there is a joyous, youthful eagerness in the way the green tendrils seem to race each other to the tops of the poles; later on, when the hops are ripe, the rustling, grasshopper-green tassels hang in graceful festoons, light as air against the darker background of their leaves.

Neither the vine nor the olive is as beautiful as the hop: and I have never seen on the Continent, or in the East, a vineyard or an olive-grove that could for a moment compare with the beauty of our Kentish hop-gardens.

I came to a place called Paddock Wood, where oast-houses are not dotted about by ones and twos, but stand together in mass formation. I counted four groups of five, and there were others some little distance away. This was the most impressive collection of oast-houses I had ever seen. Like all oast-houses at this time of year, indeed at every time except for about three hectic weeks in the autumn, they were silent and deserted.

While I was looking at them, wondering to what emperor of hops they belonged, a young man came out of the yard, and the first thing I noticed about him was that he was wearing a pair of brand-new army boots: the real old foot-slogger's boot that made you feel as if a couple of angry lobsters had got at your feet.

'Good afternoon,' I said, 'I was just thinking what a huge place you've got here.'

'It's the biggest in Kent, sir,' he replied.

The word 'sir' is heard in these days only on the lips of people who have been expensively educated. I wish elementary school teachers would tell children that there is nothing servile about the word.

'It belongs to Whitbread's,' he said, and then, noticing that my eyes kept reverting to his feet, he grinned: 'I'm breaking them in,' he explained, 'because I go into camp next week with the Anti-aircraft; and they take some breaking in, I can tell you.'

'Wait until you get a pair of puttees round the ankles, my lad!' I said cruelly.

'Oh, we don't wear puttees *now*,' he said. 'We have overalls and slacks for walking out.' Whereupon I felt as obsolete as one of Agincourt's crossbowmen.

'If you have the time,' I said, 'would you take me into a hop-field and tell me something about hops?'

'Come along,' he replied. 'I'm just going that way; but, first of all, wouldn't you care to have a look at our hoppers' huts?'

We entered a village of tin and wood bungalows. There were wash-houses with hot and cold water laid on, an all-night café, a milk bar, a crèche, a grocer's shop, a surgery, an excellent writing-room and a mission hall. I told him it was more like a holiday camp than the old-time hoppers' compound.

'That's true,' he said. 'It is really a holiday camp. We have a large waiting list for it, too. The same crowds come down year after year. Some of them have been coming all their lives. They love to go to their old huts, and even if they are offered a more modern hut – like that new type over there – they always say, "Oh, can't we have our dear old hut?" and if the dear old hut has been superseded by something better, they don't like it at all at first . . .'

We walked down the lane and entered a hop-field where the vines were in their most luxuriant mood, racing upwards to the strings. Hops, he told me, can grow six inches in twenty-four hours. The cost of cultivating an acre of hops has risen amazingly in recent times. In 1893 the average cost was £35 an acre. In 1900 this had risen to £37, and today it is nearer £60.

The hop-farmer has to put back every spring all the chemicals that the hops have taken out of the soil. He must manure the earth, first with potash, then with phosphates, and finally with ammonia. When he has done this, and the new crop is growing, he has to make war upon every kind of pest. He has to spray the hops with nicotine powder to destroy insect pests, and then with a lime and copper spray to prevent hop blight.

As if hop-farmers have not enough trouble, a new disease has developed, known by the beautiful name, Verticilium Wilt. To the hop-grower, it is worse than either aphis or blight. One day the hops look marvellous, but the next they are beyond all hope, wilted and finished. One of the terrible characteristics of Verticilium Wilt is that the germ – or whatever it is – hangs about in the soil and attacks future crops. My friend pointed out acres of wheat which last year were under hop cultivation, but it is impossible to grow hops there again until some clever young man with a microscope has found out what the germ is, and how to cure it.

I heard a smiliar story recently in Jamaica, where thousands of acres which formerly grew bananas are now either derelict or under sugar-cane. The Panama Disease, as it is called, infects the ground so that bananas can never again be grown there, and unless this germ can be killed, large areas of the island will inevitably fall out of cultivation; for the disease is terribly infectious.

It is a common experience to travel for half a mile or so with a wilted banana grove on one side of the road and a healthy one on the other; and once the germ crosses the road, it runs like wild-fire through the sound trees.

The Men of Kent use many interesting old words in the hop-fields; indeed the hop industry has a language of its own. I believe the word 'bine' may be a Kentish word, for I think in some parts of the country they call them 'wires'. A 'shim' is a horse-drawn hoe, and a 'scubbit' is a wooden shovel used by the hop-driers.

Hop-gardens are set out in 'cants', which is a word probably older than hops, for it was once used to denote any portion of corn or woodland. Each 'cant' is divided into 'sets', and each 'set' into so many 'hills' of hops, and each root is called a 'hill'. The hops are gathered in bins and are transferred to a sack, called by the good old English term, a 'poke'. When hops are doing well they are said to 'grow and blow'.

Wishing my young friend the best of luck with his searchlights, and hoping that the hops will be blowing and growing like mad when he returns from camp, I went on my way down the green lanes.

Maidstone is an ancient county town whose streets, crammed to bursting point with traffic, reflect the prosperity of the 'Garden of England'. It is not a pleasant town to enter, because every kind of wheeled vehicle contends for mastery in its streets. In the middle of the High Street a youthful version of Queen Victoria, standing beneath a little shrine that looks like as much of the Albert Memorial as the town council of that time could afford, presides with dignity over an age so different from her own.

The town is an expression of the commercial drive of the Men of Kent, as well as the Kentish Men; and having mentioned those terms, I suppose I ought to explain them. The river Medway divides the Men of Kent from the Kentish Men. The Men of Kent live on the east of the Medway; the Kentish Men on the west. This ancient distinction may go back to a time when there were two tribes in Kent, one with its capital at Canterbury, the other with its capital at Rochester. I have also heard it argued – and this topic, for some reason, is a fruitful subject for argument – that the Men of Kent earned their distinction when they went out with green boughs to meet William the Conqueror and, in return for their embassy, obtained a confirmation of their ancient privileges.

I went to an hotel to get some lunch, and the waiter, having given me an enormous plate of cold roast beef, placed a half Stilton cheese on the table and handed me, with the compliments of the management, a card on which was printed 'Sporting Events. June 1939.' It was a menu of race meetings as far away as Manchester, Yarmouth, Doncaster and New-

castle. I was, however, surprised to notice that the printer had inserted among them 'first Sunday after Trinity' and 'Second Sunday after Trinity'. But I recollected that Maidstone has never been a Sabbatarian town. Did not the Rev. Thomas Wilson make this shocked comment in 1672: 'Maidstone was formerly a very prophane town inasmuch as before 1640 I have seen morrice dancing, playing stool ball, crickets, and many other sports openly and publicly on the Lord's Day'?

I think Maidstone is more than living up to its 'prophane' reputation by including the first Sunday after Trinity among 'Sporting Events'!

I went out to see what I could find; and I was not long in finding it. The four finest things in Maidstone are the Library and Museum, housed in a grand old black-and-white manor house, the parish church of All Saints, the neighbouring Archbishop's Palace on the banks of the Medway, and, a few yards away, in Mill Street, a superb tithe barn.

Maidstone's church is like a small cathedral. It is hung with the ghostly colours of county regiments, and in the quiet building lie many of the great ones of Kent. Twelve columns, six on each side of the nave, symbolise the Twelve Apostles, and four in the chancel, two on either side, represent the Evangelists. It is a pity that many of the fine windows are ruined by stained glass of the worst Victorian kind.

One of the most flamboyant, but most interesting, monuments in the church is that of the Astley family. It is a huge architectural mass of alabaster which shows, at the top, Sir John Astley, who was Keeper of the Jewel House to Queen Elizabeth, and, lower down, his son, Sir John Astley, who was Master of the Revels to James I and Charles I.

A little slab near this monument commemorates Sir Jacob Astley, a cousin of Sir John the Second, a tough old soldier who struck some hard blows for Charles I. He was the author of the famous and beautiful prayer which he spoke on his knees before the battle

*'Maidstone's old palace is as perfect a building
of its type and period as it can be'*

of Edgehill: 'O Lord, thou knowest how busy I must be this day. If I forget Thee, do not Thou forget me,' then rising from his knees he cried, in the same breath, 'March on, boys!'

I approached the former palace of the Archbishops of Canterbury, which, by one of the merry chances not uncommon in the career of an ancient building in England, is now Maidstone's Maternity Welfare Centre. The old palace is as perfect a building of its type and period as it can be: it is a lovely silver-grey colour, and it stands proudly on the riverbank, wearing an air of quality and experience. Instead of entering by a front door in the centre of the building, you have a choice between two flights of steps which run to the left and right. The flight on the right is used by mothers and children, and the one on the left by visitors in search of the caretaker.

The bell was answered by an agreeable woman of sensible age, who took me into a number of high, snuff-coloured rooms with imposing chimney-pieces and windows which look straight down on the no longer limpid Medway. She told me a lot of history and, unlike many a caretaker I have known, had a genuine love and respect for the old place.

It was one of the many country residences of the Archbishops of Canterbury until Cranmer, who, as you remember, was always ready to oblige Henry VIII, exchanged it for some other form of revenue; and from that time until Queen Victoria's Jubilee it has passed from hand to hand. It was during the Jubilee rejoicings that Maidstone decided to buy the palace and give it a municipal purpose.

As we walked through the dignified old place, I was pleased to learn that Cranmer haunts it. I am not sure whether my guide has actually seen the ghost, but others certainly have. Pushing open the door of a sombre panelled room, she said: 'And it was here that he signed his recantation.'

I seem to remember that there were six or seven recantations, and I thought they were all signed in prison at Oxford. Nevertheless, Maidstone is convinced that he signed at least one of them in the old palace.

The room in which he is supposed to have done so is now occupied by three dissipated-looking rocking-horses. Other majestic rooms, in which once upon a time archbishops dealt with refractory monarchs, are still put to much the same use on certain days in the week, as the cots and perambulators indicate. The strangest thing about the palace is that it does not appear to resent the Maternity Centre; in fact it seems to like it.

I walked across the road to the great barn in which the archbishop's tithes were once stored, and from the size of the building, it seems that he took an adequate share of the produce of Kent. It is redolent of a thousand harvests and, as you look at it, it is easy to forget the passing cars and lorries and to see men of another age passing through its many gateways with the riches of the year.

In the days of the Canterbury pilgrimages, the Pilgrims' Way divided in the valley of the Medway, the main road keeping to the southern slope of the high chalklands, while the lower passed through West Malling, and so to Maidstone and the Abbey of Boxley. Those pilgrims not in a hurry to reach the end of their journey frequently parted from their companions and, descending into the valley, went to see the two famous sights of Boxley. One was a small stone figure of St Rumbald which declined to be lifted by an unchaste woman or a sinful man; the other was the Rood of Grace, a figure of the crucified Christ that moved its limbs, lips and eyes. This figure, which was able to smile or frown, was never approached by a pilgrim whose state of sin had been detected by St Rumbald until the sinner had confessed and been shriven by the monks.

When the commissioners of Henry VIII visited Boxley they reported that, having examined the famous Rood, they 'found therein certain engines of old wire and rotten sticks in the back of the same, that did cause the eyes to move and stare in the head like unto a lively thing; and also the nether lip in like wise to move as though it should speak'. The Rood was taken to London and publicly burned in the churchyard of old St Paul's.

I was sitting on a wall at Boxley on a May morning, with the old abbey somewhere near, degenerated into cow-sheds and fallen into ruin. It was one of those blazing days that sometimes come in May when the fresh countryside luxuriates in a silence broken only by the sound of bees, and you can almost see the leaves growing. Not far from where I was sitting, cows, defeated by the food around them, had sunk into a paddock of buttercups. The cottages stood together like gossips talking. A little girl ran to the post-office, one of those shops that sell everything, even stamps. A carter led his horse along the road. A small car stopped at the King's Arms, a young man got out, tried the door and finding it locked, appeared annoyed and, making that noise which writers spell 'pshaw', prepared to get into the car again.

I told him not to be impatient for in two minutes' time the King's Arms would open its doors, so he joined me on the wall. He was a

fruit farmer from somewhere round Maidstone. He told me what an unfortunate year he and others had had last year, when a late May frost ruined the fruit. This year might be wonderful, he said; but again it might not! A glut of fruit brings down prices and only the jam-makers get anything out of it.

While he was talking, the door of the King's Arms opened, and we went inside to a little room full of old oak and stuffed birds. They were not the kind of birds you see in Kent, but East Anglian birds, every kind of marsh bird and sea bird. The innkeeper was an Essex man and his collection had been made by his father. He knew a lot about birds and also about Boxley, so that we were soon talking about the Pilgrims' Way.

'Cows, defeated by the food around them, had sunk into a paddock of buttercups'

This ancient road, perhaps the most ancient of all our roads, is believed to be haunted along certain of its stretches, and, of course, if ever a road should be haunted, it is the Pilgrims' Way. On the high land above Wrotham, on the other side of Maidstone, where the Pilgrims' Way keeps to the edge of the downs, there are ghostly tracks of it in the woods, and you can always tell it by the yew trees. I remembered Wrotham during the War when I was stationed there with a yeomanry regiment. We had to water our horses twice daily in the woods not far from the Pilgrims' Way. The routine was to ride one and lead one up to the horse-troughs. One day, however, the horses stampeded. It was the first time I had ever experienced a stampede, and it happened in the twinkling of an eye. Panic communicated itself to the horses, there was a sound of galloping, and in an instant the whole squadron had wheeled round, the spare horses had broken away, many of the others, which were ridden bareback, had thrown their riders, and the fear that drove the animals here, there and everywhere even communicated itself to the men. No one was ever able to explain why it happened or what caused it. But the thing occurred on the following day and the day after that. It became clear that the horses refused to face the Pilgrims' Way, and we were obliged to move the horse-troughs down to the fields. The popular explanation, which may have originated in the bar of the local inn but nevertheless satisfied everybody, was that the horses, who can see spectres, had been frightened by a ghost among the yew trees.

The innkeeper said that he thought he had heard this story before, and I should not be surprised, for it was the talk of Wrotham in its time.

My fruit-grower departed on his journey,and I went up the long, green stretch of grass to the church.

I had not come to Boxley to see the remains of the Abbey, but the grave of a friend of mine

'If ever a road should be haunted,
it is the Pilgrims' Way'

who died nearly three centuries ago. I call him a friend, because George Sandys wrote a book of travel that gave me infinite pleasure long before I dreamed that it would fall to my lot to follow him at an interval of three hundred years through Greece, Turkey and Egypt.The companionship of a fellow traveller can be the most satisfactory, or the most hateful, of human relationships. To travel with an unsympathetic companion, or one without humour, tolerance, curiosity or a sense of adventure, is intolerable; and the only thing is to part as soon as possible. I am by no means sure that I should like to have travelled very far with Cobbett, Defoe or Sterne, but I have no doubt whatsoever that I could have wandered contentedly for years in company with gentle, discerning and learned Sandys.

He was the youngest son of a twice-married Archbishop of York, Edwin Sandys, who, dying a month after the defeat of the Spanish Armada, left George, then aged ten, in the care of his mother. Sandys never married, and it was not until his mother's death, when he was thirty-two years of age, that he decided to set off and see the world. He planned what was a mighty tour in days when it required real courage and resolution to visit Moslem countries: Greece, Turkey, Syria, Palestine,

Egypt, Cyprus, Crete, Malta, Sicily and Italy. The year of his departure was 1610. James I sat upon the throne of England. The Authorised Version of the Bible had just gone to press. Shakespeare, Raleigh and Bacon were still alive. The Gunpowder Plot was five years old. Milton was in his cradle, a child of two, and Cromwell was a schoolboy at Huntingdon. Sandys was abroad for two years and, returning, produced *A Relation of a Journey Begun An: Dom: 1610*, a small folio book illustrated with a number of woodcuts.

This book became immensely popular, and was still being reprinted in 1673, thirty years after its author's death. Isaak Walton mentions it in the *Compleat Angler*, and a poem written by Sandys in the Holy Sepulchre in Jerusalem helped Milton with his *Ode to the Passion*. That first copy that came my way was a worm-eaten and considerably battered version of the seventh edition that I picked up for a few shillings on a foggy afternoon in the Charing Cross Road. I saw at once that Sandys had solved the problem of beginning a book. 'I began my journey through France,' he says, 'hard upon the time when that execrable murther was committed upon the person of Henry IV by an obscure varlet.' From that moment I found myself transported into another world as I wandered the Levant with him. The London fog melted away, the domes and minarets of Constantinople lifted in his clear prose; the Greek islands lay upon a blue sea; there was a smell of rope and tar and cargo as the sails of galley and brigantine slanted into the harbours of the ancient world.

I entered the church with liveliest anticipation, hoping to see an effigy of my old friend, but I could find nothing of the sort. I could not even find his tombstone. I looked everywhere in this dim little building for his grave. I moved mats and rugs in the chancel and peered beneath, and came to the conclusion that the grave must be hidden by the choir stalls. I found, however, a wall tablet put up in 1848 to the memory of

> George Sandys, Esq., eminent as a traveller, a divine poet and a good man, who died March 4, 1643, at Boxley Abbey, aged 66, and lies interred in the chancel of this church.

His life was throughout blameless and never unuseful, its earlier part was sometimes pass'd in observing his fellow-men in foreign lands: and its latter years at home in celebrating the praises of his God and attuning the Songs of Zion to the British lyre.

'I went up the long, green stretch of grass to the church'

But what, you may ask, was Sandys connection with Boxley? It was a close and intimate one. The Abbey of Boxley had been in the possession of the famous Wyatt family since the time of Henry VIII. Margaret Sandys, a niece of George Sandys, married Francis Wyatt. It was evidently from his wife's family that Wyatt derived his interest in colonial settlement, for the Sandys were actively concerned in colonising America. When George Sandys returned from the East and wrote his book of travel, he found Francis Wyatt deeply involved in the affairs of the Virginia Company. In 1621, having been elected Governor of Virginia, Wyatt sailed off for his colony, taking with him, as treasurer, his friend and kinsman by marriage, George.

The adventures which befell Sandys in the old world were nothing compared with those encountered by him in Virginia. Within a year of his arrival the Indians rose and massacred more than three hundred settlers. The news reached London four months after, and Margaret Wyatt at once decided to leave Kent and, like a brave wife, share her husband's dangers and anxieties in the colony. When she arrived in Virginia she found that her uncle had been quietly working through all these alarms and perils at the completion of his translation of Ovid. Two books, he said, had been written 'amongst the roaring of the sea', while the others were written during the painful vicissitudes of colonial life. Thus George Sandys could claim the distinction of being the first English settler to write a book in America.

Ten years or so of colonial life were enough for Sandys, who it seems, disliked his fellow colonists and was always quarrelling with them. Returning home, he spent his life in writing those paraphrases of the Psalms which, with his Ovid, have given him a place among the Jacobean poets. He did most of his writing in a little summer-house in the grounds of Boxley Abbey. An inscription on the wall stated that in that place Mr George Sandys 'after his travaile over the world, retired himself for his poetry and contemplation'.

In one year all three of them, Margaret and her husband, Francis Wyatt, and Uncle George Sandys, were laid to rest in Boxley Church. Margaret died in March 1644. Wyatt, returning from America in the spring, was just in time to reach the death-bed of Sandys, and a few months later he followed his wife and his kinsman to the grave. Their exit was well chosen. The schoolboy of Huntingdon, who had been eleven years of age when Sandys set forth on his journey to the East, was now a man of forty-five with an army of 'Ironsides' at his back, and although the Civil War had already begun, those three devoted followers of Charles I, a prince to whom Sandys dedicated everything he wrote, were spared the knowledge of its end.

How typical it is of England, and our quiet parish churches where so many noble lives are harvested, that with some slight knowledge of a family, a man, reading between the stilted lines of a memorial, can see the minarets of seventeenth-century Constantinople rising, as in a mist, and in the peace and quiet of the Kentish countryside can catch a glimpse of Indian arrows quivering in the stockades of Virginia.

As I was motoring along the road between Maidstone and Ashford, my eye, in passing, caught sight of a notice that had been placed on a board in the hedge: 'Leeds Castle: open today.' This was lucky, for Leeds Castle is open to the public only once or twice a year. Unlike Penshurst Place and Knole, which are opened regularly two or three times a week, Leeds Castle is unknown, except to those who have enjoyed the hospitalilty of Lady Baillie, the wife of Sir Adrian Baillie, MP, who bought the estate in 1927.

Coming to the castle gates, I paid half-a-crown to some local charity and drove into a park. In a few moments, lying ahead on slightly lower ground, I saw a castle that might have been created by Tennyson or Walter Scott. It was indeed what writers of the last century were thinking of when they used the phrase 'this noble pile'. It is enormous. Its tall, turreted walls are pierced by Gothic and Tudor windows. When the sun is shining, the effect of the stone is striking: it is as white as marble. The white walls descend into still water, and are mirrored by a reflection interrupted only by thousands of water-lilies.

But to say that Leeds Castle is moated does not convey the right impression at all: a moat suggests a surrounding ditch or trench filled with water. What makes this castle so beautiful is that it lies in the centre of a lake that is anything from fifteen to twenty acres in extent. Among the lilies swim black and white swans which, against such a background, suggest the enchantments of Merlin.

I sat on the grass and thanked God that Leeds Castle does not belong to me. To have to live in such a colossal place, and to maintain there a great pack of retainers, every one of whom no doubt expects to be motored to the nearest cinema at least once a week, is just my idea of purgatory.

I should have said that the only way to live at ease in a castle this size would have been in days when it was a little garrison town with its own population. And I thought how remarkable it is in these days, when incomes can pay more than ten shillings in the pound income tax, and people are less inclined than ever to assume responsibility, that anyone can be found who loves this old castle sufficiently to keep life within its walls.

A young man, an inquisitive visitor like myself, came over to the grass where I was sitting and took several photographs across the water.

'What do you think of it?' I asked him.

'It'll make a lovely photograph,' he replied. 'It's funny to find a Leeds Castle in Kent, isn't it?'

Having once read the only book written about this castle, a book published nearly a century ago by a previous owner, Charles Wykeham Martin, I was able to tell him why.

The name has nothing to do with Leeds in Yorkshire. It takes its name from an Anglo-Saxon thane, called Led or Ledian, who built the first rude fortress on the island in the lake about the year A.D. 850.

I crossed the drawbridge to the Inner Barbican, and then walked over another bridge to the gatehouse and the porter's lodge. The space where a portcullis used to hang, and the grooves into which it fell when it was lowered, are plainly seen in these defensive gateways.

Standing there and looking back across the moat, it was obvious that before the invention of gunpowder, which literally blew the mediæval Baron out of his castle, this stronghold must have been proof against all danger but famine or treachery from within.

Beyond the gate-house is a wide courtyard, the Inner Bailey, at the far end of which stands the castle and the main entrance. Men and maid-servants were gathered in the hall, evidently enjoying the novelty of showing people round. In charge of a tall and aloof manservant, I made a progress through a series of living-rooms, where long windows provided a glimpse of the waters of the moat below.

On a fine, sunny day, life in a moated castle is attractive, but on a wet day, with the moat pricked out with falling rain, it is not the perfect cure for melancholy. Indeed, if statistics had been kept in the Middle Ages, it would probably have been found that suicides in moated castles during the winter months were more frequent than at other times of the year! Also an ill-tempered Baron, who had been living on salt fish for several months, must have been more liable at this than at any other period of the year to throw his friends and relatives into the moat which lies so suggestively beneath the windows.

The castle is not all as venerable as it looks from the lakeside. A good deal of the main structure is Victorian Tudor, and this is connected by a bridge over the moat with a smaller, more ancient portion of the building, which stands on its own little island.

My guide was unable to tell me anything that was new to me about the castle, except that it has a ghost, as indeed a castle of its size and age should have: the ghost of a little old lady in grey, who appears with a black dog. No one knows who this little old lady is, but she has been seen, I understand, by the present housekeeper. She might be a number of people, for the history of Leeds Castle teems with women, and some of them must have been little, old, grey, and addicted to black dogs.

The castle was for many centuries part of the dowry of the Queens of England. The first Queen who possessed it was Eleanor of Castile, the beloved wife of Edward I. She it was who went with her lord to the Holy Land, and is said to have sucked the poison from his wound. She also gave birth to a daughter in Palestine, who became known as Joan of Acre. It was this Eleanor also who became the mother of the first Prince of Wales, and held the infant aloft on a shield in Carnarvon Castle. When she died in Lincolnshire, funeral crosses were erected at every stopping-place of her coffin all the way to Westminster Abbey, the last one being the Cross at Charing, or Charing Cross.

Another Queen, Isabella, a meddlesome, violent woman, the wife of Edward II, caused considerable trouble at Leeds by vainly demanding entrance to what she considered her own property, after her husband had secretly bartered it away for something else. This was not fair of him, or at least he might have informed her. The end of this misunderstanding was costly and sanguinary. The occupants of the castle, having declined to admit the Queen, discharged arrows, slaying six members of her escort. The Queen then demanded vengeance, and the King, who was temporarily in a good humour with this tiresome woman, attacked Leeds Castle, subdued it and hanged the Seneschal together with eleven of his followers.

A touch of novelty was brought to Leeds by Queen Joan of Navarre, the second wife of Henry IV, and step-mother of the popular Henry V. She arrived there under escort, charged with witchcraft. That a Queen Dowager of England should have been suspected of witchcraft is interesting, but nobody was able to prove anything. The affair ended tamely enough when Henry sent her some money to buy new clothes and released her.

My guide handed me over to another, who took me to a detached building called The Maidens' Tower. The story now current with the staff at Leeds is that Henry VIII built this tower for his queens, but even Henry was not such a wholesale Bluebeard. It is more probable that he built the place for the maids-of-honour in attendance on his queen of the moment.

Beyond this tower some old steps descend to a mysterious place, now a boat-house, known as Edward I's bath. The explanation is that when he was in the Holy Land, the monarch acquired a novel taste for bathing and returned to build this forbidding cavern full of icy moat water. If there were any heating arrangements, this story might be plausible, but, so far as I could find out, there is no trace of them. The only baths that would have attracted a visitor to the East in those days were the luxurious Roman baths in the Byzantine cities, of which the modern Turkish bath is a direct descendant.

The visitors to Leeds Castle that day were not impressed by Edward's bath, but they expressed astonishment and admiration for the swimming-pool constructed by the present owners of the castle. A retainer demonstrated that it was possible to cover the water with artificial waves by turning a switch. We were

'What makes Leeds Castle so beautiful is that it lies in the centre of a lake'

also shown a cocktail bar adjoining the pool which had been murally decorated by a foreign artist. It is a grim and, I suppose, amusing political satire entitled 'Boys will be boys'. It shows Mr Neville Chamberlain skating on a pond covered with thin ice, and surrounded by a series of wintry statues, each one a buxom dame in the process of being lifted from her plinth and carried off. One statue bears the title 'The Rape of Austria', another 'The Rape of Czechoslovakia', a third 'The Rape of Abyssinia'. Hiding in the background, as two naughty little urchins, are Hitler and Göring, while Mr Duff Cooper and Mr Winston Churchill watch events from the opposite side.

That this bitter cartoon of Europe's trials should hang above an English cocktail bar completes its irony. I expect the foreign artist thought so too.

It was interesting to learn that in ancient times they made wine of English grapes at Leeds, and a portion of the garden is still known as the Vineyard. Wykeham Martin says in his book that several of the cottages in the village are covered with vines which bear peculiar small grapes known as 'cluster grapes'. He believed that they were the descendants of the grapes from which Queen Eleanor made wine in 1290.

With a farewell glance at the superb castle reflected in its lake, I went back to the main road and within an hour was in Canterbury.

CHAPTER THREE

I arrive in Canterbury, watch the feast of tea-time, see a shop that sells ARP, climb the Bell Harry Tower, and reconstruct the murder of Thomas à Becket. I visit a leper settlement, go to Walmer Castle, where I am shown the Wellington Room, and continue my journey through the 'hurst' and 'den' country of Kent.

It was delightful to walk about Canterbury in the evening, with the sun still lighting the Cathedral towers and streets warm with life and bustle. The old houses and narrow lanes were pervaded by an air of ecclesiastical peace, plenty and privilege. Everyone I spoke to – the girl at the hotel, the boots and the shopkeepers – was distinguished by that smiling affability that comes so naturally to those who are always in brief contact with strangers.

Old streets, like Mercery Lane, cannot have changed much since the Middle Ages either in appearance or in their function. They exist to sell cheap souvenirs which prove that the purchaser has been to Canterbury. These shops once sold leaden medallions of the head of St Thomas; now they sell postcards and ash-trays emblazoned with the city arms.

Chesterton might have written a good story about a bus-load of trippers from Ramsgate who came to Canterbury only to find themselves involved in a miracle. Perhaps T. F. Powys could do it even better. And I have the suspicion that an average band of Canterbury pilgrims were much the same a few centuries ago as those today who wander vaguely about the city on a day trip. Could you replace their curiosity with faith, or at least hope, I think you would have a similar crowd of people.

There was nothing wrong with pilgrimage except the pilgrim. In the East today you can still see mediæval pilgrimage in being, and I have sometimes amused myself by picking out the characters of the *Canterbury Tales* from the motley throng that fills Jerusalem in Passion Week. Still, when all is said and done, maybe one poor, simple-hearted creature with tears coursing down his cheeks, experiencing the bliss that neither wealth nor a science degree can give, cancels out all the hard-faced bargainers with God. And no doubt it was the same in Canterbury. In every pilgrimage there must have been at least one who redeemed the rest.

A bell began to ring. Becket would have called that moment vespers, a lovely word; the Dean and Chapter would call it evensong, not quite so lovely as the other; but, to the general population, it was obviously tea-time. Were I a tea-lover, I could have had a wonderful time in Canterbury, because, like most cathedral cities, Canterbury takes its tea seriously. It is rich in examples of that English institution, the tea-shop. But, alas, I am not a great tea-man. I think tea is best drunk in the early morning or in the middle of the night. I also think it extremely odd that we should call an orgy of farinaceous solids by the simple name of a harmless liquid. We might as well call breakfast 'coffee'.

I stood at the windows of those shops gazing over a rampart of cakes to the charming scene beyond, a perfect picture of an English social custom. You will never see anything quite like a Canterbury tea-shop anywhere else on earth. It is extraordinary to think what a mighty habit we have built round that dried leaf from the other side of the world, and never once for a matter of three centuries have the supplies of it failed us. At the same time I have held the belief for years that the consumption (except in Scotland, where it is the last meal of the day) by middle-aged and elderly people of large quantities of bread and butter, tea-cake, crumpet, muffin, jam, honey and cake, is a habit that originated in the nursery, for all English nurses have a passion for colossal and fantastic teas. The young, gazing at them in envious wonderment, and denied that repletion which their nurses reserve for themselves, develop the vice in later life and try to justify themselves by calling it, simply, 'tea'. It was with an almost Freudian satisfaction that I watched a well-fed, elderly parson peep greedily under the muffin lid and select a warm and buttered segment, which he carried to his mouth with juvenile enjoyment, afterwards quickly licking the butter from his fingers like a naughty little boy. No doubt he was getting his own back on nurse.

The tea-shop as we know it today is a fairly recent development. It is the feminine counterpart of the inn. Refinement is its key-note, and it has also inherited a lot from the arts and crafts period. That is because once upon a time when a lady in a chintz overall decided to go into business, it was a toss up whether she opened a tea-shop or bought a hand-loom and some herbally dyed wool. And the number of ladies who do pervade tea-shops with a tremendously lady-like air of bravery and resignation is legion. Another of my theories is that the first generation of such ladies, long ago, when it was daring and emancipated to have a tea-shop, plunged into the tea-world in order to forget an unhappy love affair, much as men of the same period are believed to have worked off their sorrow upon wild animals in India or Africa.

And even today, if you wish to find a lady whose heart is elsewhere, you have only to look for the nearest collection of home-made cakes, jam, lemon-curd and ginger-nuts, and there you will see, gazing into the distance, the wistful features of Sister Alice. I have always understood that neither Swinburne nor Burne-Jones were much addicted to tea or crumpets, nevertheless they have, in some strange way, bequeathed to the tea-shop their drooping, sad madonnas.

Having watched the ceremony of tea, I wandered idly through the streets, coming at last to the most bizarre shop window I have ever seen. It was full of rattles, hand-bells, whistles, electric torches and gas-masks. The shop called itself the ARP Information Bureau. Had it not been closed, I should have gone inside to seek an answer to the question everyone is asking, although it was only too clear that the organisers of this exhibition had no doubt about the answer. The central feature of the window was a chart setting forth the various signals to be used in air raids. Upon the signal 'action warning', people were to take cover; upon the signal 'raiders past', they were to emerge. The gas alarm would be signalled by rattles and the 'all clear' by handbells.

No one seemed interested in this window, and I was its only student. I thought it a grim contrast to the crowded, happy tea-shops of Canterbury, an ogre of a shop, something too grotesque to be comic, too improbable to be true. At the same time the rattles and hand-bells, instead of appearing the most modern of all window displays, had a queer air of the archaic, as if they were a collection of bygones in a museum. I found it difficult to imagine men running through the lovely streets of Canterbury waving rattles or ringing bells. Surely Canterbury will never know the sound of war.

As I was turning away, a man came up and looked at the window.

'Do you think we shall ever need these?' I asked him, nodding towards the grisly display.

He was a cautious, spectacled little man who peered at me carefully before he replied.

'Well, er, I don't really know,' he said, 'but I suppose it's better to be on the safe side. We're very keen on ARP in Canterbury, as you see, but it's not easy to get people interested.'

'May I ask if you are connected with ARP?'

He was apologetic about this, as if he thought I might laugh at him.

'Well, if you really want to know,' he said, 'I'm an air-raid warden.'

He peered up anxiously, and, when I did not smile, he went on.

'The trouble is that people don't think we're serious. They think this war scare is just newspaper talk, and that everything is going to come out all right. But you bet they'll get interested as soon as something happens!'

He looked round into the night, his spectacles gleaming, as if he heard already the whine of Civilisation's doom, and he went off with nothing to indicate that he belonged to a new order of knighthood – the Knight of the Twirling Rattle.

I stayed at the Royal Fountain because it looked quiet, and Canterbury is one of the noisiest cities in England. Motor bicycles, cars and lorries whine, explode and change gear in the High Street all night through, so that sleep is an impossibility. This I know, having stayed in a front room there years ago, when I swore that I would rather walk about the streets all night than do so again.

At the Fountain they are proud of the legend that the knights who slew Thomas à Becket called there for a drink before they went to the Cathedral. I suggest that they consumed several drinks, for contemporary accounts of the murder clearly describe a drunken brawl. You would hardly believe that the hotel is so old, because Georgian and Victorian plaster covers the mediæval structure, but it is worthwhile to glance at the cellars where you can see the ancient foundations, as I did in company with the boots.

Emerging from the cellar, the boots took me upstairs into a long room with a piano in it, known as the farmers' club room.

'You've heard of General Picton, sir? Well, you'll be interested in this room.'

And he told me that on 11 June 1815, General Picton, with his aide-de-camp, Captain Tyler, arrived in Canterbury on their way to join Wellington in the Low Country. Picton had been Wellington's right hand in the Peninsular War, and as soon as Napoleon escaped from Elba, the Duke asked him to leave his retirement and go out and serve under him. The citizens of Canterbury, aware of the great events on the Continent and of the importance of their visitor, entertained the General to dinner in the long room which is now the farmers' club room.

In the morning Picton departed, arriving two days later at Brussels. Wellington gave him command of the Fifth Division and the reserve, and on the following morning at daybreak, the 16th of June, Picton and Wellington left Brussels together. All that day Picton was in action with the French at Quatre Bras. His troops had no sooner formed square to repulse the enemy infantry than the French lancers charged them, greatly superior in numbers to the British cavalry. But Picton, despising the enemy's superiority, put himself at the head of his cavalry and gave the order to charge. He drove back the French, inflicting great losses on them, and his troops lay down that night to sleep among the dead and wounded upon a field of victory. But during the charge Picton had been wounded by a ball that broke his ribs. Determined to lead his division, he told no one but his servant, who helped to bandage him up. On the following morning, the 17th, Picton was obliged to fall back upon the plains of Waterloo, where that night the allied armies rested on their arms. The next day Picton's wound was more serious, still he kept it secret. Again he fought a fierce and violent action with superior French forces, and again he placed himself at the head of his cavalry and, drawing his sword, cried: 'Charge, hurrah! Hurrah!' but, as his brigade galloped into action, a cannon ball hit him on the forehead and he fell back dead. Captain Tyler placed his chief's body beneath a tree and, when the battle was over, went back and found it.

As the stage-coaches were galloping through England giving the glorious news of Waterloo, the body of Picton was landed at Deal. It rested the first night at Canterbury, in the room in the Fountain where a fortnight previously the brave soldier had been entertained by the city.

After dinner I watched twilight come upon Canterbury, and I saw the towers grow black against a sky that promised more sunlight tomorrow. Thrushes were singing in the Cathedral close, and one by one a few windows were lit, revealing books and panelling before the curtains were drawn.

I paid my respects to the Dean, who is known to newspaper readers as the 'Red Dean' because of his interest in Russia. Actually he is a pink-and-white dean, a man

'*It was delightful to walk about Canterbury in the evening*'

with a healthy, fresh complexion and two side bushes of snowy hair.

He received me in his superb panelled drawing-room, a room of most elegant and splendid proportions, and we went to his library, another equally fine Georgian room, where we talked of Russia, about which I knew little, and about the chances of war, about which I knew even less. The Dean, however, thought that only by a miracle could we escape it.

Talking of the Cathedral, he told me – and this I never knew before – that in, I think, 1511, tapestries of silk and wool depicting scenes in the lives of Christ and the Virgin were hung round the choir. They were taken down by the Cromwellians and sold to the cathedral of Aix-en-Provence, where they hang to this day.

The Canterbury Pilgrims gave a verb to the English language and a name to an English flower. The name Canterbury Bell was given five hundred years ago to one of our most charming wild flowers because it was thought to resemble in shape the little bells which the pilgrims tied to the bridles of their horses. Gerard, who wrote his *Herbal* in 1597, complained that it was not right to give the name to certain bell flowers that grew round London, because the true Canterbury Bell was a native of Kent and was to be found in great profusion near Canterbury. The habit has grown since Gerard's time, and if you open any seedsman's catalogue today you will find that all kinds of cultivated flowers of the genus *Campanula* are called 'Canterbury Bells', some of them huge exotic flowers that bear only a family resemblance to the real bell.

Then the verb to canter is, of course, a contraction of a 'Canterbury gallop', which was the easy hand gallop into which the pilgrims urged their horses, possibly when they came to level stretches of the South Downs. It has also been claimed that the word

'cant', meaning religious jargon, is derived from Canterbury, but I am not at all sure of this. But the phrase 'to tell a Canterbury', or lie, was one used by the Puritans, and though it has long since fallen out of use in this country, it was carried across the Atlantic by the Pilgrim Fathers, and may still be heard in the United States.

Soon after the Cathedral was open in the morning, I went there and made the acquaintance of Mr Wood, the Vesterer. I found him putting away the embroidered copes which had been used at the morning service. He had the keys of the safes with him, so I asked if I might see some of the treasures of Canterbury Cathedral.

The most beautiful object he showed me was a thin, handbeaten chalice of silver-gilt which was discovered in the grave of a man who was buried in the year 1205. The man was Hubert Walter, Archbishop of Canterbury in the time of Richard Cœur de Lion. When his grave was opened in 1892, those who were present at the time looked with awe as they saw for one second, before the air caused the body to fall into dust, an archbishop vested, with his crozier beside him, just as he had been buried by the monks of Canterbury 687 years previously.

It is believed that Hubert Walter took the chalice with him to the Holy Land, when he went with Richard on the Third Crusade. If so, it was used at Mass long ago, among the palm trees at Acre. It does not often fall to any man's lot to hold a relic such as this.

There is not a place to which this chalice travelled in Palestine that I do not know. I have wandered through the ruins of Acre, Ascalon, Tyre and Sidon, watching the Mediterranean rollers come swinging in from the sea, to break in foam against the piles of masonry that were fortresses in the days when Hubert Walter said Mass with the English army. He was the outstanding man of his time, and the strong man of England. He was a good man and, like many an early church-man, stood between the people and the tyranny of King and noble. It was said of him that 'he was so bountiful in providing for the poor and the wayfarer that his income seemed common property'.

It was Hubert Walter who, when Richard foolishly got himself into prison on the Continent, went round England with the hat and raised the fabulous ransom (in those days) of £100,000. I have always felt that he might have spent it to better purpose, for Richard, our dear hero, could not speak English, knew nothing of England, and, out of a reign of ten years, spent only nine months in this country!

Walter ruled England when the King was away. Among his constitutional innovations was the appointment of coroners. Few JPs know perhaps that they owe their office to him, for he appointed knights whose duty it was to enforce an oath to 'keep the peace', and such knights developed into our Justices of the Peace. When Richard died, Hubert Walter crowned John. He was the only person in England who could stand up to this King, and when he died John remarked: 'Now, for the first time am I truly King of England.'

Such was the great man whose chalice, after lying for 687 years in the darkness of the tomb, is sometimes used in Canterbury Cathedral today. There are more ornate and more costly chalices in the world, but not one, I think, of greater interest.

Mr Wood offered to show me round the Cathedral. We ascended spiral staircases to the triforium, then up again into the dark passages above the nave and transepts. It was like walking under the timbers of an old ship, dark and dusty, and with only an occasional handrail to guide one over the narrow planks which stretch across the vaulting. This is the exquisite roof which visitors admire from the floor of the church, but from this position it looks like a crop of enormous stone mushrooms growing in the darkness.

Perhaps few of those who admire the glory of Canterbury, or any other cathedral, know that between vaulting and roofing is this vast V-shaped no-man's-land where the wind whistles through slit windows, where pigeons nest, and where bats hang from rafters cut from oaks which were probably giants at the time of the Norman Conquest.

There was no beauty in this dim and unvisited region, but we explored it eagerly, discussing the marvels of thrust and counter-thrust, and admiring the workmen who made this stupendous church centuries ago.

We ascended the steps of the central tower, known as the Bell Harry Tower, but before we had gone very far Mr Wood pointed out what must be one of the few mediæval cranes in existence. It is a gigantic wheel, the size of a mill wheel, and was used by the masons of the Middle Ages to lift heavy stones from ground level to the summit of towers. It was worked by man-power. Several workmen stationed inside the wheel would walk, as if on a treadmill, which caused the wheel to revolve and wind up a rope to which stones were attached.

It is still in perfect order, although I don't suppose it has been used for five centuries. Standing inside it, I discovered that the balance is so delicate that when I placed one foot only a few inches in advance of the other, the huge wheel began to revolve.

We climbed still higher – much higher – and came out on the summit of Bell Harry Tower, where the stone, now in process of restoration, is eaten away by wind and rain. Below us lay Canterbury in the calmness of a spring morning. The trees so far below hardly moved in the breeze, though a sharp wind was blowing across the tower. Looking down, the huge cruciform building is like a giant aeroplane, the transepts its wings, and the body of the church its fuselage.

The bells, dismantled during the reconstructions, lay mouths up, the heavy clappers resting against the rim, where a spot of bright bronze marked the striking point.

I said how costly must be the task of keeping

a cathedral in repair.

'Yes,' said Mr Wood, 'but now and again a cathedral has a bit of good fortune.'

I asked him to explain this, and he smilingly told me this story. A roughly dressed man was recently in the habit of haunting the Cathedral, wearing a pair of old trousers and a shirt which opened at the neck to reveal a hairy chest. He had developed to a high degree the habit of singing loudly and out of tune. His voice was so loud and inaccurate that he began to affect the choir, which, to the consternation of the Dean and Chapter, also began to sing out of tune. The visitor, who became a daily anxiety, was tactfully asked to sit farther away from the choir, which annoyed him considerably; nevertheless, he consented to do so. Then one day he did not appear, and in a little while they heard that he was dead. When his will was proved the Cathedral received £6,000 and the Choristers School £5,000.

'And it's with his £6,000 that we are now doing this,' ended Mr Wood, indicating the restoration to Bell Harry Tower.

If there is any moral in this it is, treat every man in old flannel trousers, and with a hairy chest, as if he were a wandering god.

We descended those exhausting steps to the ground, and looked at the cathedral from the outside. Mr Wood pointed out how the Archbishop of Canterbury's Palace is joined to the Cathedral by the Great Cloister, and although it is a modern building, it stands on the ground occupied by the palace of the early primates.

'It was from that palace that Thomas à Becket took sanctuary in the Cathedral on the night of the murder,' said Mr Wood. 'And there are three stairs left in the Palace on which he must have walked that night . . .'

The Archbishop was away at Lambeth, but we were invited to step into the palace. I had no idea that the Archbishop of Canterbury lived in such a modest house. The word 'palace' is purely a formal title, for many a penurious vicar would be grateful for so small a vicarage.

On an upper floor we found the fragmentary remains of an old stone staircase, with three of the original treads remaining. It was the same kind of narrow stone tube in which we had spent so much time that morning when we climbed to the roof. In this house it is clearly seen how, when the murderers had armed and were ready to do their work, Becket left this building unseen by them, using a small, private door that once opened into the cloisters.

'And now,' I said to Mr Wood, 'let us go to the Cathedral and try to imagine exactly what happened on the night of December the twenty-ninth in the year 1170.'

Civilised adult human beings are rarely in the habit of falling into ungovernable rages, of biting the carpet in fury, and exhibiting other signs well known in badly conducted nurseries. But in early times our kings and nobles were not ashamed to give such violent exhibitions. They would roll on the floor, snapping at the rushes like dogs. They would scream. They would rave. They would weep tears of fury, and then the mood would pass, and, like naughty children, they would sometimes be sorry.

The men of that time were neither ashamed nor amused by such scenes. When Richard of Devizes described how Richard Cœur de Lion had ranted and shouted, and 'champed with his teeth the pine-rod which he held in his hand', he compared this childish display with the noble rage of a lion.

On a night towards the end of December, in the year 1170, King Henry II of England, who was then at the Castle of Bur, near Bayeux, fell into one of these royal rages. The cause of his anger was the action of Thomas à Becket, Archbishop of Canterbury, who for eighteen years had been fighting the State's attempt to dominate the Church. The King loathed Becket as only an autocrat can loathe an equally strong rival, and what perhaps made their relationship even worse was that, before Becket had entered the Church, he had been a gay man of the world and the King's favourite. It is well known that no people can fight more bitterly than old friends.

Henry had forced Becket to be Archbishop against his will, because he wished to have a complacent friend at the head of the Church he wished to attack. But he had chosen the wrong man. No sooner was Becket consecrated than he ceased to be the King's man and became God's man; and from that moment, and for eighteen years, the story of England is the fight between the Church and the State, between Becket and Henry.

On that night in December Henry worked himself into a frightful paroxysm. He called Becket 'a fellow that came to court on a lame horse with a cloak for a saddle'. He said that a man he had 'loaded with benefits' was insulting him. Then, turning to the assembled courtiers, he shouted: 'What sluggard wretches, what cowards have I brought up in my Court, who care nothing for their allegiance to their master! Not one will deliver me from this low-born priest!' He rushed from the hall.

That same night four men crossed the Channel, Reginald Fitzurse, William de Tracy, Richard le Breton and Hugh de Moreville. They crossed by different routes, two arrived at Dover and two at Winchelsea. They rode to Saltwood Castle, near Canterbury, which was held by one of Becket's enemies, Dan Randolph of Broc, and there, in a darkened room, they discussed a plan of action. It was 28 December.

As I stood in the North Transept of Canterbury Cathedral, at the place where Becket died, I thought I would try to write a plain account of his murder, rejecting all fable and fancy and using only the facts supplied by men who saw it happen, or who were alive at the time.

The murder of the Archbishop is one of the best documented events in mediæval history. He was slain in the Fleet Street of his time – if I may be forgiven the comparison – surrounded by the only reporters of that age, the monks and priests of the Church. Some who stood beside him, some who ran away and hid, others who vested his corpse for burial, have left descriptions from which it is possible to paint a true picture of that night 769 years ago.

In addition to many contemporary narratives, there are no fewer than five eye-witness accounts of Becket's death: the account of William of Canterbury, a monk; William Fitzstephen, a clerk in attendance on Becket; Benedict, another monk who was there; John of Salisbury; and Edward Grim, a clerk of Cambridge who was on a visit to Becket at the time. From these five accounts it is possible to reconstruct the murder in every detail; and this is what happened.

On 29 December, the day after the four knights had crossed the Channel, at three in the afternoon Becket sat down to dinner in the hall of the Archbishop's Palace, which was separated from the Cathedral by the Great Cloister. He sat at the high table with his household and the monks, while at the long table sat the poor people and beggars whom he entertained every day. The floor was covered with fresh hay; the smoke of burning logs ascended through the hall, and the grey light of a December afternoon shone beyond the narrow windows.

At the end of dinner, after a thanksgiving had been sung, Becket went to his retiring-room, and the servants flung themselves on the broken meats. The sound was heard of horses clattering into the courtyard. In a few moments four knights in ordinary dress strode into the hall through the crowds of departing beggars.

The servants asked if the visitors would like something to eat, but they refused and went to Becket's room. The Archbishop, seated on a couch, was leaning on the shoulder of a monk, while monks reclined on the floor near him. He was over six feet in height, handsome, and with a keen and piercing eye. He was fifty-two years of age and, though his figure was really spare, he felt the cold so acutely that he wore an incredible number of garments in order to keep warm; and these gave him a padded, corpulent appearance.

As the knights entered, he continued to talk with the monk next to him. They came in silently, without a greeting, and sat on the floor at his feet. Then Becket looked at them and spoke to Tracy by name. The knights began to talk violently.

They charged Becket with undermining the royal authority and with causing disturbances, and they demanded that he should lift the ban of excommunication from the Bishops of London and Salisbury. Becket, who was a man of quick temper, also raised his voice, and soon knights and Archbishop were quarrelling violently.

The knights flew into one of their Norman passions and stamped about the room, twisting their long gauntlets, advancing close to Becket, gnashing their teeth and waving their arms. They screamed that he had threatened to excommunicate them; he shouted back that they could not frighten him.

'Were all the swords in England hanging over my head,' he shouted, 'you could not terrify me from my obedience to God, and my lord the Pope.'

Crowds of monks and servants ran into the room and gathered round Becket. The knights roared at them to stand back if they were loyal to the King. They refused to move. The room was soon a pandemonium, and through it the knights ran to the door shouting, 'To arms, to arms!'

It was now nearly five o'clock. The winter's darkness had fallen. Beneath a sycamore tree in the courtyard the knights put on their armour. The monks bolted the doors and Becket sat down again on his couch.

'It is wonderful, my lord,' said John of Salisbury, 'that you never take anyone's advice.'

'I am prepared to die,' replied Becket stubbornly.

Some of the monks, discussing the scene together, believed there was nothing to fear because, as William Fitzstephen noted, 'the men had come drunk' and 'would not have spoken like that before dinner'. Others were not so sanguine. At this moment a frightened monk rushed in to say the knights were arming. All save a few companions fled into the Cathedral. 'All monks are cowards,' said Becket. His attendants, believing that the knights would not dare to shed blood on consecrated ground, forced Becket against his will to leave the palace. Half pushed, half lifted, he was taken through the cloisters and into the dark church, where vespers had just begun. As they gained what some of them hoped was sanctuary, they heard behind them the crash of woodwork as the knights broke into the palace.

What then happened took place in almost complete darkness, a darkness lit only by tapers burning before the shrines. A hammering echoed through the church. Becket ordered the doors to be opened, and when no one would do it he strode forward and himself flung back the bars. A terrified crowd of monks fought to enter. Becket helped them, saying, 'Come in, come in, faster, faster!'

By this time the church was full of flying and hiding men. Only three remained with the Archbishop: Robert of Merton, William Fitzstephen, his chaplain, and Edward Grim, the clerk. They tried to get Becket to hide in the crypt or in the triforium, where he would never have been discovered, but he declined to do so. At last they persuaded him to mount the steps from the north transept, in which they were standing, to the choir, but, as they did so, the knights, covered to the eyes in chain mail, broke into the church. Fitzurse came first, with a sword in one hand and a carpenter's axe, which he had picked up in the palace, in the other. He could see nothing in the darkness, and stood calling for the 'traitor Becket'. There was silence. He called again, and then Becket came down the steps.

'Reginald, why do you come into my church armed?' he asked.

Fitzurse placed the carpenter's axe against Becket's chest and said: 'You shall die. I will tear out your heart!'

'I am ready to die,' replied Becket, 'for God and the Church, but I warn you, I curse you in the name of God Almighty, if you do not let my men escape.'

The knights, fearing to commit sacrilege, then tried to hustle Becket out of the church. 'I will not fly, you detestable fellow!' he shouted, pushing Fitzurse away. Then they tried to place him on Tracy's shoulders, but Becket seized Tracy and flung him to the floor. At that moment Fitzurse came up with lifted sword, and Becket, now furious, cried out, 'You profligate wretch, you are my man – you have done me fealty – you ought not to touch me!'

Fitzurse shouted back: 'I owe you no fealty or homage contrary to my fealty to the King,' and made a blow at Becket's head. It did not touch him, but knocked back his skull cap.

Tracy then came up and aimed a blow which the clerk, Grim, who had his arm round Becket, tried to parry. The blow cut Grim's arm and grazed the crown of Becket's head, and also cut into his shoulder.

'For the name of Jesus, and the defence of the Church, I am ready to die,' whispered Becket and, with those words, fell flat on his face. Richard le Breton stood over him and delivered a tremendous blow which servered the top of the skull; so violent a blow that the sword snapped as it met the marble floor.

Hugh of Horsea, a sub-deacon who had joined the murderers, was then taunted with having taken no part in the murder. He came up and thrust his sword into the wound, scattering Becket's brains over the pavement.

So, with Becket newly slain on the floor of his church, the murderers, beside themselves with rage and triumph, ran through the cloisters, shouting, 'The King's men, the King's men!' as if they had been in battle, for that was the war-cry of the English; and as they rode away, a thunderstorm of great violence broke over Canterbury, striking terror into the hearts of the people.

That night a strange scene took place before the high altar. The monks undressed the body of Becket for burial. They took off the incredible assortment of garments which covered him. First a brown mantle, then a white surplice, then a long coat of lamb's wool, then two woollen pelisses, then – to their utter astonishment – the black robe of a Benedictine monk. At the sight of it their grief and emotion knew no bounds. It astounded them to think that the Archbishop, whom they had regarded as a great noble, fond of purple and fine linen, should have secretly assumed a monk's habit.

'See what a true monk he was, and we knew it not!' they sobbed.

A greater surprise awaited them. When they stripped the body, they saw that Becket wore a hair shirt next to his skin and that beneath it his body was marked with the weals of scourging. So he was a more austere monk than any of them!

Then they saw a thing which is nauseating to our minds today, but in those days proved beyond doubt that a man had subdued the flesh and humiliated the body in order that his soul might shine; they saw that Becket's hair shirt crawled with vermin. Their joy and amazement at this revolting sight were boundless, and they cried, as indeed I can imagine a Coptic monk of Egypt crying today: 'He was one of God's saints!'

So on the very night he died, within a few hours of his martyrdom, Thomas à Becket was hailed as St Thomas of Canterbury.

The townspeople, who had filled the cathedral during he murder, fought for pieces of his attire and, washing the bloodstains, took them away as sacred relics. Miracles were reported almost at once. No one can say that they were invented by the monks, because the cathedral, having been desecrated, was closed for a year; the altars were stripped; the crucifixes were veiled; the bells were silenced, and the offices were conducted in the Chapter House without chanting. Indeed, there was every reason why the monks were desperately anxious to hush up the growing cult of St Thomas, for fear of the King and the terrible Randolph of Broc, who had seized the Archbishop's Palace and was their nextdoor neighbour. The measures taken to hush up these miracles from motives of fear and policy, and the failure to do so, is one of the most curious stories in the history of mediæval pilgrimage. Despite every discouragement, crowds of people began to visit Canterbury to pray at Becket's tomb, to touch his garments, or to apply to afflicted portions of the body water in which the archbishop's blood had been mixed. The wave of horror that had swept over Christendom was succeeded by a feeling of amazement and wonder when stories of the cures and miracles began to get about. The Pope was obliged to send a legation to England to enquire into them. They took back with them part of a tunic stained with Becket's blood, a fragment of his brain and some portions of the pavement on which he died, relics which are still preserved in the Church of Santa Maria Maggiore in Rome. The result of the enquiry was the canonisation of Becket three years after his murder and the appointment of 29 December as the Feast of St Thomas of Canterbury. There was now no further need for concealment. Canterbury became one of the great pilgrimage shrines in Europe. Churches dedicated to St Thomas sprang up in Christian countries all over the world. And four years after the murder a wonder-stricken, but approving world, heard that Henry II, barefoot and in sackcloth, had gone on foot to Canterbury to be scourged at Becket's tomb.

This tomb was in the crypt, where the monks had hurriedly buried the martyr the day after the murder. A strong wall of hewn stones roofed with marble had been built round the tomb, with two openings in either side so that a pilgrim might kneel down and, placing his head through one of the openings, bend forward and kiss the sarcophagus. It was in this humble posture, and clothed only in a hair shirt, that Henry II offered his penance. On his knees and with his head inside the cover of the tomb, he received upon his back five strokes of a rod from every bishop and abbot present and three from each of eighty monks.

After this ordeal he spent the night, bruised and fasting, upon the floor of the crypt, and in the morning, after early mass, he went his way to London, taking with him, as all pilgrims did for centuries to come, a small leaden phial full of the miraculous water.

It was a privilege to go round the Cathedral with Mr Wood, who knows every stone of the building. He showed me the place in the crypt where Becket was buried before the magnificent retro-choir behind the high altar was constructed to hold the relics. Fifty years to the day after the martyr's death, his remains were taken up from the crypt in a chest full of white flowers and placed in a shrine behind the high altar, which became one of the wonders of Christendom.

The piety of kings, nobles and common folk covered the shrine with gifts until it seemed to be one blaze of gold and precious stones. Resting on arches of masonry, the shrine was covered by a wooden canopy which could be drawn up on ropes towards the roof. As it slowly rose, pulled upward by the monks, the tinkling of the silver bells attached to it warned pilgrims all over the church that the martyr's shrine was being shown. As the blaze of gold and jewels came in sight, the pilgrims fell upon their knees, while the Prior, pointing with a white wand, described and valued ruby, diamond and emerald in English and French.

The shrine was dismantled and the relics removed by order of Henry VIII. Several cartloads of treasure were taken away, but one jewel, the great Regale of France, Henry VIII reserved for his own use. This was a ruby or a diamond of extraordinary size, the gift of Louis VII. Henry made it into a ring which he wore on his thumb.

What happened to the bones of Becket has been a mystery ever since. There is no actual proof that they were burned, as some have believed, neither is there positive proof that the monks buried them secretly before the Commissioners destroyed the shrine. A great sensation was caused in Canterbury in 1888, when workmen discovered in the crypt, not far from Becket's first tomb, a stone coffin containing the bones of a tall man. The skull appeared to have been smashed by a battle-axe or a sword. Were they the bones of Becket?

They were photographed – and you can buy photographs of them in Canterbury today for sixpence – and the skeleton was put together by competent anatomists, but no definite conclusion was ever reached about it. The bones were replaced in the coffin and, together with a sealed bottle containing a photograph of the skull and a record of the discovery, reburied in the same place in the crypt, where they lie today.

I went off one morning to see the almshouses of St Nicholas, about a mile and a half out of Canterbury on the Faversham road. They stand on top of a steep bank which commands the most typical piece of Kent you could wish to see. It has everything in it. It looks as though an artist has grouped in a small space more of Kent than Nature would have dared to do in even her most exuberant moments.

In the foreground are oast-houses. Beyond them the ground falls away, to rise opposite in slopes which are neatly planted with orchards and with regiments of hops; to the left, chalk downs are folded one against the other, ridged with trees, and among them, I think, are belts of typical black yews. If an artist wished to paint a picture called 'Kent', all he would have to do would be to take his paint-box to the almshouses of St Nicholas and put down what he saw in front of him.

The almshouses themselves make a lovely foreground to this panorama. The old grey church stands on the top of the bank, and the ground then slides steeply towards two groups of little grey cottages, each one with a bright front garden. Like all almshouses, the place is quiet and reposed. You know that Youth is finally excluded; but flowers and young birds come gaily into this retreat, invading autumn with something of spring's beauty.

There was no one to be seen as I stood there, until a baker's boy came whistling down the path and delivered a loaf to an old woman who has sat to Rembrandt many a time. Then two old men appeared with a lawn-mower, and advanced on the curved slope of grass. One old man was unbelievably smart. He wore a bowler hat, a winged collar and tie, and grey cotton gloves. His friend had a piece of string, which he attached to the front of the mower in order to assist the machine up-hill.

I watched them for some time, and thought how strange it was to see an old man mowing grass in a bowler hat and gloves. He was, I thought, some old pensioner who had lived all his life in a town, probably some small shop-keeper of Canterbury noted for his tidiness and his sobriety, and he had carried the outward symbols of rectitude with him to the grey almshouses on Harbledown Hill.

'Good morning,' I called when they came near me. 'A notice on the door says that the Sub-Prior will show the almshouses to visitors. Will you tell me where I can find him?'

The old man in the gloves gave me a friendly smile and gladly, I thought, left the lawn-mower.

'I'm the Sub-Prior,' he said, 'and I'll show you the place. Let's have a look at the church first of all.'

So we climbed up the steep bank together and approached the church of St Nicholas. I thought it delightful that these old people should live under the protection of the patron saint of children.

We entered a church which is in parts the same building put up in 1084 by William the Conqueror's friend, Lanfranc, when he was Archbishop of Canterbury. He built it as the chapel of a leper settlement, and I think I am right in saying that this was the first leper

hospital in England. It is still a fine old church and has not been injured by earnest restorers. There is some early Norman carving on the capitals, some beautiful early glass, and a grand open wooden roof.

The peculiarity of the building is that the pavement slopes so steeply from chancel downward to the door that, if you put an orange on the floor at the east end of the church, it would roll rapidly away and, if it went in a straight line, out of the church by the west door.

'And why do you think the floor slopes like that?' asked the Sub-Prior.

'I don't know.'

'Lepers!' he said triumphantly. 'Lepers were unclean, weren't they? They were diseased, weren't they? Now then, what would they do as soon as lepers had been to church? They'd swill the church down with water; and that's why the floor slopes away to the doors, to make it easier to give it a good wash down. I don't know whether there's another church floor like this in England, but if there is, you may be sure it was a leper's church.'

He then turned to me and said, holding his bowler hat in his hands and looking at me with an expression of great seriousness: 'Lanfranc endowed this place in the year 1084. That's a long time ago, isn't it? And I'm receiving benefit today.' He pointed a finger at his waistcoat and repeated: 'And I'm receiving benefit today; and thousands more before me, going back nearly a thousand years. That's a very wonderful thing, isn't it?'

It is a wonderful thing. Few good deeds have lived so long in the world. I thought that Archbishop Lanfranc, if he were leaning out of heaven at that moment, would have been touched to hear the old man's gratitude.

'How many of you are there now?' I asked.

'Twenty,' he replied. 'Men and women. We get free quarters, and twelve-and-six a week.'

As we went outside again, the Sub-Prior began to talk about the history of the place, and an interesting history it is. Leprosy is a

'The almshouses of St Nicholas stand on top of a steep bank which commands the most typical piece of Kent you could wish to see'

disease now happily absent from Europe, but once prevalent everywhere. As the traveller in the East knows, it is still visible there in the twisted and almost unrecognisable forms of the poor wretches who crawl about and ask for alms, though most of these are now being isolated and cared for in institutions.

In the Middle Ages every town in England had a leper house outside the walls, for the lepers were forbidden to live in towns, but they could enter them to beg, always with a wooden clapper to warn people of their unclean approach. They were encountered everywhere centuries ago, limping along in the high leather boots which they were made to wear.

There is still a good deal of mystery about the cause of infection, but it seems that both rich and poor were subject to the disease in the old days. Among royal lepers were, it is believed, Henry II and Henry IV. A Queen of England is said to have been a leper – Adelicia of Louvaine, the second wife of Henry I. It is probable that Robert the Bruce died of leprosy, so did a Bishop of London, Hugh de Orivalle, who was the first Bishop of London appointed by William the Conqueror.

This bishop was consecrated by Lanfranc in 1075. He died of leprosy ten years after, so that Lanfranc must have known him when the disease first showed itself. No doubt he discussed it with him and became familiar with his attempts to become cured. I wonder whether this had anything to do with Lanfranc's decision to found the leper hospital? Did he first become interested in the problem of the leper through his unfortunate Bishop of London? Is it not significant that he should have founded the leper hospital in 1084, the year before Hugh de Orivalle died?

The old man unlocked the door of a little museum which is full of peculiar relics. He went over to the window and pointed to the downs.

'The Pilgrims' Way to Canterbury crosses that down,' he said, 'and then dips into that

bit of wood there and comes up past this place. Every time the pilgrims came to Harbledown the lepers would go out and ask for alms, and always got something, for people were very kind to lepers in the old days.'

He unlocked the safe and showed me a leper's collecting-box. He brought out a pilgrim's flask. He then produced a great and historic relic: the yellow stone from Becket's shoe.

I do not know how the lepers gained possession of this relic, if it is what they claimed it to be, still less do I know how it survived the Reformation. Throughout the Middle Ages it was so famous that all pilgrims kissed it on their way to and from Canterbury.

The shoe has long since vanished, and the present occupants of St Nicholas show the yellow stone set in a wooden maser bowl. It was this stone which roused the anger of Dean Colet, the founder of St Paul's School, when he passed that way with Erasmus in 1512. As they came near, an old man tottered out and offered the upper part of a shoe bound with a brass ring.

'What,' cried the angry Dean, 'do these brutes imagine that we must kiss every good man's shoe? Why, by the same rule, they might offer his spittle to be kissed.'

But Erasmus added: 'For my part I pitied the old man, and gave him a small piece of money by way of consolation.'

After the relics had been put away, I discovered in conversation with the old man that he had reached that stage, which I suppose we all attain some day, when the past seems infinitely brighter than the present. Nothing was as good today as it was when he was young.

I looked at his grey cotton gloves and his bowler hat and wondered what saga of shopkeeping lay behind him. Had he been a grocer or a draper? I thought, somehow, a draper. It was odd to see a man who had obviously never had anything to do with gardens spending his last years tending the earth with gloved hands. At last I ventured.

'What did you do in the old days?' I asked.

'Me? My job?' he asked. 'You've heard of Dean Farrar, of course? I was his gardener.'

When I arrived at Walmer I found it was the one day in the week, a Thursday, on which Walmer Castle, the residence of the Lord Warden of the Cinque Ports, is open to the public.

I bought a ticket and was admitted to a garden which I thought was almost perfect. It was simple and full of colour and scent and its peculiarity is that it is made on the edge of the moat that runs round the castle.

I should have been willing to while away my sixpenny ticket in the garden, enjoying the scent of the flowers and the hum of the bees, but I felt that I ought to know something about the rooms in which the Iron Duke laid down his eighty-three years.

An official took me through a fearsome-looking gateway into a house which has been made almost hysterically cheerful in contrast to the grim bastions of its exterior. The problem of making a home out of a rugged mass of masonry, constructed with the sole object of repelling first the Spaniards and then the French, cannot have been easy. Lord and Lady Willingdon were in residence, and they suffer the public to tramp through their charming drawing-room once a week, on the way to the room where the Duke of Wellington died in 1852.

As soon as I entered this room, it captured me completely. Its sternness, its simplicity, its touch of almost priggish discomfort, and its lonely pathos, seemed to reflect the life that had been lived there. It has been kept, whether by accident or design I do not know, almost exactly as it was the day he died. Nothing has been altered. You almost expect the door to open and to see the old Duke, hook-nosed and silver-haired, glide in with a frosty gleam of blue eyes.

Wellington made no concessions to old age. With the whole of Walmer Castle to live in, he preferred one small bed-sitting-room modelled on the tent of a subaltern; and a frugal subaltern at that. His bed was an iron camp bed three feet wide. He allowed himself no luxurious blankets, but only a German quilt. The one sybaritic touch is a horse-hair pillow covered with chamois leather, and this he used to take about with him whenever he spent a night away.

A mahogany desk, a few books, a few engravings, a reading-desk, at which he wrote his letters standing, and one or two chairs, complete the furniture. An ivory statuette of Napoleon sitting astride a chair used to stand on the mantel-piece.

'That was how he commanded at the Battle of Wagram,' Wellington once told a certain Mr Tucker as he pointed to the statue. Such was the simple room in which the hero of Waterloo spent much of his life from the age of sixty until his death.

'He was always called at six of a morning,' said the guide in an appropriate military voice. 'He went for an early morning walk, ate very little breakfast, came up here and read, or wrote letters, standing at that desk by the window. He answered all his letters himself, and people used to write to him about all sorts of silly things, just to get a reply. Sometimes they got ticked off good and proper. At eleven-thirty at night he used to light a candle and come up here to bed.'

This grand old Tory, who resisted every

reform with the stern formality of his native century, the eighteenth, remained a national hero all his later life, with one brief exception. When he opposed the Reform Bill, he rode slowly through London, high-nosed and bleak, to the jeers of a mob and to a hail of brickbats and mud. As he reached Apsley House in Piccadilly, he turned and said to the police constable by his side: 'An odd day for them to choose.' He had remembered that it was the anniversary of Waterloo.

As he grew older, his rôle merged naturally from that of Achilles into that of Nestor. They consulted him about everything. When the Crystal Palace was first erected in Hyde Park, the London sparrows failed to show proper respect for the assembled works of art, and with so much glass about, it was impossible to shoot them. So the Queen sent for the Duke: the dear Duke would know what to do.

'Try sparrow-hawks, Ma'am,' he said instantly.

'It was Wellington's last victory,' commented Mr Philip Guedalla, in *The Duke*.

Perhaps his last victory was the conquest of age. At eighty he was as bright and sprightly as a robin. To the public, he was always a tight-buttoned, reserved figure, aloof from the warmer passions of life, and great would have been the astonishment could the public have seen the Duke now and then behind the ramparts of Walmer.

He loved children to stay with him. Before dinner he would dress, always in the uniform of Lord Warden, a blue coat with red facings and tight, white overalls strapped under the boot, and would sit reading the newspaper. The children then played a game which they called 'the Battle of Waterloo'. This began when one of them threw a cushion at the Duke's paper.

Lord Stanhope, in his *Notes of Conversations*

'I felt that I ought to know something about the rooms in which the Iron Duke laid down his eighty-three years'

with the Duke of Wellington, tells how on one occasion the old man learned that the small children of Lord and Lady Robert Grosvenor, who were staying with him, loved to receive letters by post. Every day he took the trouble to write to each of them a careful little letter which was posted and delivered by a Castle servant.

He was kind not only to the children of friends, but also to those of strangers. One day a woman and two children were being turned out of the Castle grounds when he rode up and apologised to them.

'Never mind, never mind,' he said. 'You're quite welcome to go where you will. And, by the way, bring the children here tomorrow at one o'clock, and I'll show them all about the place myself.'

They found luncheon ready and, after showing them round the gardens, Wellington took from his pockets some half-sovereigns which he had tied up in blue ribbon, and he hung one coin round each neck.

He was fond of filling his pockets with surprises, and it is recorded that on one almost unbelievable occasion he appeared to the children who were staying at the Castle dressed up like a Christmas tree, with toys tied all over him! No one living at the time would have believed this, for in public he never permitted one hint of human feeling to escape him. He was an icy, forbidding old man, high-handed, formal, and bitingly candid in his comments about men and affairs.

He died in the little bastion room after only a few hours' illness. 'I feel very ill,' he said to his valet. 'Send for the apothecary.' Those were his last words. He had a fit in the night, and died the next day, aged eighty-three. He was buried to the sound of a nation's grief, and when the guns boomed across London as his funeral car swayed through the hushed streets to St Paul's, England said farewell to the eighteenth century.

The guide took me downstairs to a room fitted up as a museum. I saw the last coat worn by Wellington and the telescope he used at Waterloo.

There were two gruesome relics; his death-mask and the silk handkerchief which was used to tie up his jaw. A certificate attached to the handkerchief, signed by James Kendle, the valet, stated that the handkerchief slipped from the jaw but the knot never became untied, and so remains today the knot which was made on 14 September 1852.

While I was looking at these things, a huge man, almost as wide as he was tall, came into the room. He was bubbling over with vitality and high spirits. Buried in the flesh of his huge face was the mischievous countenance of a boy aged ten.

He swept up the guide and myself in his terrific enthusiasm, and soon we were listening to a lecture about the Iron Duke. It was a good lecture. We tried to interrupt it once or twice, but without success.

When I got this large man alone in the garden, I told him that I had enjoyed his discourse and we sat beneath a tree.

'Wellington was a grand old boy,' he said. 'Although I don't agree with any of his politics, he was a grand old boy. I'm writing a book to be called *Pattern of English Life*, in which I have a lot to say about the old man. You heard some of my book inside, didn't you?'

'I was interested to hear you call Wellington the first modern English gentleman.'

'I think the modern idea of the Englishman as a quiet, silent, stoical bloke, who considers it bad form to show his feelings, dates from Wellington. His influence on English life was so terrific that the public-school Englishman copied his unemotionalism. "Behaving like a gentleman" was Wellington's contribution to English manners.

'As a nation we are by nature emotional to a degree. We're sloppy and sentimental, and it's only within the last century that crying in public has gone out of fashion. Think of the Elizabethans! They were always in tears. The whole House of Commons used to burst out crying! Think of Nelson, an Englishman of the old type, emotional, sentimental, bombastic. How different were Nelson and Wellington; what worlds apart they were! On the only occasion they ever met, in a waiting-room in Whitehall, Wellington thought Nelson was no gentleman. Why? Simply because Nelson talked too much. It wasn't done! 'Kiss me, Hardy!' Can you imagine Wellington saying that? Of course you can't: it was the voice of good old dramatic, tearful Elizabethan England. Nelson was the last Elizabethan. Wellington was the first modern English gentleman.'

'I shall buy your book.'

'That's the way to talk!' shouted my large friend, and, wringing my hand heartily, he rushed like a frolicsome elephant through the garden.

I once met a Turkish diplomat who had just arrived in this country for the first time. He spoke English almost perfectly, having, as he said it, belonged to the class of Turk which forty years ago was much 'governess-ridden', the governesses being English.

I asked him if England were not a surprising change from the mountains and plains of his own country; and he thought a moment.

'Yes, England is delightful,' he said. 'But when I go out into the country, I have the feeling that I have fallen into a plate of spinach.'

To one accustomed to the hard outlines of mountains covered in snow in winter and burned brown in summer, or to plains that lie to the sky, stone covered and almost bare of herbage, I suppose the neat greenness of the English landscape is at first unbelievable. The Weald of Kent is perhaps what my Turkish friend would call spinach country: incredibly green, incredibly neat and – incredibly English. This is the part of Kent that has gained for the county the title of the 'Garden of

England', and on a sunny day in summer you could find no better name for it.

Even a casual glance at the map of the Kentish Weald reveals a remarkable number of villages ending in 'hurst' and 'den'. Penshurst, Ashurst, Speldhurst, Lamberhurst, Hawkhurst, Goudhurst, Staplehurst, Shadoxhurst, and many another lie within a comparatively small area. So also do the 'dens': Bethersden, Smarden, Standen, High Halden, Tenterden, Biddenden, Benenden, Frittenden, Rolvenden and Marden. You can go on for miles in this part of Kent, passing through village after village with the same termination.

These names mean that once upon a time all such villages, now in open country, were dotted about in a thick forest. 'Hurst' is the Anglo-Saxon 'hyrst', a wood, and 'den', or 'dene', is a hollow, or clearing in the trees. No matter where you find 'hursts', 'dens' and 'holts', places that contain the words 'oak', 'ash', 'birk' or birch, and 'elm', you can be sure that the country was densely wooded at some time, even though today it may be as bald as a billiard table.

Many people do not realise that the English countryside is always changing its appearance. I have met some who will take their stand on a hill and believe, as they look around them, that they are gazing upon the same scene which met the eyes of our remote ancestors. Except maybe on the chalk downs of Kent and Sussex, and on Salisbury Plain, this is not so. An Elizabethan would see

'Smarden'

enormous changes in the appearance of the country, while a Saxon and a Norman might have some difficulty in recognising their own lands.

When the Romans came to Britain they saw a forest lying everywhere in the lowlands, covering the Weald of Kent, much of the Midlands, many of the river valleys, and stopping short only at the marshes and fens. Above this sea of green rose the smooth outlines of the South Downs where primitive man, lifted above the dangerous forests, had lived his life.

How much of the forests the Romans cut down during the four hundred years of their occupation is unknown, but it is no doubt right to imagine Roman Britain as a land in which straight paved roads ran through forests and across marshes to well-planned walled towns.

Both Saxon and Norman inherited the forest, and the story of the country's transformation during those periods is that of the woodman and his axe; the making of fields from forests, the clearing of the 'hyrst', and the planting of wooden shacks in the 'dens'.

Physical changes such as forest clearance, the draining of fens and marshes, changes in agriculture and in land tenure, and the use of brick in building, have each made some difference to the appearance of England. Our grandfathers contributed the railway, the telegraph and tree-planted landscape; and we have added the electric cable, the grid, the bypass and the arterial road. It is not, therefore, right to talk about the 'natural beauty' of the country; it is a beauty that is anything but natural, the result of centuries of hard work and innovation.

If I had to give a prize to a 'hurst', I should award it to Goudhurst, and if to a 'den', to Biddenden. Goudhurst stands on a hill, and is well worth going to see as an example of a fine Kentish village. I suppose the highest point is only four hundred feet above the sea, but the view over the Weald might be from the top of

Sinai. The church at Goudhurst is fine, and contains an Elizabethan sculptured tomb, a life-sized man in armour, a Culpeper, and his wife, kneeling in prayer face to face, and below them, on a smaller scale, their regiment of children.

'If I had to give a prize to a "den",
I should award it to Biddenden'

It is remarkable that the Elizabethans could make such devout and touching tombs, while the Jacobeans, only a few years afterwards, perpetrated almost comic memorials, such as the Selby tomb in Offham Church. This shows Sir William Selby and his nephew, life-sized and in armour, reclining in a hideously uncomfortable attitude on a marble shelf, one above the other, as though they are having an uneasy night in a sleeping-car.

Biddenden, though only a few miles away, is as unlike Goudhurst as it can be, lying in flat country. A striking signpost at the entrance shows what appear to be two Cretan maidens joined together at the shoulder, and they remind the traveller that he has come to the village of the Biddenden Cakes.

I went into a cake-shop and asked the girl for a Biddenden Cake, expecting to be told that they are produced only at Easter-time. To my surprise, she went to a tin and produced a flattish biscuit, about four inches long and two inches wide, on which is a primitive raised design showing the Siamese twins of Biddenden, joined at the shoulder and hip. Above their heads are the words 'Eliza and Mary Chalkhurst'.

*'Two Cretan maidens
joined together at the shoulder'*

'How many would you like?' the girl asked.

I said that I was surprised to be able to buy even one.

'Oh, we're often asked for them,' she said. 'We keep them in stock all the year. They are exactly the same as the Biddenden Cakes that are given away on Easter Day.'

The tradition is that about the year 1100 Siamese twins were born at Biddenden and were named Eliza and Mary Chalkhurst. When they reached the age of thirty-four one of them died, and the survivor refused to be separated from the body of ther sister, a feat, incidentally, far beyond the power of mediæval surgery. 'As we came together, we will go together,' said Eliza or Mary; for I do not know who was the survivor. In a few hours she too was dead.

The sisters are said to have left certain land to the parish, still known as the 'Bread and Cheese Land', and from the revenue an annual Easter 'Dole' of Biddenden Cakes and bread and cheese is distributed to all and sundry on Easter Monday. I believe the 'cakes' were once thrown down to the crowds from the church tower.

Although the gift is still distributed and the money comes in as steadily as ever, the antiquarians have cast doubt on the story of the Siamese twins. Hasted, the Kent historian, who was born in 1732, believed that the land was given by two apparently normal ladies named Preston. He said that the rough drawing of the two women on the Biddenden Cakes was only about eighty years old in his day, and that they represented, not Siamese twins, but two of the poor widows for whom the 'Dole' was originally established.

It is strange that this very ordinary bequest has taken such a hold on popular imagination and given Biddenden so wide a fame. No doubt the story of the Siamese twins has had a lot to do with it.

From Biddenden I went south and was soon over the border into Sussex.

CHAPTER FOUR

I enter Sussex and go to Battle to see the field of Senlac. In Alfriston I see a fine church and, in Lewes I find the last ironworks in Sussex. Crossing the Downs, I come to Pyecombe, where they make shepherds' crooks, and, by way of pretty Fittleworth, I go to Bignor, to see the Roman villa, then south to Arundel and Chichester.

'Why is it that the oxen, the swine, the women, and all the other animals, are so long-legged in Sussex?' asked John Burton in 1771. 'May it be from the difficulty of pulling the feet out of so much mud by the strength of the ankles that the muscles get stretched, as it were, and the bones lengthened?'

The worker in Wealden clay still knows that 'Sowsexe is full of dyrt and myre', and to our ancestors that was the distinguishing feature of the county.

Until almost modern times the roads in Sussex were so unspeakably bad that judges on circuit rarely ventured beyond the border towns of Horsham and East Grinstead, and when Defoe was in Sussex only a little over two hundred years ago, he saw a lady of 'very good quality' going to church in a coach drawn by six oxen. He also noted that felled trees sometimes lay for a year, until the muddy roads were dry enough for them to be dragged away by ox teams.

It was undoubtedly the horror which the roads of Sussex inspired in the minds of our ancestors which enabled the county to keep to itself, and retain that rich dialect and mass of local custom and superstition which delighted the people who wrote about Sussex even as recently as fifty years ago.

Since that time Sussex has suffered an invasion almost as complete and overwhelming as that which transformed the northern towns during the first stages of the Industrial Revolution. But the Sussex invasion was not of workers, but of retired people and wealthy weekenders. The Sussex squire has been replaced by the London stock-jobber, and the Sussex cottage has become the paradise of the London financier. It is interesting to notice, as you motor through Sussex today, that while the old squire, like Charles II, took a long time in dying, the new squires are dying by the score, as the 'To be sold' boards which are to be seen outside so many large houses clearly indicate.

The Sussex coast probably contains more thriving and populous towns than any similar coastal area in England. They lie in a long chain: Hastings, St Leonards, Eastbourne, Brighton, Worthing, Littlehampton and Bognor Regis. Those Sussex seaside towns alone have a resident population of nearly half a million.

Some of the settlements on the Sussex coast are among the most hideous objects in modern England. They have been run up by speculative builders and amateur builders, and have ruined large parts of what was once a superb stretch of coast. The only consolation is that already they seem to be falling down.

Towns like Eastbourne and Brighton should increase in dignity with the years, if local authorities will keep a keen watch on architects. Eastbourne is already pleasantly Edwardian, and Brighton is, with the exception of Regent's Park in London, the most perfect example of the Regency period in England. But already in Brighton the rot is setting in with box flats; and if it goes on, no one with any taste will ever go there.

The Sussex invasion still continues, and is having its effect on that older agricultural Sussex which carries on unobtrusively in the small towns and villages. The famous Southdown sheep are being driven off the Downs, for the growth of the huge seaside towns has created a tremendous demand for milk, with the result that cows are now becoming more profitable than sheep.

Another factor in the dwindling of the Southdown flocks is the disturbance caused to sheep by the advance of suburbia and the appearance of weekend horsemen, and, worst of all, hikers with their dogs.

If towns lived up to their names, Battle would be a place where men went red in the face with rage, gnashing their teeth and pushing

'The Sussex cottage has become the paradise of the London financier'

people off the pavement. But in reality it is one of the drowsiest and most peaceful little towns in Sussex. It has its share of the cafés and antique shops which establish themselves in all places where visitors assemble, and the only danger likely to be encountered in Battle today is the prices of the antiques.

Only in England perhaps could Battle Abbey become a girls' school. Indeed it might seem to a foreigner to be one of the baffling inconsistencies of English life that the place where the future of England was changed should be devoted to the education of young ladies; for here, if anywhere, is a sacred national shrine. But when you approach the fine gateway of Battle Abbey it is soon made clear to you that Battle is a girls' school first and a national shrine a long way after.

As you go in, it is true that the gate-keeper will ring a bell to summon a guide. But the guide may, or may not appear. He did not appear for me. But better than any guide would be a few intelligently written notices near the site of the high altar and on the Terrace which overlooks the scene of the Norman advance. It would be a compliment to the public if a little of the gate money were used for this purpose.

The stranger is obliged to follow a 'visitors' route', which leads him here and there and roundabout. Now and again his meditations are pleasantly interrupted by maidenly cries of 'love-fifteen' and the phut of a tennis ball against a racket; but the girls of Battle remain carefully invisible behind hedges.

Every schoolboy knows that Battle Abbey was built by William the Conqueror in fulfilment of a vow made before the Battle of Hastings. He did not like the look of the Saxon army. In spite of the fact that it had been drinking and making merry the night before, it had a tough appearance as it stood on the well-chosen hill, and the Conqueror vowed that should victory be granted to him, he would endow an abbey on the battlefield.

The abbey he built was a tremendous place

about a mile in area and endowed with lands stretching for three miles round its walls. The abbot had a seat in Parliament, and among the abbey's privileges was the right to give sanctuary to all unhappy wretches and fugitives from justice who gained the safety of its doors.

The Abbey was pulled down by the orders of Henry VIII, but the foundations still remain and it is possible to see where the altar stood and where the apse of the church ended. It is recorded that William chose for the high altar the exact place where Harold fell.

'Battle Abbey was pulled down, but the foundations still remain'

I should like to see a notice here telling people that they are standing on the place where the Saxon army camped on an unlucky day, Friday, 13 October, in 1066. There were about twelve thousand of them, mostly rough countrymen, badly armed and ill disciplined, slovenly, careless, but without fear. It is said that they drank and danced round their fires all night, crying 'bublie' and 'wassail', 'laticome' and 'drinkhail', while in the opposing camp the Norman army confessed to its sins and attended Mass. It seems that once, years before, Harold had sworn on the bones of a martyr not to contest William's claim to the English crown, and those relics the Duke had brought with him and now carried into battle in a bag round his neck.

His army was not much greater in numbers than Harold's, but it was infinitely superior in its weapons and theory of warfare. It was completely up-to-date. Even cross-bows, which had just been invented, had a place in it. Most important of all, the Norman cavalry was the last word in shock tactics.

In the hazy autumn morning of 14 October, the two armies faced each other over a mile of Sussex: Harold and his Saxons securely posted on the hill that ever after was to be known as Battle, a forest behind him and steep slopes guarding his flanks: William and his Normans on Telham Hill, with the ground sloping down to Senlac Bottom, then up again to the place where the Saxons stood shield to shield.

They fought from nine in the morning until the shadows of afternoon began to fall. Then victory came, not perhaps to the bravest, but to the most efficient. The Saxons fought as their ancestors had fought, on foot, behind the shield-wall, but the Normans came charging at them on dray horses, crying 'Ha Rou!' and hurling spears before they hacked at the footmen with their swords. As twilight fell, the last desperate fight was waged round the Red Dragon of Wessex, where Harold and his thanes died one by one.

Duke William pitched his tent among the dead on the hill of Battle. Three horses had been killed under him, yet he was unhurt. And on this tragic field he marked out the great abbey that was to rise there in order that God's pardon might be asked for the blood that had been shed there.

If you walk down from the place of the high altar and come to the terrace, you will see a few fields, some cows grazing, and trees, a quiet English scene. It was across those fields that the Normans charged to victory, and it seems strange that the destiny of England could have been settled in a few small meadows. What a noise the Battle of Hastings has made in the world, yet what a minor brawl it was! What minor brawls all wars were in ancient times: a few men trying to kill each other in a meadow. It is only today, when Man calls himself civilised, that whole nations go to war, and even include their women and children in it.

When I returned to the entrance the gatekeeper was waiting for me, and during my absence he had learned my name.

'You're one of the old families, sir,' he said waggishly. 'You must see your name on the Roll.'

He led me to an illuminated parchment which is framed beneath the arch and, running his finger down, stopped at the name 'Morton'. This was the Battle Abbey Roll; and for the first time I knew that I had come over with William the Conqueror.

'You'd be surprised,' he said, 'by the number of people who come to see their names in the Roll. They come from all parts, even America.'

Unfortunately for us noble Normans, the Battle Abbey Roll is not what it pretends to be. A list of William's followers compiled from Domesday, and other contemporary material, does not agree with it at all.

Still the gatekeeper of Battle is always glad to recognise an old boy.

I left the admirable town of Eastbourne with the intention of visiting the Long Man of Wilmington. As I approached him, rain began to fall and continued to fall with such vehemence that the Long Man was blotted from view. Still, for a moment I saw him in white against the downland, an immense figure two hundred and forty feet in length, walking with a staff in each hand.

Like the White Horse on the Berkshire Downs and the Cerne Giant of Dorset, whom he greatly resembles, the Long Man of Wilmington is an outlined figure formed by the removal of the downland turf. Who first removed the turf is one of the mysteries of England. The figure has been attributed to Ancient Briton, Dane, Saxon and mediæval monk, but no one seems to know why one or other of these people should have gone to the trouble of putting the Long Man on the hill.

'The Long Man of Wilmington'

Until sixty-five years ago the figure's outline was merely a shallow trench cut in the Downs, and the Long Man was visible in those days only at early morning or at sunset when an oblique light fell upon him, or during a thaw in winter when the snow lay longer in the trenches than on the surrounding grass. But in 1874 enthusiasts outlined the Long Man in white bricks, thus making him one of the famous landmarks in Sussex.

I went on to that pretty bit of country where the Cuckmere winds through meadows to the sea, and, overlooking the stream, I saw the fine flint church of Alfriston and the pretty village, which is one of the most delightful and best-known in the whole of Sussex.

People go there in thousands in the summer to see how beautiful and how natural an old Sussex village can be. I have no doubt that Alfriston is to many of them a sentimental haven, the ideal village which most Englishmen keep in their hearts. Without appearing to be deliberately antique, Alfriston lives up to its reputation with dignity and grace. The old houses gaze at each other across the narrow street without self-consciousness, like old people who have done their job in life but are by no means in the grave. Indeed, from their willingness to provide tea and sell fudge, it is clear that the old houses of Alfriston fully appreciate the profit to be made from those who are so starved of beauty that they will go miles to look at a thatch.

The Star of Alfriston is one of the best mediæval inns in England: an old striped house, with an overhanging storey and a roof of patinated Horsham stone. It is said that it once belonged to Battle Abbey and was a pilgrims' rest house on the road to the shrine of St Richard of Chichester. I should think this is very likely so, for the Star, without the Garter or the Crown, is an ancient religious symbol, though not the Star of the Magi. It was the mediæval symbol of the Virgin, just as the Pole Star was the symbol of the Church, a sign that generally carried with it the motto in Latin, 'He who does not look at me goes astray.'

I was surprised by the size and shape of St Andrew's Church at Alfriston, a splendid flint church in the form of a Greek cross. It is not, like so many old churches, a mass of architectural styles, but is the creation of one period,

'The pretty village of Alfriston'

about 1370. I have rarely seen so fine and large a country church with so few tombs in it worth looking at, but it has something even more interesting. It is one of the few churches in England – I think there are not more than three – in which you can see the hooks that used to hold the Lenten Veil in pre-Reformation days.

In the days of Roman Catholic England a veil which hid the altar from the congregation was hung in churches during Lent. It was drawn only during the reading of the Gospel at Mass and on Saturdays and remained in position from the first Sunday in Lent until Wednesday in Holy Week. How old was this custom can be guessed when King Alfred in the year 878 imposed a fine of 20 shillings as the penalty for tearing down a Lenten Veil.

It is probably that the veils were a relic of the once universal custom of hiding the altar,

'I was surprised by the size and shape of St Andrew's Church at Alfriston'

not only in Lent, but all the year, a custom which the Eastern Church still observes. Anyone who has attended a Greek, Armenian, Syrian or a Coptic Mass, will recollect that the altar is hidden by a permanent wooden screen with a small central opening, and that, at the moment of consecration, the deacon pulls a curtain across it, so that the celebrant is concealed from the congregation.

The Lenten Veil in the Western Church was perhaps the last memory of the *ikonostasis*, or screen, which was once common to the whole of Christendom; and Alfriston should be proud of this relic.

In the north wall of the chancel I noticed another interesting thing: a deep niche rather like a tomb, which bears, at one side, the sculptured figure of a curled-up dog and, at the other, the head of a woman. In an excellent little sixpenny guide which I bought in Alfriston it is suggested that this niche may be 'the tomb of the founder'; but it is nothing of the kind, it is an Easter Sepulchre, and this again takes us back to the rites of the Roman Church.

'The sculptured figure of a curled-up dog'

It was the custom on Maundy Thursday, when the altar was stripped, the images shrouded and the whole church in mourning, for the priest to place the Sacrament in a tabernacle and carry it in procession to this recess in the north wall of the chancel. Members of the congregation watched beside it day and night. Then the priest would come early on the morning of Easter Sunday and, taking up the Host, would go to the altar singing the anthem, 'Christ is risen'.

This beautiful custom, which is still observed in the Roman Church, is seen also in various forms in the Eastern Church. It is a symbol of the Entombment and the Resurrection. The Greeks, the Syrians, the Armenians and the Copts each have their own traditional rite. On Maundy Thursday or Good Friday some of them bury an ikon, or a crucifix in a coffin, some place a picture of Jesus in rose leaves, and these are brought forth in triumph on Easter Sunday to shouts of joy.

The rain was still beating against the windows and gurling into the gutters, so I settled down in the church to read my sixpenny *History of Alfriston* (seventh edition) and first published by the author, Florence Pagden

(Mrs Hubert Winstanley) in 1899. I wonder how many topographical books will read as well in forty years' time.

I learned that Alfriston, despite its deceptive air of innocence, was once a desperate place for smugglers. A famous gangster of the period was named Stanton Collins, who had a feud with a Mr Brooker. It appears that Mr Brooker, who also had his weaknesses, fell in love with his deceased wife's sister, which so horrified the minister of the chapel, a worthy man called Mr Betts, that he refused to solemnise the marriage.

Mr Brooker, who was a person of power and influence, deposed the minister by the simple process of arriving early for chapel and placing an itinerant preacher in the pulpit. Poor Mr Betts arrived to take the service and found his rival there before him, and he sensibly made no fuss, but took a seat in a pew and waited to see what would happen.

It happened quickly. Stanton Collins and his boys, drinking over at the George, heard what had occurred and, scenting an excellent chance to get even with Mr Brooker, broke into the chapel, dragged the alien preacher out of the pulpit and reinstated poor Mr Betts, demanding that he should resume the service while they stood guard round him. Mr Betts gave out the hymn, 'God moves in a mysterious way'.

There are one or two excellent little pen pictures in this book.

'During the incumbency of one of our numerous vicars,' says the author, 'an old woman was employed to ring the bell for the week-day services, and an odd sight it was. She was a masculine-looking woman, very tall and thin; her face, drawn into a perfect network of wrinkles, was surrounded by a poke bonnet, her gaunt figure attired in a dress of faded green rep curtain, and an apron of coarse sacking, which was tied at the waist and knees. The bell being heavy, each time she pulled the rope she was lifted off the ground, displaying thus at intervals a pair of beautifully clean white stockings and men's hobnailed boots. Her severe expression and loud grating voice caused her to be spoken of as repulsive; but, as I knew her, she was ever kind and good-natured.'

The sun appearing, as miraculously it did, I took the lane behind the church and, crossing a bridge over the Cuckmere, went up a curved field to Lullington, which boasts 'the smallest church in England'. This is not quite honest, because it is not a church at all, but only the sixteen-foot long chancel of a church, the rest of the building having vanished in some cataclysm.

I believe that the smallest church – and, of course, I mean a complete church – is that of Culbone, near Porlock, in Somerset, which, if I remember rightly, is about 35 feet by 12 feet; and I am sure Sussex cannot beat that. Still, Lullington among its buttercups with the big rain-clouds curving overhead, and Alfriston with its beautiful old houses and its church, are the kind of places that make one thankful to be alive in England.

I walked up the hill into Lewes, a town that has always been the pride of Sussex. Though new-comers like Brighton, with its population of 147,000, have established themselves in the neighbourhood, Lewes, with its 10,000 inhabitants, remains the capital and the sentimental heart of the county.

The older I grow, the more I appreciate towns like Lewes. There is nothing meretricious about them. They have roots as well as branches. They have weathered storms and dangers in the past, and they survive to prove to us that, while life is often dangerous, it need not neccessarily end fatally.

There is both courage and experience in the stones of Lewes and among the qualities of such towns is detachment, not from life but from hasty judgments; a quality gained perhaps in the process of watching so many generations go past; so many brides riding in their happiness, so many babes lifted to the windows, so many old men going for the last time to church.

And through it all runs the connecting link of a local spirit: the feeling that sheep-tracks, which became lanes and then grew into roads, still carry men to the old town on the hill, men who are not unlike their fathers or their grandfathers. As long as you can meet someone called Verrall or Vidler in the streets of Lewes, there's nothing much wrong with the town.

I walked, as everyone does, to the ruins of the old flint castle which stand on top of the hill. It is not an interesting castle to look at, but the view from its tower is magnificent. You can see the low country all round and below you the red-tiled houses cluster almost in terraces, lying in a bowl whose rim is the smooth green contour of the Downs.

The Sussex Archæological Society, which is one of the best organisations of the kind in England, has preserved in a house below the castle, and also in the castle itself, that queer assortment of articles which tells how many extraordinary things have happened in the long life of our country.

I looked at a Roman altar which some remote inhabitant of Britain had erected to Constantine the Great. It was discovered in a garden at West Worthing. There is a Spanish gun found in Newhaven Harbour, also a cannon ball, made possibly for the ships of Francis Drake; a Roman paving tile; village stocks; and a trolley used on Bonfire Night to draw tar barrels through the streets of Lewes. In the gardens of the castle are long, old-fashioned guns forged in Sussex, and round the wall, or rather let into it, are some of the original railings from St Paul's Churchyard, which were removed from London in 1874 during a street widening. These railings were made of good old Sussex charcoal iron in the reign of Queen Anne. When they were taken

'I walked up the hill into Lewes'

*'In the gardens of the castle
are long, old-fashioned guns'*

down from the churchyard some of them crossed the Atlantic, and can be seen today in the High Park at Toronto. The story is that they were shipped in a vessel that sank, but they were recovered by divers.

Later in the morning I was lamenting the complete disappearance of the Sussex iron industry to a friendly and knowable stranger in the White Hart.

'Oh dear, no!' he said. 'We have the last ironworks here in Lewes. You turn to the left by the traffic lights and go straight down until you come to the Phœnix Works. If you're interested, they'll be only too glad to show the place to you.'

I took his advice, and found a modern, prosperous-looking works humming with activity. They were making lamp-posts, iron manhole gratings, and a casting for linotype machines. It was good to see Sussex men still working iron as their fathers did long ago. The

horses that charged to death at Bannockburn were shod with Sussex iron, and the first cannon forged in England was made at Buxted, in Sussex.

'Why did the iron trade leave Sussex?' I asked.

'It was the first industry to go north and west to the coalfields,' I was told. 'Sussex iron used to be smelted with wood and charcoal. As you know, Sussex was a thickly wooded county in the old times, but the iron works ate up all the forests. Not only did wood become scarce, but laws were made to prevent deforestation, and in Elizabeth's reign new forges and furnaces were prohibited by Act of Parliament. It's difficult to imagine what Sussex must have looked like in those days. The iron stone was mined here, it was then crushed and smelted at the foundry, and "fined" at the forge.

'Whole districts were cleared of trees to feed our furnaces. Thousands of miners, hammer-men, foundrymen, charcoal burners, forge hands and smiths were at work until about three hundred years ago. But the trees couldn't keep pace with the furnaces. Then people began to grow wood for the furnaces. Even that didn't help. And gradually the Sussex wood-fired industry died away and the coal-fired industry of Wales, the Midlands and the North took its place.'

As we were walking round the yard, we encountered a pile of pig-iron.

'One thing good old Sussex has given to the world is the term "pig-iron",' said my guide. 'Have you wondered why a bar of iron should be called a pig? Well, this is the reason. In the old days the metal, after having been heated for a fortnight, was allowed to run out of the furnace upon channels which had been made to receive it. There was one main channel, and a lot of smaller ones leading from it. The resemblance to a sow and her piglets was pretty obvious to anyone brought up in the country. So the word "pig" for a bar of iron has passed into the English language; but I don't think you could find many people who could tell you the origin of it.'

Upstairs, over the modern works, is perhaps the best collection in the world of Sussex iron: cannon, firebacks, wrought iron, pots, and even tombstones. It is obvious that most of the 'genuine antique Sussex firebacks', which are now sold at great price by antique dealers must be fakes: nothing could be easier than to take a casting from these old specimens.

Although the iron industry has left Sussex, the art of the smith lingers in the county. We can look upon the Sussex blacksmiths, who still make beautiful wrought-iron gates, as the last vestige of a great mediæval industry.

One other thing interested me in Lewes. This is a house known as Anne of Cleves House, whose picturesque appearance is marred by a shop sign that invades its ancient roof-line with the words: 'Stop here. Finest fish frying nightly.'

Anne of Cleves, the fourth wife of Henry VIII, whom he so rudely described as 'the Flanders mare', was the only one of his six wives who retired safely with a pension of £3,000 a year and the official title of 'sister'. Living in placid retirement, Anne not only outlived Henry by ten years, but had the satisfaction of watching him blunder twice again into matrimony. Her solid figure and placid, homely face were observed at the Coronation of 'Bloody' Mary as she rode in a coach with Princess Elizabeth. Indeed, Anne of Cleves seems to have been one of history's few perfect step-mothers. Both Mary and Elizabeth were devoted to her, and she to them. What talks they must have had about 'your poor dear father'.

I was not much interested in the house itself, except in so far as it helped to pay this admirable woman a part of her alimony, for there is no proof that she ever lived there. There are a number of smiliar houses in Sussex linked vaguely with her name, and when caretakers cannot prove that she inhabited them, people go away thinking the association is pure invention. But they probably were part of Anne's rent roll: the price she gladly accepted in exchange for Henry's dangerous affection.

It is a little late in the day to sing praises of the Sussex Downs. They are among the most written of and walked over portions of England, and it is right that they should be so, because they are superb. Their attraction is twofold: their curved contours are as restful as a day in bed, and the sudden way they loom straight out of agricultural country is one of those dramatic geological invasions which give our English landscape its character.

It is almost as though the Downs are the mighty outline of some prehistoric monster whose bones lie below in the white chalk; a body clothed with soft turf, powerful even in death. I have felt, and no doubt you have, the eerie character of the Downs. I came upon a reference to them the other day as 'the jolliest hills in England'. To me they are not jolly hills: they are rather sinister, melancholy hills, as I think anyone will agree who has stood in Cissbury Ring at twilight, during this lachrymose summer.

While it is true that their shape is restful to the eye, their bare expanses are haunted by dark, far-off things, and even in Sussex, within hail of Eastbourne and Brighton, I seem to see the shadow of Stonehenge across the grass.

Most of England has been tramped upon by history until the footprints of Briton, Roman, Dane, Saxon and Englishman form an almost indistinguishable mosaic; but the chalk Downs are almost as smooth as Crusoe's strand, marked by only one startling footprint, the bare mark of Neolithic Man. Sometimes you find in the chalk the flint arrow-heads which he made, or his polished stone axes; and in several places in Sussex are tunnels in the chalk, the flint mines, where he dug his way with a pick made of a red deer's antler, and on the roof of the tunnels you can see to this day the smoke of the lamps he burned four thousand years ago.

The Downs are haunted by the ghosts of hairy men, men grasping stone axes, men driving their little sheep before them over the sweet chalkland, peering now and then towards the black forest of the now peaceful Weald as into some jungle of the Amazon.

It is easy to forget such thoughts when larks are singing and the Downs lie warm in the sunlight; but when the shadows fall, or a thin rain blots out the distant map of fields, leaving you alone with the grass and the wind, a little shaggy Piltdown Man seems to be trotting at

'Cissbury Ring at twilight'

your side. So in a land empty of any but the most grotesque and ancient memories, the lonely figure of a shepherd looming through the rain with his sheep has all the dramatic possibilities of a man met in a fog. It is almost with relief that you find he is alive and clothed in an oilskin, a man from your own world and your own time, and not a figure conjured up by the Downs from beyond the mists of history.

In a farmhouse near Poynings, where I stopped to shelter from a violent shower, I met a man who talked to me about sheep and the diseases of sheep. Centuries of close feeding on the Downs have bred a minute worm, or snail, in the grass, which gives sheep a liver disease called fluke. For this reason large portions of the Downs are being 'rested'.

I saw in a shed a beautifully formed shepherd's crook made of steel and set on a wooden haft.

'That's a Pyecombe hook,' said the man. 'They're still made by the blacksmith over at Pyecombe, but not in quantities as they used to be in the old days, for there's few shepherds on the Downs now.'

The rain cleared up and I went on, thinking that sheep-herding in Sussex is perhaps the most ancient occupation in England still carried out on the same spot. It is older than agriculture, for Stone Age man wandered with his sheep long before he settled down and was content to wait for the results of farming.

I thought, too, what a wonderful thing a shepherd's crook is, the humble, common implement of most pastoral people, but also, after the Cross, perhaps the most significant emblem of Christianity. I do not know when Christian bishops first took a crook as the symbol of their care of souls, but it must have been early in the first Christian centuries. I have never seen an Arab shepherd with a crook, although nearly every Christmas card or child's book of Bible stories shows the shepherds at Bethlehem leaning on crooks. The Palestinian shepherd, who has probably not changed in his habits since New Testament times, carries a club like a shillelagh, and a long straight staff.

I think Roman shepherds used crooks, and certainly Pan was often pictured with one. Therefore it is probable that the European shepherd has given the Church its symbol, and not the Eastern shepherd, which may explain why the symbol is used only by Western bishops. In the Eastern Church it is unknown.

I went to Pyecombe to see the crook-makers, and found a tiny village tucked away on a hill above the broad sweep of the London–Brighton road, where it comes over the Downs from Clayton. Although so near the main road, Pyecombe is a little bit of old Sussex: a few farm buildings, some cottages, an old partly Norman church and, a few yards from the church, the blacksmith's forge.

Two brothers named Mitchell run the forge and make the crooks and shoe about forty horses a year. They are both, I should think, over sixty, and their father, who is ninety-five, is still alive and gave up work only the other day. The old man remembers travelling down to Sussex from London on the Brighton Coach, long before anyone thought of motors.

In the dark forge, with the fire glowing and the beams hung with horse-shoes, the brothers told me about the making of shepherds' crooks. The head of the crook is of iron or steel, and nothing makes a better crook than an old gun barrel. The haft of the crook must be formed of unpeeled hazel for the shepherds will not have ash. They polish the hazel until it looks like mahogany.

As the purpose of a crook is to catch a sheep by the leg, and as the various breeds of sheep in England vary in size, there are many patterns. A Sussex crook would be of no use to a Kent shepherd, and a man herding Dorset Horns would require still a different pattern. The Southdown sheep is a small creature with a small leg, and so the typical Pyecombe crook is an elegant curve of metal with an opening about an inch in width, just the right size to admit the animal's small leg-bone.

'A man came here t'other day to ask us to make a crook for a cross-bred sheep,' said one of the Mitchells, 'and we had to make a much bigger crook than usual. The Kent people use a tremendous big crook. The sheep get into the dykes, and when they can't see their legs they get 'em out by the neck, or where they can. In Scotland I've heard tell they make wooden crooks, but I've never seen one.'

Pyecombe crooks last more than a lifetime, but as there are fewer shepherds than ever on the Downs, there is not much genuine demand for them today. Instead, the Mitchell brothers are generally busy making crooks for bishops and hikers!

'Young fellows and girls come along here and buy crooks,' I was told. 'So do bishops. When a big conference was on up at London recently, the forge was full of bishops wanting crooks. We made crooks for the Archbishop of Cape Town and the Bishop of Uganda, and also for the Bishop of Tristan da Cunha, who told us he was the loneliest bishop in the world.'

So we got talking about foreign parts, and I was told that the younger Mitchell had served in the South African War and in Egypt during the Great War. He had been to the Fayûm and to a lonely place on the west coast of Egypt, Mersa Matruh. He could hardly believe that I had been there too, and I could hardly believe that he had been there, so we stood in the forge swopping stories while the other brother looked at us in admiration, as if Stanley had at last encountered Livingstone.

'Oh, bless me, the heat in the Fayûm!' said Mitchell. 'Miles of sand, miles of it, and the sun beating on it, day after day! Fellows round here won't hardly believe what life's like out there. But what a relief it was to get back home and to see that, after nothing but sand and more sand . . .'

And he waved his hand towards 'that', which was a dome of green grass, a great curve of the Sussex Downs.

So I left the Brothers Mitchell near the London–Brighton road, but spiritually as far away from it as any two men could be.

When a man has knocked about the world, it goes without saying that he must have talked to a number of barmaids on a variety of subjects: but, looking back over many years, I cannot recollect one such conversation which has left any impression on my mind. I may have had the bad fortune to encounter dull barmaids, or I may not be the kind of man to whom barmaids confide their more memorable thoughts.

It was in the little village of Fittleworth, in Sussex, or, to be more precise, in the snuff-brown bar of the Swan, that Fate suddenly relented and decided that it was time I should have an interesting conversation with the girl behind the bar. It began, ordinarily enough, with a talk about the beauties of the local countryside, and then diverged at some point to the difficulty of photographing wild animals in their natural haunts.

The girl told me that she had been getting up at six o'clock for the past few mornings in order to photograph a family of foxes living on Fittleworth Common. It was a difficult job, she said, and it was necessary to creep up step by step, praying that a twig would not snap beneath her feet: then she had to wait as still as a stone until the little foxes came out and played in a patch of early morning sunlight. They were just like puppies as they chased each other about and rolled their little red bodies over in the bracken.

The light had been deceptive that morning, but she thought she had taken a good picture. Just when she had done so, the vixen became

*'The typical Pyecombe crook
is an elegant curve of metal'*

aware of her and, with a 'most peculiar bark', called her young ones to cover.

I thought that no one, except perhaps Thomas Hardy, could have imagined a barmaid in the bracken, watching for little foxes. Indeed, sitting there under the black beams, I began to feel that I had somehow got into a Wessex novel.

'Oh, how I should love to photograph a badger!' she sighed, with a longing which barmaids are commonly supposed to lavish upon more metropolitan delights.

She came, not from Sussex, but from the grand county of Suffolk, and she told me she felt almost like a foreigner when she first arrived. The Sussex dialect is still strong, and some of the words in use are difficult to catch at first. They call a lane a 'twitten', and they call a dyke a 'dick'. While she was talking, the figure of a huge man with an apron of sacking round his waist loomed in the shadows of the bar in the act of drinking a tankard of beer. At her words, he removed the tankard for a second and said in a deep voice, as though proposing a toast, 'Good old Sussex!' and then immediately lifted the tankard again and put it down empty.

We talked about otters and badgers, and about a grasshopper warbler which had been heard in those parts; and I went to bed with the pleasant knowledge that I should always connect Fittleworth with the only interesting conversation I have ever had with a barmaid.

The village is among the recognised beauty spots of Sussex. It is an irregularly grouped cluster of sleepy little cottages, some white and thatched, some half-timbered: and it looks, as most old villages do in England – and this is the true secret of their beauty – as if it had grown up as naturally out of the soil as the oak trees and hedges.

There is an old mill and a mill race that comes tumbling out of bushes to form a dark pool near a grey bridge; there is a good Early English church dedicated to St Mary, there is

an old yew tree in the churchyard. There are other less tangible beauties, such as the fall of light and shade which has enchanted many artists, who have left what I trust is not their best work on the wooden panels of the smoke-room at the Swan.

As I wandered round the village, I thought how silent and reserved such places are. Visitors come to them, look around and say how 'pretty' this is or how 'nice' that is, but of the great procession of humble human life that has been passing through them for long centuries they know nothing; neither is much to be known. We know that the knight of the Hall went on the Crusades, or that he died in the Wars of the Roses, or that, in more recent times, the squire had sat in Parliament; but of the hundreds and thousands of common people who have been born and have died in the place there is no record.

Now and then a painstaking vicar, or someone interested in the history of a village, will go to the trouble of searching the Record Office, the parish registers, and the Manorial Rolls, in the hope of gleaning one ear of local corn, and the result is always worthwhile. We cannot have too many village histories, and Fittleworth is lucky in having found its local historian in the Hon. Lady Maxse, whose little book, *The Story of Fittleworth*, came into my hands by chance: I commend it to all who would like to write the annals of their parish.

Having read this book, I know why a place near Fittleworth is called Plumpudding Corner. It seems that from 1279, when Fittleworth was already an old village, a weekly fair used to be held at the neighbouring village of Egdean, then an important place, and it was at Plumpudding Corner that the crowds attending the fair purchased plum puddings,

---

'There is an old mill and a mill race that comes tumbling down out of bushes to form a dark pool near a grey bridge'

'The wooden panels of the smoke-room at the Swan'

cooked for them in a row of ovens which have left their mark in the meadows.

It is well known that small communities everywhere love a bit of scandal and gossip. Lady Maxse tells a story about village gossip in the days of Henry VIII which not only suggests that gossip is eternal and unalterable but also casts a revealing light on the government of England in those days. Henry's reign, and the period of the Republic, when England was ruled by Cromwell's psalm-singing generals, were probably the two most sternly disciplined periods of our history. There were spies everywhere, even in little Fittleworth, as the story shows.

One day, in the year 1538, two tax collectors arrived in Fittleworth to take away the pig of a man named Hamlyn, for non-payment of fourpence, taxes due to the King. Hamlyn was out, but his next-door neighbour, a kindly woman named Margaret Keynard, asked the men why they were driving away the hog, and, upon learning the reason, offered to pay the fine. They took her money and put the hog back in his sty.

When Hamlyn came home, instead of being grateful, he was furious with the woman. He said he was as able to pay the money as she was, and when she pointed out that the money was the King's, and had to be paid then and there, he burst out with these fatal words: 'The King will have all our money and all that we have. I pray God a vengeance on the King and his Council. I would they were all hanged!'

It may seem incredible to us today (but not perhaps unbelievable to citizens in spy-ridden countries) that the words of an enraged rustic in Fittleworth soon reached the ears of the King's Council in London. The process was this. First the village gossips got hold of the story and wagged their chins off, and, as the story grew with every telling, Margaret Keynard was so certain that she would be implicated, her name having been coupled with that of Hamlyn, that she sought out the local spy and turned King's Evidence.

This man went straight to the squire, who went straight to the local knight, who held an inquiry and sent the report – the evidence of four village women! – up to the Council in London. The order came back to fling Hamlyn into prison. What his fate was we do not know, but for lesser crimes men have died.

Is there not a moral in this which all who love to enlarge on the affairs of their neighbours might take to heart?

Another thing which impressed me while reading the slender records of a village like Fittleworth, is the way towns have drained such villages of their industries during the last two centuries. When roads were bad and communications difficult, and before factories catered for the many, each village, no matter how small, was a nest of trades. These little places were almost self-supporting. They had their own shoemakers, weavers, tailors, carpenters, builders, and so on, while the cottagers made their own bread, grew much of their own food and brewed their own ale. All these talents have vanished and those who practised them have long since departed.

No village was complete without its witch, whose rhymes and remedies were respected by people who would readily pour doctor's medicine down the sink. Fittleworth's witch lived under three pine trees on the top of Wyncombe Hill, and it is said that on cloudy nights her charms worked wonderfully, but if the moon broke through and revealed the spire of Fittleworth Church, they just fizzled out and her power departed. The last wise woman of Fittleworth was a Mrs Cooper, who was curing adder's bite and giddiness in cattle well into the last century.

So, as I walked about Fittleworth looking at the sleepy old cottages, I thought: you've seen quite a lot of life since Saxon times, but your story is not, as a sentimentalist would like to think, that of dear old ladies cutting flowers in the front garden, but of men and women with their full share of generosity and kindliness, of malice and villainy, of bravery and cowardice, of wisdom and stupidity, for, small as you are, you are an adequate fragment of the great world.

In quiet lanes about three miles south of Fittleworth, a cottage stands by itself near the village of Bignor. I knocked at the door and asked if I could see the Roman Villa.

A pleasant, smiling woman gave me a ticket and removed a bunch of keys from a hook; and we crossed the lane and mounted a rising path that ran on the edge of a wheat-field.

When we had walked a hundred yards or so, the woman turned round and pointed with the keys towards the way we had come. The landscape is dominated by the South Downs, whose smooth northern slopes descend in gentle sweeps to the fields and the meadows of the Rother Valley.

'There's Stane Street,' she said. 'Can you see it coming down towards us?'

And I saw, like a straight line drawn in apple green upon the darker emerald of the Downs, the ghost of the great Roman road that once joined Regnum, which is now Chichester, with a port on the Thames called Londinium. We turned and went on beside the field of wheat.

The Roman villa we were approaching was discovered by a ploughman in the year 1811. His ploughshare struck something large and hard, which turned out to be a coloured pavement. As he scraped away the soil, Ganymede, borne godwards in an eagle's claws, looked at him out of the Sussex mire; being a Saxon, the man did not recognise him and ran off to ask Mr Tupper, the farmer, to come and have a look. Then came the discovery of more coloured pavements, of dining rooms and reception rooms, centrally heated, of baths, bedrooms, barns, stables and outhouses. It was one of the three finest Roman villas in England; as fine as the Woodchester villa in Gloucestershire, and the villa at Brading, in the Isle of Wight. Experts think

it was built about A.D. 79, the year the Emperor Vespasian died.

When we came to the highest part of the path, we saw a tall yew tree ahead of us, standing like a sentinel at the entrance to a group of thatched barns.

'The barns have been built over the pavements to save them from the weather,' said the woman. I thought that a more convincing Saxon village could not have been constructed, though a curiously barbaric covering for so much Roman elegance.

We went round unlocking doors and unpadlocking wooden shutters, and through each opened door and shutter shot a beam of light which streamed down on the coloured mosaic pavements. The pavements of seven rooms have been preserved in a fragmentary condition, but all the fragments are large enough to give a good idea of the complete design.

It was interesting to see patterns which I have seen in Pompeii and Herculaneum, and in more remote places of the Roman Empire, lying in a Sussex meadow. One pattern seems to have been a monotonously popular one with Roman artists. It must have occupied the place in Roman interior decoration that 'The Monarch of the Glen' occupied in Victorian dining-rooms. This is 'The Four Seasons', a geometrical design with allegorical heads in the four corners, representing the Seasons of the Year.

A fine head of Winter is to be seen at Bignor, a human face in a hooded cloak, wearing an expression of gloomy hopelessness, as if asking: 'Is this weather *ever* going to improve?' The finest pavement shows a stately head, probably of Juno, flanked by peacocks, an emblem of immortality. Below the usual geometrical borders is an interesting strip which shows twelve cupids playing at gladiators.

But the most interesting thing about this work, apart from its fine quality, is the nimbus or halo which Juno wears. I should think that this is the only pre-Christian halo in England.

But who lived eighteen centuries ago in this great house beside Stane Street, and what did the house look like in Roman times? I imagine it had an immense walled outer courtyard rather like a large modern farm, in which were the stables, the barns, the farm wagons and the oxen. At the far end of this stood the villa, built round an inner courtyard, the rooms running round three sides of the quadrangle.

The house must have been elegant and rich. All the rooms were centrally heated by hot air from a central furnace which circulated beneath the floors and in wall flues, and there was a fine swimming-bath, which was filled with heated water. In a remote and still largely barbaric island, the villa reproduced something of the ease and comfort of a Roman country house.

Roman travellers, on their way from London to Chichester, have paused at its gates in admiration, anxious perhaps to present letters of introduction to the owner, hoping to be asked to stay the night there, or at least to have reclined in civilised surroundings for a while and to have enjoyed dinner in one of the spacious rooms whose pavements have survived.

'A beam of light which streamed down on the coloured mosaic pavements'

It would be interesting to know who lived in the big house on the side of Stane Street, but that, I suppose, we shall never discover. Mr S. E. Winbolt, the archæologist, has put forward the interesting and likely theory that it may have belonged to Cogidubnus, the British chief of the Sussex tribe of Regni, who was so pro-Roman that he was allowed to retain his chieftainship.

'Can you imagine what England was like when people lived in this house?' I asked the woman.

'Well, they knew how to make themselves comfortable,' she replied, like a practical housewife, 'with their central heating and swimming-pools and such like.'

No doubt they did, but I imagine that comfort was unevenly distributed. I think if I could make a brief exploration into the past I should choose to travel for a week or so through Hadrian's Britain. I should give much to see what London was like, what a country town such as Silchester or Chichester was like, and what a British village was like.

It would be interesting to see where Romanisation ended, and to know if the peasants bore any ill feeling towards the upper-class Romanised Celts. I should expect to find wealthy landowners, townsmen and shopkeepers priding themselves on their Roman habits and fashions, assembling in the forum, going to the theatre, even maybe trying hopelessly to cultivate the olive and the grape; but I should expect to find the British villagers still primitive and Celtic-speaking and looked down upon, possibly with a touch of patronising affection, by the Romanised Britons of the towns. Perhaps some young upper-class Briton in a toga might be seen exploring the villages with the object of studying the folklore of his countrymen, and of copying down for the delight of a sophisticated public the simple stories told round wood fires in stockaded encampments.

While we were locking up the barns, I saw one of those unforgettable little relics of the past which are sometimes more revealing than pillar or mosaic. Firmly printed on a Roman tile, and impressed upon it while it was still soft, are two sets of prints made by two dogs eighteen centuries ago.

One dog, evidently a big fellow with long claws, stood with his front legs so closely placed together that his prints overlap. Facing him stood a smaller and lighter dog, for his pads have not sunk so deeply into the tile. This smaller dog stood with his weight on his left foreleg and his right leg barely making an impression at all.

Looking at these paw marks, I seem to see the picture clearly: the big dog, feet together, his head lifted, was skittish and playful, as big dogs sometimes are: the small dog approached suspiciously, with one foot barely touching the ground, ready to run away if necessary! I should like a naturalist to examine these prints and tell me if I am wrong. I should also like to know the kind of dog that made the deep marks; he must have been a Roman Alsatian.

Looking again at the photograph which I

took of this distant encounter, I am beginning to wonder whether the smaller prints may not be those of a cat. Can this be the record of a cat and dog friendship in Roman Britain?

Locking up the villa, we retraced our way beside the field of wheat, and high above us on the Downs we saw the apple-green streak of Stane Street running on into the distance as straight as a spear.

The name of Arundel is so fine a one, and so famous in history, that I have always imagined the town to be a busy place full of life and markets, and perhaps even of ships. But I came down a steep hill into a quiet little town lying in the shadow of a mighty castle. A river with a fairly stiff current – for I watched a young man trying to row his girl up stream – runs through the town, but there are no signs of cargo-boats or barges on the Arun. It is a river which has retired from business and now amuses itself with punts and young men who row boats.

'We used to do a bit of trade in the old days,' said a local inhabitant, 'but now the port has gone, so has the market, and the town lives on the castle.'

High above Arundel, like a trumpeter on a hill, rises the tremendously embattled castle in which lives the Earl Marshal and Hereditary Marshal and Chief Butler of England, Bernard Marmaduke FitzAlan-Howard, 16th Duke of Norfolk, Earl of Arundel, and Premier Peer of the Realm.

His Grace is a Roman Catholic, and about a third of Arundel's population of 2,700 also profess the old faith; but that is not, in my opinion, the reason why the town has a faintly Continental look about it. The Calvinist who hopes to see pale Jesuits flitting about and plotting in corners, or who expects to hear the groans of a tortured heretic greengrocer rising in the night, will be disappointed, for Arundel takes its faith with nothing of a convert's fanaticism.

I think the foreign appearance of Arundel is explained by three things: the way the town clusters round the castle, the French look of the Church of St Philip Neri, and the castle itself. It is only a faint resemblance, to be noticed in certain lights, as if Arundel might have had a French grandmother.

The Howards are kindly and well-liked in Arundel. They no longer come down into the town and sweep the men away to some inconvenient battle-field; instead they present it with public buildings. An atmosphere of benevolence strays down from the battlements into the streets.

The kinder side of feudalism still lives there, and who but a fool would deny that feudalism had its softer moments? The late Duke, who was once Postmaster-General, gave the town its nice red post-office.

It was late afternoon when I arrived, and I was told that the castle is not open to the public until August, but whatever I did, I must see the park. So late on a summer's evening, I walked beside the Arun round the castle hill until I came to a shaded and obviously enchanted pool near a bridge; and here was an entrance to the park.

I walked for some time on the shores of a lake, a beautiful and natural lake with plenty of weed in it, where wild fowl were swimming with their downy families. The lake is fed by a number of springs which rise within a few feet of the bank. They come oozing and bubbling out of the earth, discharging into the lake a quantity of beautiful blue water, and though I am no chemist, I wondered whether they were nitrogenous springs, for the water is the same colour as the mineral water of Buxton in Derbyshire.

I turned inland from the lake up a steep path through a majestic beech wood, and soon the lake was lost to sight. The park stretched apparently for miles, a gentle undulating expanse of grass and tall trees. Herds of deer grazed in compact brown companies, slowly passing out of the shadow of glades to stand

'*Wild fowl with their downy families*'

golden brown in the late sunlight. The Georgians did not dot the park with classical bowers, and its later owners have wisely left it to Nature and the deer, which keep the grass as closely clipped as if a regiment of gardeners was at work on it.

If ever a foreigner asks me to show him something which is typically English, I shall run him down to Arundel and walk him through the park. I approached as close as it was possible to the castle, but little of it is visible. Although it is so famous in history, I am ashamed to say that I could remember nothing about it except the charming reference in Lamb's essay, 'In Praise of Chimney-

Sweepers'; but whether the story of the sweep's little boy who was lost in the castle and discovered at last asleep in a ducal bed, is true or not, I do not know.

Nevertheless, Lamb wrote that 'the little creature had alighted upon this magnificent chamber; and, tired with his tedious explorations, was unable to resist the delicious invitement to repose, which he saw exhibited; so, creeping between the sheets very quietly, laid his black head upon the pillow, and slept like a young Howard'.

Then there is, of course, the story of the North American eagle owls which were presented to Charles, Duke of Norfolk in the eighteenth century. The birds were encouraged to breed in the old keep of Arundel and became a famous sight of the castle. It was the ducal fancy to give these birds the names of prominent politicians and other distinguished men of the time. One day a visitor was looking at the owls when the keeper, pointing to a singularly old and ruffled specimen, said: 'We call that one Lord Eldon.'

'Oh, do you?' replied the visitor. 'Well, I happen to be the real Lord Eldon.'

The best story of the Arundel owls is that of the butler who gravely entered the breakfast-room and approached the Duke.

'Please, your Grace,' he said, 'Lord Thurlow has laid an egg.'

After a night in an admirable new hotel near the riverside, I climbed the steep high street and saw the sights of Arundel. I saw the large, cold, but impressive Roman Catholic church of St Philip Neri, which was built by the late Duke about sixty years ago. The architect was that interesting person, Joseph Aloysius Hansom, who designed several fine churches, and also invented and gave his name to the hansom cab; an invention which should have made his fortune, but I think he received no more than £300 for it.

Opposite the Catholic church is the old parish church of St Nicholas, which is, of course, Church of England. The Duke of Norfolk attends St Philip Neri, but his Protestant Duchess attends the parish church, whose vicar comes from her parish at home.

Before the Reformation the parish church was served by a college of secular priests, and in the chancel of this church the Dukes of Norfolk were buried. When you enter this church today, you are at once struck by the peculiarity that the chancel is cut off from the body of the church by a fine mediæval iron screen, which is backed by a hideous modern brick wall. The screen was always there, but the brick wall dates from the famous quarrel between the late Duke of Norfolk and the vicar at that time, the Rev. G. Arbuthnot, a quarrel which ended in a celebrated law case in 1879.

The Duke was a remarkable man, and was the first Catholic layman since Sir Thomas More to play a distinguished part in the public life of England. It is a curious and interesting reflection on the swiftness with which religious toleration has come to this country that as recently as 1860, when the late Duke was a boy, Roman Catholics were not allowed at Oxford or Cambridge. He was educated under Cardinal Newman at the Oratory, Edgbaston, Birmingham, and throughout his life championed the cause of his fellow Catholics.

The quarrel with the vicar turned on the relationship of the FitzAlan Chapel to the rest of the church, of which, architecturally, it is of course a part.

'They were both hot-tempered men,' said the verger, describing this last clash between Puritan and Cavalier. 'Neither of them gave a brass farthing for anybody. But the Reverend Arbuthnot angered His Grace one day by referring to the FitzAlan Chapel as the chancel of *his* church. Do you see the meaning of that? Why, it meant that if it was part of the church, the screen ought to come down and the chapel

OVERLEAF *'I came to a shaded and obviously enchanted pool'*

on the other side ought to be part of the parish church!

'So what did the Duke do? In order to make it clear to the vicar that the chapel belonged to him and not to the parish, he took workmen there one night and, working all night through, bricked up the entrance, as you see it today. And what did the vicar do? The next night he got workmen and knocked down as much of the wall as he could in the time. So then the fat was in the fire! The case was heard in 1879 and the Duke won it. It was proved that the FitzAlan Chapel was the private property of the Dukes of Norfolk. But the vicar appealed, and again he lost his case. So here we have a church without a chancel, or at least a church with a chancel that doesn't legally belong to it.'

And on the eastern side of the partition Masses are sometimes said for the souls of the Howards, while on the western side of the screen is a Church of England.

I was fortunate to be in Arundel on a morning when the FitzAlan Chapel was open to the public. Knocking at one of the lodge gates, I was taken by the lodge-keeper's wife into the burial-place of the Earls of Arundel and Dukes of Norfolk.

I entered one of the most wonderful tomb chapels in England, a place that, though it was badly knocked about during the Civil War, is still the loveliest thing to see in Arundel. I know few burial-places in which the fear of death seems less present.

The nobles of Arundel, separated by many centuries and ending with the late Duke of Norfolk, lie, their feet to the altar, resting on the FitzAlan horse; their heads are on marble cushions, and their hands are clasped in prayer. The South Chantry, which was built about 1498, is one of the most beautiful tombs in England. Petworth marble has been carved to resemble the finest lace.

In the centre of the chapel, surrounded by a screen of mediæval iron work, lie Thomas FitzAlan and his Countess, the daughter of John, King of Portugal. They died in the fifteenth century. She is sculptured in her best clothes, a horned headdress on her head, a gown sewn with pearls, and the tight sleeves seamed with pearls. The guide told me that when a Requiem Mass is celebrated, ten candles of unbleached wax are burned on the ten prickets of the screen which surrounds their tomb.

Nearby is the grave of John FitzAlan, who lost a leg and died at the siege of Beauvais in 1435. For centuries there was a mystery about his body. It was brought home by a man called Elton, who demanded 1,400 marks, which the family refused to pay. Elton therefore kept the body in pawn for a number of years, and it was not definitely known to have been redeemed and buried in the family vault until 1859, when the tomb was opened and the bystanders saw the old warrior lying there with only one leg.

Old William Camden, writing about Chichester, said: 'The city hath four gates, opening to *the four quarters of the world.*' I like that fine flourish, which seems to link the homely outskirts of Chichester with Trebizond and Samarkand.

Although the gates have gone, the four main streets of Chichester are called North, South, East and West Streets, and you will not find a better example in England of a city that was planned eighteen centuries ago by the legions of Rome.

The American grid-iron cities, which we think so modern and sensible, were, of course, the rule in the Ancient World. No Greek or Roman would have been surprised by New York. Alexander the Great built Alexandria three hundred years before Christ just as a modern American architect would do; and all the Hellenistic cities of the period were designed on the rectangular principle.

When, therefore, did the winding street and

the narrow alley begin? I remember once sitting among the ruins of Ephesus, looking at the marble bones of the old city, which lie under the grass and the shrubs. Shepherd-boys were wandering through the ruins with their goats, and I noticed that, as the animals wandered here and there in search of grass and herbage, they trod winding paths which cut across the plan of the city.

I have an idea that goats and sheep are the architects of the mediæval lane! When the Romans left this country, the defenceless inhabitants of the cities fled or were massacred by Saxon war-bands. As the marauders were pastoral people, they feared and disliked cities and preferred to see them fall into ruin rather than face the claustrophobia of life within walls. They built their villages round about in the fields, but nevertheless adventurous herds-men must have wandered curiously about the cities with their animals, as they do today in Ephesus.

Is it not possible that, when the cities were reoccupied, the new streets were not the Roman streets, but the winding paths and short cuts made by the sheep and goats?

If there is anything in this theory, cities like Chichester can never have been entirely ruined or deserted, because their Roman street plan is too perfect. Either citizens with a Roman municipal education survived to carry on through the Dark Ages, or the Saxons conquered their dislike of a town wall and consented to live within it.

As soon as I entered Chichester, I felt it to be a comfortable and friendly place, which I should like to visit again and for a longer time. So far as physical appearances go, it would seem to have a greater affinity with Gloucester than with any town in Sussex; although I had only to listen to the people who crowded the narrow pavements and entered the shops (not yet, thank Heaven, entirely chain stores or combines) to realise that Chichester is to West Sussex as Lewes is to East Sussex.

Let us hope that nothing will ever persuade Chichester to remove its wonderful Market Cross, the best in England, planted in the very heart of the city, where the four points of the compass meet.

It stands in what was once the middle of Roman Regnum, the beginning of that North Street which, as soon as it left the gate of Regnum, became the famous Stane Street that flew to London over Down and across Weald, as the crow flies. It reached London Bridge, a little over fifty-five miles away, with a divergence of only about a mile and a half. What a marvellous engineering feat this was!

The dignity and pride of Chichester resides in its cathedral, a huge mass of worn, elephant-coloured stone lifting itself from grass on the side of West Street. Where, I wonder, did I gain the impression that Chichester was small and uninteresting compared with other cathedrals? I was surprised to learn that it has a greater total length than Exeter, Hereford, Worcester, Lichfield, Chester, Ripon or Southwark.

It has one unique feature: the only detached cathedral belfry in England, a tall fifteenth-century tower in the north-west corner of the churchyard, which visitors may enter and ascend. Suspended in the darkness there you see 'Big Walter', the hour bell, which weighs 74 hundredweight, and a peal of bells of various ages, the oldest bearing the date 1583.

As soon as I entered the beautifully kept cathedral, I was impressed by its extraordinary width. The nave is nineteen feet wider than those of Westminster Abbey and Canterbury Cathedral, and with the exception of St Paul's and York Minster, it is the widest cathedral nave in the country. This peculiarity is caused by double aisles. I have seen these only in old churches which have been enlarged to accommodate an expanding parish.

How exquisite is the calm dignity of the architecture, chiefly Norman, of this church, and how fortunate it is that no one has blocked the view with a hideous organ; you can see straight down the church from the west door

to the east window.

Behind the high altar I saw the place where the shrine of St Richard of Chichester used to stand, at one time a great place of pilgrimage, as famous, almost, as the shrine of Thomas of Canterbury. An inscription in the retro-choir says that St Richard's body was moved there from the nave on 16 June 1276, in the presence of King Edward I and the chief people of the realm.

Richard's life is proof that violence and murder print a name on the future more securely than goodness and sanctity. Most people can tell you something about Thomas à Becket, but few could describe the life of Chichester's bishop, who was the most saintly character of his time. Unlike so many early Churchmen, he was not a statesman; he was just a good and pure man who, though he was a bishop in a materialistic world, lived like one of the Apostles. Perhaps he is the only Englishman who might be compared with St Francis of Assisi.

He was called Richard de Wyche, or de Droitwyche, for he was born at Droitwich in 1197. He was elected Bishop of Chichester when he was about forty-eight, but his see had been ravaged by Henry III, who had confiscated the estates and declined to restore to him the temporal rights, or, to put it more bluntly, the money.

Undeterred by this, for no man ever cared less for money, Richard tramped Sussex for two years, staff in hand, visiting his clergy, comforting the sick and doing what he could for the poor, gaining the love of all by his humility and his simplicity.

His great friend was Simon, the priest at West Tarring, near Worthing, a man who shared his meagre possessions with his penniless Bishop; and it is said that those two

'Let us hope that nothing will ever persuade Chichester to remove its wonderful Market Cross'

worked in the fig garden at West Tarring, which still exists. It is the only fig garden in England, I think, and still bears a grand crop of figs in good years.

A charmingly written booklet about St Richard, by Caroline M. Duncan-Jones, is sold in Chichester, and from it I learned that when he was a little late in rising, the Bishop would listen to the birds and say: 'Little birds of heaven, irrational though ye be, ye have been before me in singing your praises to God.'

When he was eventually restored to the state of a bishop, Richard continued to live with the simplicity of a hermit. He was obliged to entertain and to keep a cook, but he ate sparingly and seemed to have a positive horror of meat dishes. Sometimes, unable to control himself when luscious dishes were carried in for his guests, he would apostrophise bird or joint with the words: 'Poor innocents, what have ye done worthy of death?'

He was a cause of some anxiety to his steward, for he was always giving away his money. On one occasion he went to see a prisoner in jail, and on his departure took good care to leave the door open! He was always descending upon his unfortunate steward, ordering him to sell something and give the proceeds to the poor.

'The horse I ride is better than I need,' he cried one day. 'Sell him, I beg, and let Christ's poor be fed with the price.'

Soon after Richard died, he was proclaimed a saint. His festival on 3 April was one of the most important feasts in Sussex until the Reformation, when his shrine, which pilgrims had covered with silver, gold, and jewels, was dismantled by the order of Henry VIII and the treasures removed to the Tower of London.

Caroline Duncan-Jones gives the odd piece of information that the honour in which St Richard was held at Droitwich, his birthplace, survived the Reformation and existed until Cromwell's day when a Puritan Parliament sternly forbade the people of Droitwich to decorate St Richard's Well with flowers and branches of trees.

In this cathedral I came across a memorial to the first person who died in a railway accident, William Huskisson, MP for Chichester, who was run over by the *Rocket* in 1830, at the opening of the Liverpool and Manchester Railway. The unfortunate man left his coach to speak to the Duke of Wellington, who was in another coach, when the *Rocket*, dashing past on the adjacent rails at a good twelve miles an hour, caught him and drew him under its wheels.

A memory of Chichester which will not easily fade is of St Mary's Hospital. This perfect mediæval building is now a charity which supports a few old people. The hall, with a magnificent timber roof, was once a sick ward, and the room was so arranged that while patients lay in bed, they could see the priest at the altar of the adjoining chapel.

Another of Chichester's sights which interested me is the Minerva Stone. It is built into the outside wall of the Council House in North Street. It is a Roman inscription, which was dug up in Chichester in 1723, taken to Goodwood House, where the Duke of Richmond built a classical summer house in its honour, and brought back to Chichester in 1907.

It records the fact that an unknown Roman, whose name ended in 'ente' and whose father was Pudentinus, had given land for the building of a temple. Eager theorists have jumped to the conclusion that the name ending in 'ente' was Pudente, and that this man was the Pudens who married Claudia and is mentioned in St Paul's Epistles.

And who was Claudia, they say, but the daughter of Cogidubnus of Chichester, a British chief who was so pro-Roman that if he had had a daughter he would certainly have called her Claudia, in compliment to the Emperor Claudius!

Well, who knows? It is a pretty story, and it is pleasant to think that 'a blue-eyed Briton born' and a Roman who had lived in Chichester may have been among St Paul's first converts.

CHAPTER FIVE

I buy waistcoats at Midhurst in a storm of rain, move into Surrey at Farnham, where they have lost King Charles's Cap, and cross into the hop country of Hampshire, where I see how sheep hurdles are made. I visit Alton and White's Selborne.

The town of Midhurst, in Sussex, cannot be too highly praised, even on a wet day. The rain was falling in vindictive sheets, yet the place looked lovely. It is an old-fashioned town which has known how to grow up without filling itself with ugliness. Like most old English towns, it contains something of everything, Tudor, Georgian and Victorian: and the cellars of Midhurst, what they don't know about smuggling is not to be known.

I took refuge from the rain in the oddly dedicated Church of St Mary Magdalene and St Denis, the headless patron of France. The church has suffered almost as drastic a mutilation as its saint, for restorers and enlargers have had their way with it. I had read somewhere that it boasts an ancient notice asking women not to wear pattens during divine service, but I could not find it.

I asked the verger, who was cleaning the church, what had happened to the notice, and he told me that, as such a big board was in everyone's way, it had been moved to the museum at Cowdray Park, just outside the town.

'I wonder if there is any place left in England where pattens are still worn,' I said.

'Not one now, I should think,' he replied.

'That church notice is evidently the last visible relic of the muddy condition of Sussex a century or so ago.'

'Mud?' said the verger. 'I've seen more mud where I was born than ever I'll see in Sussex. I'm Lincolnshire. We've got the most affectionate mud in England there. When I was a boy, I well remember the women wearing pattens. You know what they're like, don't you? They're thick wooden soles raised about four inches off the ground, on iron hoops. Women used to slip their feet into them before they went out in the mud, and they took some walking in, I can tell you. And when I was a lad I can remember old men wearing smocks, but it's many a long year since I've seen one of them!'

As I left the church it was still raining, and now and again came a dull rumble of thunder. Still seeking refuge, I entered the shop of an antique dealer, and, after giving him a lot of trouble, which he did not seem to mind at all, spent a few shillings on two Georgian seals, one a quadriga in full gallop, the other a minute coach and four, and both of them beautifully engraved.

Instead of resenting the time I had taken up, this quiet, gentle man showed me all his treasures and told me how he had found them.

'This house used to be a depôt for smugglers,' he said. 'It must have belonged to someone very respectable, and probably because of that, it was one of their hiding-places. Come and look at the cellar!'

The house, like many in the town, had a bland and blameless Georgian exterior, but the interior was a mass of old ships' timbers, the colour of snuff and as hard as iron. The cellars were like the crypt of a church.

'That is where they hid the stuff,' said the antique dealer in his mild voice. 'Over there. Just here is the place where the look-out man stood. Come and stand here and see what a wonderful view he had of the stairs.'

It was true, he had a wonderful view of old, white steps creeping down into the darkness.

'Now, suppose someone came down those stairs,' continued my friend in a cold, blood-curdling voice. 'Suppose a revenue man came down, and you were the look-out man, what would you do?'

'Offer him a bottle of brandy,' I said, trying to laugh off the feeling of creepiness that was coming into the cellar.

'Oh, no, you wouldn't,' replied the smooth voice. 'Look here! You would just open up this flag-stone and underneath is a passage. You would just disappear! Simple, wasn't it?'

We climbed to the attics, where he had discovered a priest's hole tucked away

---

*'Still seeking refuge, I entered
the shop of an antique dealer'*

amongst the rafters. He had found it by tracing a mysterious hatchway in the basement, which proved to communicate with a shaft that runs up the house beside the chimney-stack. There was a pulley and the remains of a rope in the stack, and it had clearly been used to send up food to anyone hiding in the secret room.

In an attic full of old furniture, he took from an oak chest a mass of beautiful brocades, dresses and garments worn two hundred years ago by long-dead and forgotten beauties and their dandies. The gowns and the silk petticoats were indescribably pathetic as they drooped ghostly curtsies on the floor; and the rain came sliding down the little attic window and the thunder rumbled nearer and nearer.

There were several gorgeous sprigged Georgian waistcoats with flap pockets and with rows of miniature silk-covered buttons running down them; some were made of velvet, with raised patterns all over them, and all were splendid. Impelled by goodness knows what influence, I solemnly slipped off mackintosh and jacket and tried them on; and they fitted as if they had been made for me.

'You can have them for five shillings each,' said the quiet voice, and I thought that this was just the way Time would sell you something if Time could come to you in the shape of a man in a dark attic during a thunderstorm.

'All right, wrap them up,' said a voice, which I suppose was mine, 'and I'll wear them sometime in the evening, just for fun.'

I had never before bought anything like them, not being much given to personal vanities, and I thought, as I did so, what a good story someone could write about the spirit of a dandy who was determined to have his waistcoats worn again. Out in the rain the feeling of strangeness wore off, and I went back to my car faintly ashamed of my absurd parcel.

The stark ruin of Cowdray House outside Midhurst is a testimony, so the story goes, to the fulfilment of a family curse. Once the rival in size and splendour of Hatfield and Audley End, Cowdray is today as spectacular a ruin of a great Tudor house as you will see anywhere in England. For more than 130 years it has stood as a devouring fire left it in the eighteenth century; and no attempt has ever been made to rebuild it.

The caretaker who conducted me through the ruins pointed out the remains of great banqueting halls, enormous courtyards, vast galleries and towers, and told me the best known story in this part of Sussex, the story of the Curse of Cowdray. It goes back a long way and the curse lay dormant for two centuries, striking down with shocking unfairness the innocent descendants of those who had been cursed.

The story is that Sir Anthony Browne, a friend of Henry VIII, was one of those Catholics who managed to reconcile his conscience with the possession of estates taken from the Church. Among Henry's gifts to his friend was Battle Abbey. Browne pulled down the church, the chapter house and the cloisters, and established himself in the abbot's lodgings. It is said that one evening when he was feasting at Battle, a monk appeared and pronounced a curse upon him and his family, concluding with the words: 'By fire and water thy line shall come to an end, and it shall perish out of the land.'

Browne inherited Cowdray, and after his death his son, who became the first Lord Montague, left Battle and took up residence at Cowdray. Seven lords Montague were born and died, most of them in their beds, and none of them by fire and water, yet it seems that the fear of the curse was always present in the family. Although it had not operated, there was a feeling that it was a delayed action curse that might at any moment come to life and exact its awful penalty. This happened in 1793.

'The eighth Lord Montague, a young man of twenty-four, was travelling on the Continent with a friend and an old family servant named Dickinson,' said the caretaker. 'In Germany the young men decided to shoot some rapids on the Rhine in a small boat. The servant, Dickinson, became very frightened and tried to pull his master out of the boat, crying: "My Lord, it is the *curse of water*!" But Lord Montague only laughed and waved his hand, and the boat started. It entered a cloud of spray and – that was the last ever seen of it, or of Lord Montague.

'Dickinson came home to tell of the death of his young master, and when he got there he found that Cowdray House had been burned down. And that was the curse of fire! The estate then passed to the dead lord's sister, who had two small boys. The mother was always haunted by the fear of the curse, which only affected the male members of the family, so that she took tremendous care of the boys.

'In the summer of 1815 the children were having a holiday at Bognor. It was a lovely summer's day, with not a ripple on the water. Someone suggested that they should go out boating. The boat heeled over on a smooth sea and both boys were drowned. There was no one to succeed. The family had ended, as the monk said it should, in water and fire.'

After this impressive recital, I asked for the later history of the estate. In 1843 it was bought by the Earl of Egmont, from whose family it was purchased in 1909 by Sir Weetman Pearson, who became the first Lord Cowdray. The modern mansion stands some distance from the ruins of old Cowdray House.

If you wish to see a perfect picture of a haunted grange, go to Cowdray on a wet day, or better still, by moonlight.

Any man who has seen Farnham on a sunny day must think of it as a town of singular brightness and warmth. It is a town of red brick which looks from the outside as though

'If you wish to see a perfect picture of a haunted grange, go to Cowdray on a wet day'

it had been built in the reigns of Queen Anne and the first of the Georges, but inside it is often darkly beamed with Tudor oak.

I think Farnham must have broken with its ancient past, and made itself fashionable, about two hundred years ago, when it was the biggest wheat market in England. There was a good deal of money about at that time, and no doubt the merchants of Farnham were only too glad to pull down the black-and-white Tudor house-fronts and to rebuild them in the elegant red brick of the day.

When Defoe passed that way in 1724, a resident told him that on market-day he had counted eleven hundred teams of horses drawing carts and wagons loaded with wheat, and you can still see, leading off the main street of Farnham, what were once yards where the wagons were parked. Most of these are now built over with small brick houses.

*'Farnham is a town of red brick which looks
from the outside as though it had been built
in the reigns of Queen Anne and the first of the Georges'*

Farnham's fame as a wheat market was due probably to the Dutch war, which made it dangerous to send wheat to London by sea; but, as soon as the war was over, the custom began of grinding the wheat and sending it as flour to London by boat; and so the great market gradually died away.

Farnham then took seriously to hops, which had been grown in the district since Tudor times, as every reader of Farnham's great son, William Cobbett, knows. And today, Farnham, and the neighbouring Hampshire town of Alton, preside over a sudden and rather surprising area, where some of the best hops grown in England follow the Upper Greensand.

As soon as I arrived in Farnham, I climbed the steep hill to the Castle, which in its time saw quite a lot of the Cavaliers and the Roundheads. It is now the abode of the Bishop of Guildford.

The remains of a circular mediæval keep are shown to the public, but there is nothing much to hold the attention except a superb view from the top, over the surrounding country. The bishop's park looks beautiful, and is open to the public.

I then asked the way to the museum, and was told, to my astonishment, that Farnham has no museum! It is surely almost unbelievable that a town with a long history, whose main street is part of the Pilgrims' Way, a town which sheltered Charles I in his distress, which gave birth to that lovable mass of indignation, William Cobbett, and also to Augustus Toplady, the author of 'Rock of Ages', has not had sufficient intellectual curiosity to gather together the relics of its past.

I asked to see the Vernon Cap, a relic which those who take any interest in such things believe to be preserved at Farnham, either privately or with the Town Council. But no one seemed to know where it was!

This is the story of the Vernon Cap. In West Street stands an old house, now empty, once known as Culver Hall, but for at least a century called Vernon House, after a Cavalier family which once lived there.

When Charles I was being conveyed as a prisoner to London, from Hurst Castle on the Solent, he spent one night with the Vernons at Culver Hall. This was on 22 December 1648. In about five weeks' time, the King walked through the snow of a January morning to the scaffold in Whitehall.

Before he departed Charles said to his host that he had nothing to leave but a white quilted cap which he was in the habit of wearing in the morning. This cap became a treasured relic, which was handed on to successive owners of the house.

In 1926, the owner, Mr Duncan Bethune, died, leaving the house and the Vernon Cap to his cousin, Mrs Rose Emily Morrison. His will contained the following clause:

I declare that the cap, of King Charles I, contained in a case with an extract from George Vernon's will, and now in Vernon House, are always to go with the said Vernon House, and, if Vernon House is sold, to still go with it, but, if the said house is pulled down, the said cap, etc., is to be presented to the Town of Farnham to be placed in the Council Chamber as a memento of the King's visit, on condition that it is always kept there and that a plate is placed on the case inscribed as follows:

'The Cap of King Charles I, given by him to Henry Vernon as a memento of his stay at Vernon House on the 22nd day of December, 1648, on his way from Carisbrooke Castle to London.'

I was told that the house has been bought by a retired local builder since this will was made, but the cap did not go with it. So, for the first time for 290 years, the Vernon Cap has been separated from the house and from the town of Farnham.

I have heard three theories as to its whereabouts: that Mrs Morrison still has it; that it is in a Cambridge College; that it is in the possession of a peer in Wiltshire. No one doubts that it is still in existence and carefully preserved, but how extraordinary it is that a town should have allowed a romantic and valuable Stuart relic, to which it has a clear and ultimate claim, to pass out of its sight.

On each side of the main road from Farnham to Winchester, narrow lanes lead to the little villages of the Hampshire hop country. Oast-houses, which they call hop-kilns, remind you of Kent, and so do the neat lines of growing hops; but there the resemblance ends.

This country is on a larger scale, is wider, windier and generally less cosy, and there are long views eastward over Surrey, and south, over a network of green fields darkened with woods and varied by steep wooded hills, called hangars, to the Downs beyond Petersfield.

The villages off the main road, each one with its old church, have not changed outwardly for many a century. Some of them are long, strag-gling villages, whose farms and cottages follow the wells in the Upper Greensand. The coming of mains water is a recent event in their lives, while in some of them many a cottager still goes to bed by candle-light.

Among the population of these villages are a few remarkable old men who began life herding sheep over sixty years ago, but nowa-days sheep are almost extinct in this part of Hampshire. They are among the last expo-nents of the ancient country crafts of England, thatching, hurdling and sheep-shearing. When they go, such arts will also become extinct, for the young men will not learn them.

Binsted, on a hill about five hundred feet above the sea, is typical of the villages in this part of the world. It has a fine, late Norman church, and in the churchyard stands the war memorial, in the form of one of the few outdoor crucifixes in England. The church is one of eighty-three old churches in England dedicated to the Holy Cross.

The blacksmith's forge is still alive in Binsted, and when I wandered there, the smith was shoeing a pony, an act which nowadays has a certain antiquarian charm about it.

A few yards from the forge a man was wrestling adroitly with long wands of hazel, engaged in one of the oldest crafts in England – hurdling. He was Jim Clements, who looks a youthful sixty, but is really seventy. He told me that he began life as a shepherd, starting work at five o'clock in the morning and ending at seven in the evening. Then he moved from job to job round the calendar: 'In the winter it was thatching, in the spring, lambing; in the summer, sheep-shearing; then came hurdling, making hay-ricks and thatching them; and so on until the hopping.'

Making hurdles is a skilful job that requires a lot of practice. They are made of hazel cut before Christmas; and a good hurdler likes to cut his own hazel. A hurdle is made of stout uprights called steeples, between which are woven lighter split lengths of wood called rods. There are generally ten steeples to a hurdle, and a sufficient number of interlaced rods rammed down one on top of the other to make the job sound.

The hurdler works with a mould or frame, which is simply a heavy wood block, some-times a tree trunk, in which ten holes have been made to take the ten uprights, or steeples.

The stakes are put in the frame with the sharpened ends uppermost, and the hurdler starts his weaving, ramming the rods tightly downward with his foot, layer upon layer. This is an old South of England craft, for in the North and in Scotland hurdles are unknown. A mountain sheep would take them in his stride.

As long as records exist, hurdles have been a feature of the English countryside. The Ancient Britons ringed their camps and vil-lages with hurdles, the Saxons used them for every conceivable purpose, and the wattle and daub walls of ancient houses are merely a

*'The blacksmith's forge
is still alive in Binsted'*

'This country is on a larger scale,
is wider and windier and generally less cosy'

form of hurdle plastered over to form a solid surface.

'Hurdles cost a shilling each, and I can make eleven a day,' said Jim Clements. 'But that's taking it easy. A man who sets his mind at it can make twelve.'

I left Binsted, glad to have seen that a bit of old England still lives there, and in four miles I came to the market town of Alton. This town was once notorious for its thieves and robbers, but the modern inhabitants are peaceful and kindly, and, so far as I could see, bear no resemblance whatsoever to their ancestors.

The robbers of the Alton district were in the habit of haunting the thick neighbouring woods, a part of the Alice Holt forest, which has now shrunk to a few acres of woodland, and they were such a terror to travellers that a portion of the forest was cut down in the Middle Ages. The main street of Alton, and also that of the village of Bentley, are said to be stretches of the Pilgrims' Way, so that the robbers of Alice Holt never lacked victims.

In the old days Alton was famous for barracan, a coarse kind of woollen or goats' hair cloth, an industry which employed five hundred workers in 1738. They make no cloth in Alton today, but they have brewed excellent beer for two centuries. The saccharometer, an instrument used in all breweries for measuring sugar in solution, was invented by an Alton brewer.

Someone told me that I should go to the church of St Lawrence, to see the bullets which Cromwell's troopers shot into the door when Colonel Rolles and eighty Cavaliers sought refuge there in 1643. I found them, as they had been described to me, round holes drilled into the thick oak doors, a grim relic of the horrible slaughter which took place in the church when the Roundheads eventually forced the doors and saw the Cavaliers lying there, shooting across their dead horses.

This fine old church, which badly needs money spent on it, has a number of remarkable features, notably the early Norman carving on some of the capitals, and three painted frescoes on a pillar. Among the memorials, I was interested to read a brass which commemorates a certain Christopher Walaston, who was groom of the chamber, and one of the 'Yostregere' to Henry VIII, Edward VI, Mary and Elizabeth.

Those four reigns occupied only ninety-four years, and it is therefore obvious that an old man, if he were good at keeping his job, might well have served all four monarchs. But the word 'Yostregere' interested me. I had never seen it before. I find that it is a novel spelling of 'Austringer', the ancient name for a falconer, or a keeper of goshawks.

Walking round Alton, I noticed these words on a doorplate. 'Here Lived Edmund Spenser, poet, 1590.' So far as I could discover, Spenser's 'residence' was a shadowy visit during one of his absences from Ireland. There is another famous name above a shop in Alton: residents can have their hair cut by no less a one than Julius Caesar!

Spenser's vague connection with Alton caused me to reflect how many literary associations are scattered round the countryside, within ten miles of the town. There is Cobbett at Farnham; from Waverley Abbey, not far away, Scott is said to have taken the name of the Waverley Novels; at Moor Park, Dean Swift, when secretary to Sir William Temple, first met 'Stella', whose name was Esther Johnson. Selborne is linked for ever with Gilbert White; Alresford is the birthplace of Mary Mitford, who wrote *Our Village*; and just outside Alton, at Chawton, lived Jane Austen.

Alton saw something of a famous writer during the war scare of 1757 and onwards, when the Militia Act embodied an additional 32,000 men for national defence. This man was Edward Gibbon. At that time he was a young man of twenty and was living with his father at Buriton, about a mile south of Petersfield. Both father and son joined the Hampshire Militia. Gibbon took over his company at Alton, and marched them to Alresford. On another occasion he treated his company to some Alton ale, 'which they received with great cheerfulness and decency'.

Who can doubt that two years of soldiering

in Hampshire helped Gibbon to understand the military problems of the declining Roman Empire? I would give a lot to put back the clock and see Captain Edward Gibbon marching through Alton at the head of his legion!

Before I left this interesting town, I visited the Curtis Museum. It is too crowded and deserves better quarters, because it has the making of a really good local collection. All kinds of objects familiar to the fathers, the grandfathers, and the great-grandfathers of Hampshire are to be seen there: harvesters' barrels, which in the old days were taken into the fields during that thirsty time of year; clogs and pattens as worn by girls and women a century or two ago; hour-glasses, man-traps, black-jacks; a flageolet once used in Selborne Church, two clarinets played in Bentworth Church; and wood blocks used in marking hop sacks, including some fine lions, for that was the mark of Alton hops in the old days.

Farnham, which is doubtfully considering the possibility of a museum, might well take a hint from Alton. Here is a much smaller town which had the vision to build up a collection with a real educational value, and one that is bound to become more valuable as time moves on.

I went to the little village of Selborne, to see the place where Gilbert White was born, and where, in later life, he wrote so lovingly of birds, animals and flowers.

White was a parson, born in 1720, and, as he never allowed his portrait to be painted, we know nothing of his personal appearance except that he was thin, upright, and only about five feet three inches in height.

He was a man whose life seems to have been free from the ridiculous, the fantastic or the romantic. Although he rode a lot on horseback, he never, so far as we know, fell off. He never married, and it is even doubted whether he was ever in love.

This placid little man has charmed generations, because he was an acute observer who possessed not only the ability to make small things seem important, but also of communicating his enthusiasm to others. Day by day he set down descriptions of the wildlife around him, in his garden, in the fields, in the woods near the little village in which he lived; and so he built up the only natural history book which has become an English classic.

In this, he was like a man who died thirty-seven years before him, Izaak Walton. Both of them managed to cast a rare beauty, a thrilling air of discovery, a freshness and a charm, about their hobbies: Izaak Walton about fishing, and Gilbert White about the sights and sounds of the Hampshire countryside.

Their books, *The Compleat Angler* and *The Natural History of Selborne*, although so unlike in style and matter, stand together as unique creations of the English mind. They are books about subjects which can be as dull as ditch-water, as we all know to our sorrow, yet even readers who have no interest in angling or in natural history have found them completely absorbing. One reason is that Walton, with his artful artlessness, and White in his earnest simplicity, have contrived, without meaning to do so, to paint an intimate portrait of themselves.

White, for instance, could never describe an owl or a bat without, at the same time, calling up in the reader's mind a picture of himself, a small, spare man in a black suit, standing intently in Selborne churchyard, watching and listening as the twilight falls.

This is a rare gift. It is much the same as the quality in an actor which causes everything he does to seem important, which makes an audience look at him the moment he comes on the stage, even though he may not appear to have made the slightest bid for their attention.

I arrived at Selborne through East Worldham and Kingsley, and then up the long, steep hill to the village. Selborne Hanger, which Gilbert White knew so well, is a dense beech wood climbing an abrupt hill and overhanging the village and the surrounding country, and is a notable landmark.

The village is small and neat, and as silent as a village can be when it is some distance from a railway station. It is an almost shopless village, and I was going to say an apparently childless one, but I suppose the children were all at school. During the hours I was there, I saw only one small boy and he was helping to toss soggy hay in a meadow.

I noticed a strange black cat with withered ears and an almost circular face sitting outside the post-office. I wondered whether his ears had been lowered in battle or frost-bite. As I expected, he dropped his habitual air of battered dignity under the influence of a few kind words, and, while I was stroking him, the postmaster came out. 'I see you like my old George,' he said. 'He's a funny cat. A soldier brought his grandfather home in his pocket from Siberia.' So it must have been frost-bite!

I thought this was an admirable introduction to Selborne. If Gilbert White were living, old George would now be purring his way to immortality. How eagerly the naturalist would have observed him, anxious to discover how a Siberian grandfather might influence a cat's reaction to Selborne.

A little farther down the street I came to the village green, which slopes gently up to the ancient church. A notice on a wall stated that charabancs and buses are forbidden to park on the 'Plestor' by order of Magdalen College, Oxford.

What a puzzling notice for the innocent stranger! What is a 'Plestor'? And what has Magdalen College, Oxford, to do with this Hampshire village?

Anyone familiar with the life of Gilbert White will remember that the living of Selborne, which the College still holds, was once the land of the long-vanished Priory of Selborne, and came into its possession in 1484, when Bishop Waynflete received papal sanction to transfer it to his college. With regard to 'Plestor', perhaps White's explanation is the best: it is the ancient play-stow, or play-place, of the village.

As soon as I entered the churchyard, I saw the famous yew of Selborne. It is a colossal tree, with a girth of about twenty-five feet, and in the twilight of its vast limbs, which are supported everywhere with wooden crutches, perhaps a hundred men might stand in comfort. I do not know whether, as Selborne claims, this is the oldest yew tree in England, but it is one of the most majestic. I think the yew in the churchyard at Darley Dale, in Derbyshire, can be its only possible rival.

The church, like many in this part of Hampshire, has a sturdy little Norman nave and mediæval windows. In the chancel is a grey stone with the words 'Gilbert White' on it, and this is assumed by nine visitors out of ten to be the tomb of the naturalist. But it is not: it is that of his grandfather. White is not buried in the church, but in the churchyard near the entrance to the vestry.

The most beautiful thing in the church is a modern stained glass window, a memorial to the naturalist, which shows St Francis and the birds. Every kind of bird known to Gilbert White is beautifully and faithfully represented. While I was looking at it, two masterful women came in and examined it minutely.

'As soon as I entered the churchyard, I saw the famous yew of Selborne'

'The most beautiful thing in the church is a modern stained glass window'

'Why have they put in a hoopoe?' asked one. 'I'm sure that has nothing to do with Gilbert White. You only see them in Egypt.'

I admit that for a moment I thought they were right. I have never seen a hoopoe in this country, but I have seen them in Egypt by the hundred.

However, I slunk away to a pew and brought out a copy of the *Natural History*, which I had in my pocket, and there, in Letter XI, I came across the following:

> The most unusual birds I ever observed in these parts were a pair of *hoopoes* (*upupa*), which came several years ago in the summer, and frequented an ornamental piece of ground, which joins to my garden, for some weeks. They used to march about in a stately manner, feeding in the walks, many times in the day; and seemed disposed to breed in my outlet; but were frightened and persecuted by idle boys, who would never let them be at rest.

The masterful women had departed by the time I had found the reference, otherwise I might have summoned up courage to tell them that the hoopoe has every right to be in the window, odd, as I admit, he looks there.

What a readable book it is! It is almost impossible to look up anything in it without reading more than you intended.

In the old churchyard I found a grey head-stone almost buried in the earth, bearing only the letters 'G. W.' I thought how right it is that no spectacular memorial is erected over White's grave, for, wherever you look in Selborne, every tree, blade of grass, every bird, every field-mouse, every flower, every shadow that passes across the sun, is in a true sense his memorial; and he would have wished for no other.

White was never vicar of Selborne, as many people seem to think. His grandfather was vicar, and White was born in the vicarage, which still stands near the church. In his thirties, White became curate at Selborne for a short time, but he did not begin his intimate association with the village until he was over forty, when he inherited from an uncle a house called The Wakes.

He lived there until his death at the age of seventy-three, fulfilling the duties of curate at Faringdon, about two miles away, and latterly at Selborne again. The Wakes was in recent years occupied by Mr Pears, of Pears' Soap, and is now occupied by Mrs Bibby, whose name is known in the steamship world. It is not shown to the public, though the gardener will kindly conduct visitors round the garden in which Gilbert White made so many of his immortal observations.

Like every stranger to Selborne, I climbed the Hanger by the Zig-zag Path. It is a short, steep climb through a beech-wood as hushed as a deserted cathedral. The trees, which are tall and straight, are almost free from under-growth. I have rarely seen a more silent wood, a wood more free from rustlings and scurryings, or one in which a man felt less conscious of watching eyes. But I suppose Gilbert White found it overcrowded with life.

At the top of the Hanger is the Wishing Stone, with a path worn all round it by the feet of many generations who have encircled it, pretending, no doubt, to make a joke of it, yet, in their hearts, wishing hard and heartily.

I was slightly disappointed by the view, which is not as good as I had been led to expect. The vista downward to Selborne through a tunnel of leaves is attractive, but the true beauty of the Hanger is its silence, its greenness, and the soft carpet of beech mast which crunches beneath the feet of the climber.

'Like every stranger to Selborne, I climbed the Hanger by the Zig-zag Path'

CHAPTER SIX

I see the ruins of Silchester, pass on to Oxford, spend the night at Godstow, and go to Cumnor, where Amy Robsart was murdered, or not as you must decide for yourself. Passing through Woodstock, where I see Bleinheim Palace, I go to Fotheringhay, the scene of Mary Stuart's execution. At Peterborough I conclude my glimpse of pre-war England and return home to await the outbreak of war.

Silchester was once a Roman city with a three-mile circuit of walls. There is nothing to be seen today but fields and country lanes, which here and there cross the site of the vanished town.

When Mr Frederick Davis wrote about the discoveries at Silchester in 1898, he estimated that the buildings in the centre of the ruins covered 9,699 square yards, or an area greater by 1,409 square yards than the space occupied in his time by Reading Town Hall, the municipal buildings, the covered market, the corn exchange, the museum, library and art gallery. So Roman Silchester, or *Calleva Atrebatum*, to give it its old name, was one of the important towns of Roman Britain.

'There is nothing to be seen today but fields and country lanes'

Turning into a narrow lane miles from anywhere, I knew that I had arrived at *Calleva Atrebatum* when I saw, in a field near the road, a mouldering stretch of Roman wall, decayed and broken, but in parts still firmly set with indestructible Roman cement.

I climbed the gate, and I was alone in *Calleva Atrebatum*.

Above the streets of the dead city, above the site of temple and basilica, main road, forum and baths, waved a field of corn. The foundations of the houses, dyers' shops and markets, which I had hoped to see, were hidden under a tall blanket of green.

I sat there with a clearer idea of *Calleva* in my mind than ever I have gained from books. The city occupied a key position, a logical creation of the road system of Roman Britain. It was like a star with five rays. From its five gates, five important roads led to great cities of the time: east to *Londinium*; north to Alchester; north-west to *Corinum* (Cirencester); and two to the south, one to *Sorbiodunum* (Salisbury), the other to *Venta Belgarum* (Winchester). Every traveller from the West Country, and as far north as Gloucester, must have passed through *Calleva* on his way to London. It was one of the grand junctions of Roman times.

For four hundred years, while Britain was part of the Roman Empire, *Calleva* was a great city. Generations of Romanised Britains were born there, lived and died where the corn now waves, gazed with pride at the temples and the basilica, and could not imagine in their wildest dreams that a time could come when *Calleva* would vanish from the earth; when a man would sit, as I was sitting, watching the corn rippling over the space within the walls. It would seem that civilisations, like individuals, do not find it easy to contemplate death.

And why did *Calleva* die? What happened to put an end to four hundred years of thriving life? The archæologists, who have dug there for the best part of a century, found only one clue. In late times some of the city gates had been blocked up and narrowed, obviously to make them easier for a declining population to defend. While Rome was strong, peace reigned in Britain and the gates were wide; but no sooner had Rome begun to totter than the Continental pirates became bolder and more numerous, rowing their war galleys up the British rivers, landing and raiding the helpless towns and isolated villas; and one city at least narrowed its gates in defence. The end of *Calleva* was probably a slow paralysis leading to abandonment. Nowhere in the whole city area did the excavators find one trace of fire or slaughter.

Calleva seems to have been quietly evacuated and left to its fate. Soon the city walls would be overgrown with brambles, the streets thick with grass; under the snows of winter and the spring rains the roofs would leak and eventually fall in; and it would not be long before the Saxon war-bands, coming through the dense forest which in those days stretched almost to the eastern gate, would stand in silence and in awe as they saw the dead city of *Calleva*, like a white ghost at the edge of the forest.

Leaving Silchester, I traversed lanes and furze-scattered commons and little woods until I left Hampshire and crossed into Berkshire. To the left I saw a distant line of chalk downs, smooth and curved, against the sky, and when at length I came to houses, and saw above a public-house a sign, The Horse and Jockey, I knew that I had arrived at Newbury.

About eight miles north-east of Newbury, in a marvellous tangle of lanes, I found the little hamlet of Aldworth, which boats a gigantic yew and a church filled pew high with a series of extraordinary tombs. The De la Beche memorials have given to the old church the appearance of a mortuary. Stiff stone men and women lie everywhere in attitudes of prayer, their feet to the altar. They rise above the pews and lie in the window niches. Never have I seen a small church so dominated by one family. Most of the

'Calleva *seems to have been quietly evacuated . . .*
soon the city walls would be overgrown with brambles,
the streets thick with grass'

RIGHT '*Stiff stone men and women lie everywhere in attitudes of prayer'*

men are in armour, and some have brought their wives to church with them. During long centuries the villagers of Aldworth have expressed their disapproval by knocking off an arm here and a nose there.

This race of stone men ended, appropriately enough, with a famous geologist, Sir Henry Thomas de la Beche, the founder of the Royal School of Mines, who died in 1855, and brought a distinguished family to its end. The tombs were one of the 'sights' of Elizabethan England and it is recorded that Queen Elizabeth went to see them, riding pillion behind the Earl of Leicester.

Through the falling dusk I went to Streatley, and on the way I came to a place where the fields seemed to slide off into emptiness; looking down, I saw lights shining in the valley of the Thames.

Oxford is one of those places which encourages the art of valediction. How natural it is that a young man, or a young woman, having spent some years in its shelter, should address a few polite words of farewell before turning towards the bleaker regions of reality.

Strangely enough, this custom of saying goodbye to Oxford seems to have been inaugurated by Queen Elizabeth. When Her Majesty was leaving Oxford in 1592, she stopped her coach before it went down the hill to Wheatley, and, turning to the dreaming spires, she addressed them: 'Farewell, farewell, dear Oxford,' she said. 'God bless thee and increase thy sons in number, holiness and virtue.'

It would be impertinent for a stranger to presume to judge the holiness or virtue of Oxford, but he is at liberty to say that Her Majesty's other command has been obeyed: Oxford's sons have increased in such numbers, and each one possesses either a motor-car or a bicycle, that it is now difficult to cross the road except at a hunted run. No other town of its size in England leaves upon the

mind such an impression of congestion.

It may be possible to find in the remote depths of some college, possibly in its cellars, a place where one might be tolerably safe from assassination, or at least out of earshot of bicycle bells, motor horns, motor bicycles, and those sudden harsh rending noises, as if an eighty-foot giant has torn his trousers, which indicate that a motor omnibus is changing gear.

It is surely remarkable that no one has persuaded Lord Nuffield to move the town of Oxford to some adjacent site, where it might carry on its thriving business with greater efficiency. If only as an act of expiation, the creator of so many motor-cars should restore to the University her ancient peace.

I went to the Trout Inn, which stands in the shadow of Godstow Bridge. The sound of water rushing down between the gates of the weir ceases neither by day nor night. Among the beauties of this old building is a moss-grown roof of Stonesfield slate, perhaps the most attractive roofing material ever used in England. I would rather see it than the finest thatch or the most mellowed tiles.

One of the pleasures of travelling in England is the crossing of geological boundaries into new scenery and to fresh styles in ancient architecture.

After travelling for some time, as I had done, through the chalk, clay and Upper Greensand counties of Kent, Sussex, Hampshire and Berkshire, it was delightful to enter the limestone district of Oxfordshire, a part of that great band of oolite which runs across England, beginning in Dorset and going, by way of a part of Somerset, Wiltshire and the Cotswolds, through Oxfordshire, Bedfordshire, Northamptonshire and Lincolnshire, right up to the moors of North Yorkshire.

All the old villages in this limestone belt are made of fine stone, some of them dark, some honey-brown, and those buildings which, like the inn at Godstow, are also roofed with stone, seem to me the most perfect of all. Mellowed by centuries of wind and rain, they collect the seeds of many mosses and even ferns, which thrive until they form a soft greenish-yellow carpet through which the silver-grey of the stones can still be seen.

The inn at Godstow is familiar to generations of Oxford men, and it is good to know that popularity has not spoilt it. There is a touch of Alice in Wonderland about it. The rooms are low, dark and heavily beamed. The bar, full of old oak and settles, is crowded like a museum with rustic objects and sporting relics: portions of foxes, hares and otters, spurs, prints of horses and game-birds, old china, pewter, cases of butterflies and stuffed fish; all are lying about or hung on the walls in an easy and natural way.

Generations of undergraduates have filled the place with laughter and talk, with exuberance and a youthful extravagance of mind, so that I did not know whether the old house itself, or the people who run it, were responsible for the impression that it is a quaint repository of much that is precious and lovable in the English character, among which I would mention humour, toleration, and a casual acceptance of eccentricity.

The place overflowed with hearty young men, pint pots in hand. Across the meadows came others who had walked from Oxford, and still more came by car and bicycle, until the terrace by the water was crowded with a new and, in my opinion, satisfactory generation.

I went to look at the remains of the nunnery of Godstow, which lies opposite in a meadow. This is the place where Rosamond Clifford, the 'Fair Rosamond' of romance, was educated and where she was buried. The nunnery is now a shapeless and untidy ruin, a pen for cattle, and even the site of Rosamond's grave is no longer known. Her story is the earliest of our royal love tragedies, and I suppose there is no one who is not familiar with it. English writers, from early historians and ballad writers to Scott, Swinburne and Tennyson, have been attracted by it, and so indeed have the writers of other nations. There is a Spanish opera about Fair Rosamond, and there are poems about her in French and Italian. Her immortality hangs literally by a thread, for without the incident of the ball of silk which, unwinding itself as she fled into the maze at Woodstock, led the jealous Queen to her hiding-place, there would be precious little to remember about her.

All the early accounts mention this thread, and it seems possible that there may be some truth in the legend and also in the belief that, in order to conceal his love of Rosamond from the Queen, the King smuggled her about the country discreetly, and perhaps made Woodstock her special hiding-place.

Eleanor of Aquitaine was eleven years older than Henry II, and if the date of Rosamond's murder is correct, she would have been a woman of fifty-five when she discovered her husband's infidelity. She was a remarkable woman, a noted beauty in her time, a woman who as the wife of King Louis of France had accompanied him on a crusade to the Holy Land, and had then fascinated and married the young King of England and became the mother of Richard the Lion Heart.

Legend says that when Henry discovered that Rosamond had been murdered, he sent the Queen to prison, but she survived him and lived to a great age. During Richard's imprisonment in France, she set herself, at the age of seventy-two, to raise an immense sum for his ransom; and then, worn out, she died.

Rosamond slept in Godstow under a remarkable Latin pun, which, according to the coarse feeling of the time, was probably one often engraved upon the tombs of Rosamonds. A free translation is:

Within this tomb lies the world's chiefest rose;
She who was sweet will now offend the nose.

*'I went to the Trout Inn, which stands in the shadow
of Godstow Bridge . . . and to look at the remains of the nunnery'*

Long before the inn was awake in the morning, I let myself out into the garden. The sun was shining, dew was thick upon the grass, and the sound of water coming into the weir was almost thunderous in the hush of the early morning.

From the curve of a rustic bridge, I looked into the water, where a number of large barbel swam, motionless but for a flick of tail or fin, their heads held to the stream. In the bright garden opposite, sunlight touched clumps of summer flowers, and a peacock walked among them solemnly, lifting and rattling a great blue and green fan of tail-feathers, apparently for his own pleasure and vanity.

I saw a pole moving among the willows, and a punt came slowly into view, holding the sleeping forms of three or four young men, while a figure in shorts and blazer stood slowly thrusting the pole into the water. He climbed on the terrace and came running across the bridge to ask me where the lock was. He said that, as the night had been such a lovely one, he and his companions had decided to spend it on the river. They had come slowly up from Oxford by moonlight.

It was nothing, I suppose, that brief encounter in the unawakened morning, with the dew on the grass and the birds singing, but there was something about it which, even at the time, I knew I should always remember, as one remembers a tune or a verse. And I think perhaps that young men, born into a dark world, may also some day recall with pleasure the nights they spent punting up from Oxford by the light of the moon, to come cold into the sweet morning by Godstow Weir.

Because Walter Scott took some liberties with fact in *Kenilworth*, many people will tell you that Amy Robsart, Lady Dudley, met her mysterious death in that famous castle. Actually, Kenilworth did not come into the possession of Robert Dudley until about three years after Amy's death. She was accidentally killed, or murdered, in a gloomy old house called Cumnor Place, now pulled down, some three and a half miles to the south of Oxford, just over the Berkshire border.

When I saw the village at Cumnor at the end of a sunny afternoon, there was no atmosphere of mystery about it, nothing to indicate that it had been the scene of a tragedy that once caused all the courts of Europe to whisper and gossip. It is a pretty village, composed of stone houses, some thatched and others roofed with stone, and in the centre stands the old parish church.

I asked a villager if anything remained of Cumnor Place. He replied that the building had been pulled down by the third Lord Abingdon over a hundred years ago, for it was so badly haunted by the ghost of Amy Robsart that no one would live in it. And this I find is true. After the death of Anthony Foster, who was in residence at the time of Amy's death, the hall was never again occupied and so in the course of centuries it gradually fell into ruin and decay. A determined attempt to lay the ghost was once made by ten Oxford clerics, but apparently without success, for the hall remained, until its demolition in 1810, one of the most eerie and shunned ruins in England. I could find no trace of it at all to the south of the church, where I was told it once stood, therefore I was obliged to reconstruct in my imagination a gloomy, mediæval building of stone pierced by many slender lancet windows, austere and church-like. In Cumnor Church you can see an admirable engraving of the hall as it looked just before it was pulled down.

In September 1560, Amy Robsart went to stay there with her husband's steward, Anthony Foster, and his wife, who had rented the hall. This was characteristic of her lonely life after scandal had coupled the name of her husband with that of the Queen. Poor Amy was the one obstacle to the marriage which foreign ambassadors and the gossip of the Court believed to be on the way. So scandalous were the stories that it was commonly believed that Elizabeth and Dudley were the parents of a daughter.

Elizabeth was twenty-seven years of age at this time; Robert Dudley and Amy were the same age, twenty-eight. Months before Amy's death the Spanish Ambassador, who had reason for keeping his ear close to the ground, reported to Philip of Spain that 'I hear from a person who is accustomed to give veracious news that Lord Robert has sent to poison his wife', which, whether true or not, indicates the impression which the affair created in the contemporary mind. There can be no doubt that Dudley had no further use for Amy and that she alone stood firmly in the path of his ambition; she was pushed into the background and spent her miserable life travelling round from country house to country house, her only pleasure a pathetic passion for fine clothes. Her surviving correspondence consists of tailors' bills and notes to tailors and dressmakers. Perhaps the poor girl, like many another triangular wife, was determined not to let herself 'go to pieces'; maybe she dreamed in front of her mirror, for she is said to have been good-looking, of reconquering the unscrupulous ruffian whom she had married.

However, in September 1560 she found herself in gloomy Cumnor Place. In addition to her servants, the household consisted of the tenant, Anthony Foster, his wife and two guests, Mrs Owen and Mrs Odingsells. On 8 September, which was a Sunday, Abingdon Fair was in full swing and Amy rose early with the intention, apparently, that the whole household should have a holiday and go to the fair, leaving her alone with old Mrs Owen. But the other two ladies, Mrs Foster and Mrs Odingsells, did not fall in with this plan and some words followed. Mrs Odingsells thought that Sunday was no day for a gentlewoman to go to a fair. Amy retorted with anger that Mrs Odingsells could choose what day she went to a fair, but servants could not do so. Therefore only the servants went, leaving at home Amy,

the three women, and perhaps Foster, although there is no evidence that he was at Cumnor at the time. Indeed, in the absence of any account of his actions that night, it seems possible that he was not there.

What happened is not clear. It is believed that Amy dined alone in her apartments with Mrs Owen, and that after dinner the four ladies played some table game together and then presumably went to bed. Late at night, when the servants came home from the fair, they found the body of their mistress lying at the bottom of a spiral stone staircase that ran from her apartments to the hall beneath. Someone noticed that, although her neck was broken, her hood had not been displaced, the suggestion being that her dead body had been put there.

Her death caused a tremendous sensation, as well it might. What malicious gossips had been whispering had actually come true, and the word 'murder' sprang naturally to the lips. Of this Dudley was well aware and he was alarmed by the danger to himself. But he had nothing to fear. The coroner's jury unearthed no evidence of murder and a verdict of mischance was returned.

But the verdict had no effect on contemporary opinion. People continued to whisper that Lady Dudley had been murdered by her ambitious husband, or, driven to desperation by his actions, had committed suicide, a possibility revealed by Lady Amy's maid, who said that she had once heard her mistress 'pray to God to deliver her from desperation'.

A writer of detective fiction could make a great point of the victim's desire to be alone that night, of her desperate anxiety to empty the house, and of the significant fact that she was wearing a hood when she was found, as though she were going out of doors, perhaps to meet someone. But such speculations only serve to deepen and confuse the mystery of her death. One fact I do think is important. Amy Robsart was not, as many of her partisans have imagined her to have been, a healthy young woman: she was suffering from a disease which may have been cancer. The Spanish Ambassador, De Feria, wrote to his monarch eighteen months before Amy's death these significant words: 'People talk of this so freely [Dudley's affair with the Queen] that they go so far as to say his wife has a malady in one of her breasts, and the Queen is only waiting for her to die to marry Lord Robert.'

Were this true, the poor girl, suffering from a fatal disease, mentally affected by the tragedy of her marriage, childless, lonely and unwanted, must have been in an abnormal state of mind, and this is amply born out by Sir Thomas Blount, who was sent hot-haste by Dudley to enquire into the tragedy. Writing from Cumnor while Lady Amy's dead body still lay there, he said: 'I have heard diverse tales of her that maketh me to judge her to be a strange woman of mind,' and, again in the same letter, 'the tales I do hear of her maketh me to think she had a strange mind in her; as I will tell you at my coming.'

If only we could know what these 'strange tales' were which Blount promised to tell Dudley, we might be better able to judge her mental condition. And I think, could we know them, they would prove that she was suffering from melancholia or worse, induced by her disease and by her husband's cruelty, and that, in the almost empty house on that Sunday night in September 1560, moved by restlessness and misery, and with no one to take care of her, she left her room for some reason and met an accidental death. I do not for one moment think she committed suicide. People bent on self-destruction do not use spiral staircases for this purpose. They descend them with the utmost care, carrying daggers or phials of poison, taking every precaution not to slip. I also suggest that while women can write earnestly to dressmakers they do not often commit suicide.

I entered Cumnor Church and found it full of relics associated with the mystery. A life-size statue of Elizabeth, an extraordinary object to find in a church, stands against a window, holding the sceptre and the orb. In a place of such memories, there is something exceedingly sinister about it. A notice says that the statue is supposed to have been originally made to Dudley's orders, and placed in the gardens of Cumnor Place as a compliment to his mistress, but is it not more likely to have been one of Anthony Foster's gestures of loyalty?

The church contains the tomb of Anthony Foster, the one man who must have known the true story of Amy Robsart's death. Hanging on a wall near the door are several pictures of Cumnor Place. There is also a letter from Amy Robsart to a tailor named William Edney, who lived at Tower Royal, which was not in London, but near Bucklebury, in Berkshire.

Two tailor's bills for clothes are hung in the church. Amy Robsart was fated never to wear these garments, which were delivered after her death. The bills include the following items:

for makynge a petecote of skarlet with bodyce and
stockes of crimson velvet   10/-
for makynge a Spanyshe gowne of velvet with a fringe
of blacke sylke and golde   8/-

Amy Robsart's tailor's bills, and the statue of Queen Elizabeth, are perhaps the strangest relics of an unedifying triangle to be found in any church. But Time has cast over them the impersonality of museum exhibits, and, as long as history is read, people will go to look at them, puzzled and interested by the unsolved mystery of Cumnor Place.

Eight miles or so to the north of Oxford, reposing in June sunshine, was Woodstock. Here is a town that in some almost miraculous way has escaped the vulgarities of our age and lives in calm and dignity, a standing memorial to the virtue of patronage, for it has grown up in the shadows of kings and dukes. Stone houses gaze at each other across wide streets:

some are Tudor, some Queen Anne, others are Georgian or Victorian; and all these styles harmonise and show their relationship one to the other, so that they remind you of a family of several generations gathered in the same room.

There are corners of Woodstock in which it is easy to imagine Elizabethan horsemen dismounting in old stable yards; there are others in which you might hope to see a six-horse coach of the Stuart period lumbering down the street, while no imagination at all is required to see the mail coach emerge from the archway of the Bear, the guard lifting his horn to salute the miles ahead.

Woodstock is, of course, a name famous in history, for in the neighbouring park once stood the Manor of Woodstock, one of the most ancient royal residences in the country. It was the traditional scene of 'Rosamond's Bower', and almost all the sovereigns of England visited the place until the time of Queen Anne, when the old palace was pulled down.

Before Elizabeth was queen she was imprisoned at Woodstock, suspected of plotting against her sister, Queen Mary, and she visited the town on happier occasions after she had ascended the throne. On one such occasion she was presented with the best pair of gloves that Woodstock could make.

The most noted industry of the town in the old days was delicate steel work made from the nails of old horseshoes. These were melted down, and the metal apparently treated in some way before it was wrought into a variety of objects. A chain of Woodstock steel weighing only two ounces was once sold in France for £170.

It was the rise of the cheap metal industries of Birmingham and Sheffield that killed the Woodstock·steel work, of which not a trace now remains.

'The archway of the Bear'

I was interested to see, as I walked round the town, that the old craft of glove-making is still carried on. Several shops advise the visitor to buy his gloves there, but who could fail to buy a pair of Woodstock gloves? I was told in one of the shops that the industry is still a handicraft. Doeskin, buckskin, pigskin, chamois and suede are cut and sewn in the town and all the best gloves are made entirely by hand. It is still the custom, as it was in Tudor and Stuart times, for cottage women to take the cut-out gloves and to return them sewn and finished.

The great sight of Woodstock is the Palace of Blenheim, which belongs to the Duke of Marlborough. The park is always open to the public, and the entrance to it is in the town. I passed beneath a vast triumphal archway into a deer park of nearly three thousand acres, where miles of grassland are varied by giant oaks and cedars. After walking for some time down a long avenue, I saw Blenheim Palace ahead, and, although I knew roughly what to expect, the sight shook me. That enormous mass of Renaissance stone planted with a terrific air of emphasis and conviction in an English park, and looking from a distance like a town that has lost its way, is one of England's most splendid fantasies. The scale on which Blenheim is built exceeds anything I have ever seen. Even photographs give no true idea of it. And as I drew nearer, I gazed in still greater astonishment, thinking that no better proof exists in all the world of the things an architect can do, given a great patron, a moment of national emotion, and a free hand.

I remembered a sentence, one that implies a profound and pessimistic knowledge of architects and their ways, in Mr Winston Churchill's great book, *Marlborough, His Life and Times*. 'According to a deep law of nature,' says Mr Churchill, 'the architect's estimate of £100,000 fell far short of the realised expense.'

I wondered how many of the people who were walking in the park and gazing, as I was, with dazed surprise through the railings, knew the remarkable story of this gigantic structure. I approached one man and asked him if he could tell me the history of Blenheim Palace.

'I'm sorry,' he said briskly. 'I'm a stranger about here.'

I approached another man.

'I saw Blenheim Palace ahead'

'I can only tell you that it belongs to the Duke of Marlborough,' he replied, 'but you'll find a lot of writing on the gate over there.'

A third, full of good intentions, was more than slightly muddled. He ventured the suggestion that the place had been given to the great Duke of Marlborough for his services in fighting Napoleon.

So it would appear that the story of Blenheim Palace is not known to everybody; and here it is.

Few people will dispute that Marlborough was the greatest military leader in English history. He took the field at the head of the allied armies to oppose the determination of Louis XIV to dominate the world. He humbled the power of France in four great battles: the first was at Blenheim, in Bavaria, in 1704. When the news of this victory reached England, the country, wild with joy, decided to reward her captain-general with some great memorial. It was the wish of Queen Anne that the offering should take the form of the old royal Manor of Woodstock, in whose park it was further decided by Queen and Parliament to build, at their joint cost, a grand house to be called the Palace of Blenheim.

The architect chosen to design this house was John Vanbrugh, a man intoxicated by stone. He was not only a great architect, but also a great dramatist. Some people would rather see one of his plays than one of his palaces.

Sarah, Duchess of Marlborough, was one of the most decisive and managing women of her time, and upon her fell the responsibility of watching this gigantic palace rise from the ground, for her husband was usually abroad winning battles. Sarah did not really like the idea of Blenheim. She would rather have had something to live in. But she knew that her husband's heart was set on the scheme; she knew that he thought of it, not as a house, but as an enduring monument that would last, if Vanbrugh built it, for a very long time. So she loyally superintended the building of Blenheim

Palace, opposing the architect whenever possible, and watching with alarm the operation of that 'deep law of nature' noted by Mr Churchill, which steadily drove the cost of Blenheim from £100,000 to £300,000.

The palace took seventeen years to build, and the man for whom it was built never saw it completed. The seventeen years were years of quarrels between Sarah and the architect and between the architect and the workmen, whose pay was often in arrears or not forthcoming at all.

Seventeen years is a long time for national gratitude to endure if there are bills to be met all the time, and it is not surprising therefore that Parliament refused to pay up. The relationship between Sarah and the Queen, once so intimate, did not help matters, for those ladies were not on speaking terms. So the work ceased. The angry unpaid labourers and the stonemasons, many of whom had helped to build Wren's St Paul's, departed from the scene, leaving the colossal house derelict, yet never slept in.

The Duke, still winning battles abroad, heard with dismay that his national memorial was likely to be burned down by angry workmen, and Vanbrugh sent him a note of the financial position: £220,000 had been paid to the Treasury; £42,000 was due to the workmen, and another £25,000 was needed to carry on; but no one was willing to advance a penny.

It is difficult to say what would have happened to Blenheim if Queen Anne had not succumbed to a fit of apoplexy in 1714; and no sooner was she dead than George I was in England, Marlborough was back in triumph, and the first man to be knighted by the new monarch was the architect, John Vanbrugh.

Work started again, this time at the Duke's cost and Vanbrugh once again flung himself with irrepressible vigour into the erection of his life's most monumental effort. For eight years the work continued. Immense new sums were spent; still the Palace was not completed. Then the Duke of Marlborough died! The man for whom all this magnificence was made never lived there, never enjoyed it, never got anything out of it except a grandiose dream of posthumous fame. Whenever he thought of his great, troublesome palace, he thought also of you and me (and of the man in the park who thought he had beaten Napoleon!), and it was for our sakes that he built Blenheim; it was of us he liked to think, the children of the unborn age, who would some day stand in front of the monument and say: 'This is the house of the great Duke of Marlborough, a house almost as great as he was.'

Among such are the extraordinary weaknesses of genius. The end of the story is that the Duchess Sarah, having been left a fortune by her husband (as Vanbrugh said 'to ruin Blenheim her own way') got rid of him and employed another architect.

Although she never liked the idea of Blenheim, so great was her devotion to Marlborough that she carried out the scheme to its bitter end, as he would have wished her to do.

She was a forbidding woman in all but her love for Marlborough, and he returned her affection to the full. They were two middle-aged people who were still deeply and truly in love. He once wrote to her from one of his battlefields: 'I do from my heart assure you that I should be much better pleased to live with you in a cottage than in all the palaces this world has without you.' And after his death, though she was sixty-two years of age, two great and wealthy noblemen asked her to marry them. To one she was kind; to the other she made this reply:

'If I were young and handsome as I was, instead of old and faded as I am, and you could lay the empire of the world at my feet, you should never share the heart and hand that once belonged to John, Duke of Marlborough.'

For his sake she carried on with the orgy of building. She put up the great Corinthian archway beneath which we enter the park. She also erected the pillar, still standing, with his statue on its summit, and upon the plinth a description of his ten campaigns.

I had a grand afternoon dodging the main roads and seeking sanctuary in the lanes of Oxfordshire.

Leaving Woodstock, I soon found myself in Kirtlington, a lovely grey village, then came Bicester, a peaceful nineteenth-century town anchored to the modern world by a common little cinema; and so by a stretch of main road into Buckinghamshire and to a village called Grendon Underwood, which remembers Shakespeare.

There are not, to my knowledge, many legends of Shakespeare, even in his native county, but the village of Grendon Underwood is absolutely certain that the poet wrote *A Midsummer Night's Dream* there. I asked an old lady in a white apron where Shakespeare used to stay, and she pointed out a black-and-white house, as if he were still at work there.

'It's empty now,' she said, 'but if you want to see it go up the road to the council houses and ask for Mr Hine, the gardener.'

Mr Hine was mending an upturned bicycle and was not pleased to see me. He was a big Viking of a man and plain spoken.

'Six o'clock's a funny time to come looking at houses,' he said. 'You Mr Smith?'

When I said I was not Mr Smith he brightened and I could see that he sometimes smiled. He left the bicycle and, taking some keys, conducted me to the old black-and-white house, which used to be the Ship Inn. There was a 'to let' board outside. Many years ago, he told me, it had been turned into a farm called Shakespeare's Farm, and then into a private house, but no one living could remember when it had been an inn.

Upon the top floor is a small timbered room with an oblong window called Shakespeare's Room, because, as Mr Hine said, 'he used to sleep there.' When I asked if he wrote a play there, Mr Hine was emphatic.

'Go up the road to the council houses'

'He never wrote a play there!' he said in the voice that he reserves for the unknown Mr Smith. 'He wrote in the church porch, as everybody in Grendon Underwood will tell you. And it was while he was writing in the church porch that two constables came and arrested him.'

'Why did they do that?' I asked.

'Because they thought he was up to summat else,' replied Mr Hine shortly.

This is a strange and provoking story, and I wonder why and when this remote little village began to associate itself with Shakespeare. Even if he did not perform the incredible feat of writing *A Midsummer Night's Dream* in a church porch, there must surely have been some connection between Shakespeare and Grendon Underwood to explain the start of this legend. It is interesting, too, that one of the few Shakespeare stories is localised only twelve miles away at Oxford, so that Shakespeare has a firm hold on this district. The Oxford story is that when Shakespeare travelled between London and Stratford-upon-Avon he always stayed in Oxford, at an inn kept by a sedate and melancholy individual

named John D'Avenant, who was married to a witty and charming wife. Their son, who was christened William, became Sir William D'Avenant, poet and dramatist, and was whispered by his contemporaries to be the natural son of Shakespeare, a story which, by the way, is said not to have displeased Sir William in the least.

As we continued to explore the house and then the garden, I developed a regard for Mr Hine, for a servant may be truly judged in the absence of his master. The owner being abroad, Mr Hine was keeping the lawns mown, the flower-beds weeded, the hedges clipped, and the outhouses were full of chopped logs, the labour of wet days. When there was a moment to spare he mounted a ladder and thatched one of the immense barns. He is one of the last thatchers in the district.

'My son can thatch too,' said Mr Hine.

'Where does he work?' I asked.

'He's an engine-driver,' said Mr Hine.

So somewhere in England a train is being driven by a thatcher, which reminds us how close we are still to the village and the country.

I stayed that night in Buckingham, visited Stowe in the morning, a school that makes Eton seem like a slum, lunched with an otter and a badger in the Swan at Newport Pagnell, and went on to Bedford, having firmly resisted the temptation to see the house at Olney where that poor tortured poet, William Cowper, kept tame hares and wrote some of the most graceful letters in the English language.

Bedford is perhaps the only large town in England that knows how to make the right use of its river. The Ouse is the pride of Bedford, and, instead of flowing through the centre of the town, carrying on its banks a dreary assortment of factories and warehouses, it is the town's chief promenade. On Sundays and holidays half the population gathers to sit there as if at the seaside, to walk on grass and under trees in Russell Park, or to embark on the broad bosom of the Ouse itself and exhibit skill, or the reverse, before the assembled townsfolk.

I saw Bedford on a Sunday evening when the sun, appearing in April bursts, lit up a scene of extraordinary animation. Rowing boats, canoes and punts moved here and there on the Ouse, while people on the banks recognised their friends and commented on their handling of the oar, paddle or pole, and also, I surmise, on their choice of companions. Love affairs cannot for long be kept secret in Bedford. It is obviously every young man's fancy to take his girl on the river, so that a gossip on the embankment misses nothing.

I thought this scene charming. It would hardly be suitable, even in an unguarded moment, to call Bedford the Venice of England, but wherever there is water on which people pass in pleasure-boats, there is always an air of grace and gaiety. What a pity it is that other towns, whose rivers are now deformed by nineteenth-century industrial developments, cannot clear them away and make their

make their streams, like Bedford's Ouse, the playground of the people.

In Russell Park I watched an amusing device which I have never before seen. It may be quite a usual thing on boating rivers, but I have not much experience of them, and to me it was a diverting novelty.

It is a long, sloping double ladder which allows boats and punts to descend over dry land from the Ouse to a lake at a lower level. In the centre are rubber rollers over which the boats going down slide on by their own weight, and on which boats going up are dragged by their occupants.

This is evidently a sight of Bedford, for the rustic bridge above was never without its crowd, eagerly watching the punts sliding down, sometimes to the alarm of their occupants, to hit the lower water with a mighty splash. The process of going up the ladder is a much tamer proceeding. It was interesting to see in Bedford a classical device for moving ships over dry land. The Greeks and the Romans made use of a similar invention. There was a famous tramway of rollers five miles long across the Isthmus of Corinth, which saved ships days, perhaps even weeks, on their voyage.

One morning I set out to learn something about Bunyan in Bedford. I had been told that every man, woman and child in the town is familiar with Bunyan and his association with the town, but I had the bad luck to encounter either the proverbial stranger or the person to whom Bunyan is hardly a name.

A bookseller in a country town told me recently that *The Pilgrim's Progress* was, after the Bible, the best-read book of the time. I knew that this was once so, but I was surprised to learn that it is so today.

Unfortunately Bedford has demolished all the buildings in which the famous tinker might have preached, or in which he languished in captivity, and the only place where you will come across any visible relics of him is the Bunyan Meeting House in Mill Street.

And these relics are well worth going to see. Bunyan was born at Elstow, a village near Bedford, in 1628, the third year of the reign of Charles I. He died in 1688, at the age of sixty, three years after the death of Charles II, and the year that James II was dethroned. He lived therefore throughout the Commonwealth and the Restoration, and missed the Revolution and the landing of William of Orange by only a few months.

He belongs to an extraordinarily vivid and crowded time in history. When he was born, Shakespeare had been dead only twelve years and Ben Jonson, who knew the Poet, was still alive. Milton was his contemporary; so were Samuel Butler, Dryden, Pepys, Rubens, Van-dyke, Peter Lely and Christopher Wren. Among the great events which occurred during Bunyan's lifetime were the execution of Charles I, Cromwell's Republic, the return of Charles II, the Plague, the Fire of London, the death of Charles and the succession of James II; and then the flight of James and the coming of Dutch William.

But Bunyan, a humble tinker of Bedford who spent twelve of the most exciting years of this period in jail, was not interested in politics, and probably had no idea that he was living in such a vivid world. His one entry into active life was his soldiering during the Civil War on the side of Parliament.

A man whose thoughts were entirely with God could have only a slight interest in mundane affairs, but even if the actual events of the time have no place in his writings, his work is soaked in contemporary atmosphere. Bunyan is a museum of the Puritan mentality in the Stuart period. Like the Oxford Groupists and other self conscious sects, he loved to exaggerate his past errors. He delighted to magnify and boast about his sins, which seem, on investigation, to boil down to dancing on the village green, playing tip-cat, bell-ringing and swearing.

'Even as a child,' he wrote, luxuriating in imaginary sin, 'I had few equals in cursing, swearing, lying, and blaspheming the holy name of God'; and he said that, as he grew up, these habits grew also, so that a 'woman who was a loose and ungodly wretch protested that it made her tremble to hear me, as the ungodliest fellow for swearing she ever heard in all her life, and that it was enough to spoil all the youth in the whole town.'

I went to Elstow to see the place where he committed the monstrous sin of tip-cat; and it was just as I had imagined it would be, having scarcely changed since his time. I saw the Moot Hall on the village green, where he danced so sinfully, and when I went to the grey church, whose bells are in a detached belfry, the verger pointed to many deeply-cut grooves in the stone of the arch.

'Those were made by Bunyan's bell-rope,' he said. 'He got the idea that it was sinful to ring the bells because he enjoyed doing it, and he thought that perhaps as a punishment the bells would come tumbling down on him. So he used to stand outside the belfry, where you're standing now, and pull the rope from the outside.'

A cottage in which Bunyan is said to have lived with his first wife, and to have mended pots and pans in a lean-to shed which is no longer there, still stands in the main street. But Bedford, not Elstow, was the true scene of his life. When he was converted, he discovered that he possessed a marvellous gift for preaching.

Like many humble, unlettered men, he had a fine choice of words, and to this he joined an absolute sincerity which illuminated his whole life and shone in every word he spoke or put down in writing. That was the secret of his power while he lived and of his popularity after death.

He was safe while the Commonwealth endured, for Non-conformist preachers were allowed to say, within reason, what they liked, but as soon as Charles II came back they were

'I saw the Moot Hall on the village green, where Bunyan danced so sinfully'

forbidden to preach and the public was ordered to return to the parish churches. Bunyan refused to be silenced, and that was why he was cast into prison.

He had just married a second wife, his first wife having died, and this gallant woman, who was looking after his four children, made a brave attempt to set him free and even travelled up to London to put his case before the House of Peers.

Bunyan could obviously have received his liberty if he had promised not to preach. As it was, his imprisonment was often merely a matter of form. He was allowed to attend meetings and even to go to London! But regulations were tightened up from time to time, and then the prisoner had to stay behind the bars.

During the twelve years (with the exception of a brief release in 1666), Bunyan wrote innumerable books and pamphlets. To most people he is the author of one book, *The Pilgrim's Progress*; to a few he is the author of three books, but only a student would dream of reading the surviving copies of the fifty-nine works which this fluent and energetic author poured forth during his captivity.

When release came he was a man of forty-four. He was given full freedom to preach, and he took it. His meeting-house was a barn in an orchard – the present Bunyan Meeting House in Mill Street – but he also toured the country, preaching and visiting nonconformist ministers, known jocularly to the country-people as Bishop Bunyan.

He enjoyed fame in his lifetime, not only as a preacher but also as an author. Charles II once said to his chaplain, Dr John Owen, that he could not imagine how a man of his learning could listen to an illiterate tinker. Dr Owen replied: 'If I could have the tinker's power, I would give all my learning to hold it.'

Bunyan's death took place at the unnecessarily early age of sixty, for he was a strong, robust peasant. He caught cold riding from Reading to London on a wet August day in 1688. He sank into a fever from which he never recovered, and was buried in Bunhill Fields, Finsbury.

I was shown over the Bunyan Meeting House, which is a chilly chapel, and was taken into a room where all relics connected with the great man have been lovingly assembled. It is appropriate that one who spent twelve years in jail should be commemorated by so many massive old gates. They show with pride the wicket gate of Elstow Church, the gate of the belfry, and two nail-studded gates from the old Jail of Bedford.

There is a wonderful collection of Bunyan first editions, his chair, his walking-stick, his cabinet and jug, and what is claimed to be the only known metallic fiddle, a strange thing surely for Bunyan to have made.

'And this is the door he used to lean against while he listened to the bells ringing in Elstow belfry,' said the caretaker. 'Even when he had renounced bell-ringing as sinful, he loved it so much that he used to go to the belfry and watch someone else pulling on his rope.'

I went away to walk through the streets of Bedford and think of the genius of Bunyan. What explains it? He had enormous vitality. He was utterly sincere. His words were simple. He never tried to be clever. He did not know that he had a literary style, but he strove only to tell a story and deliver a message. Above all, he was that rare thing: a great preacher whose spell did not desert him when he took up a pen.

As I travelled north from Bedford into Huntingdonshire and north-west to Northampton-shire, I thought how large a part of England is still happily unknown to the advertiser. Someday the whole problem of private profit, and what crimes against good taste a man may commit in the search of it, will have to be faced, but how I do not know. Well-meaning societies do not even begin to tackle the problem. Perhaps a Ministry of Taste might be able to do good by educating the public and formulating laws limiting the amount of harm a financier and a speculator may inflict. But until ordinary men and women recognise as offensive the ghastly little foreign cinemas standing so ostentatiously in the main streets of English market towns, until they learn to hate the numerous shoddy deformities of speculative building and the countless crimes against local architectural traditions everywhere committed, even by the Ministry of Health and the Post Office, we shall never get very far.

Northamptonshire is a wonderful Midland county. Like many of the agricultural shires, it is more in the nineteenth century than the twentieth. Its market towns are, generally speaking, un-Woolworthed and de-Spencered; you never encounter in its lanes the man on a tricycle peddling ice-cream, whose presence in the south these days is the sign of a frequented thoroughfare; there are no road-houses and the countryside is entirely free from advertisements. The lanes of Northamptonshire, with wide grass verges on each side, the sheep grazing in the meadows, the spires of distant churches rising above woodland, the grey stone farms, and the little Tudor manor houses standing among old trees, form an unforgettable picture of an unspoilt England.

I have said something about the villages of Oxfordshire with their stone houses and stone roofs. In Northamptonshire you have the same type of village, only much of the stone is darker. The most characteristic sight in a Northamptonshire village is a row of sturdy old fortress-like cottages, their roofs of mossy stone undulating in the prettiest way as the old rafters have bent under the weight. Of all the roofing stone I have seen since I entered the limestone country, I think the Colley Weston slates are the most beautiful to look at. This is a stone which was quarried in the old days, and may even be quarried today for all I know, in the north of the county, near the Rutland border.

I have been told that the stone is taken from quarries in huge slabs, and then exposed to the action of frost. It is even watered on winter nights to give the frost a greater hold of it. When this has happened, a single tap from a hammer will split the stone into thin uniform layers, admirably adapted for roofing purposes. I noticed that the stone roofs of Northamptonshire are cemented on the outside, not on the inside, as you see them in Gloucestershire.

Northamptonshire was the scene of the most tragic execution in English history, the death at Fotheringhay Castle of Mary, Queen of Scots. The village of Fotheringhay lies about ten miles to the south-west of Peterborough, and I approached it by way of Oundle, a dark scholastic town of almost black stone.

In a few miles I came to broad, flat meadows traversed by the Nene, a slow and placid stream running its course through country that reminded me strongly of Warwickshire. There was a grey stone bridge, and in open fields on the river-bank a huge Perpendicular church with flying buttresses and a tower from which rose a graceful octagonal lantern. I crossed the bridge and found myself in an avenue of horse-chestnut trees. The village street was wide, empty and silent. A few stone houses stood dotted along its length. There were no shops and only one inn, the Falcon, and an old farmhouse turned into an hotel.

The door was opened by a man in a white mess-jacket who greeted me in a Scottish voice.

'Heavens, man, have you been here since the execution?' I asked.

'Och, no; I'm no' sae antique as a' that,' he said.

'It's a strange thing to come to Fotheringhay and hear a Scots voice the moment one arrives.'

'Aye, mebbe. I've heard that before,' he replied, taking my bag and leading the way upstairs.

My first impression of Fotheringhay was one of ineffable peace and quiet. No sound louder than a horse going past on the road or a dog barking disturbed the small, retired village. Sensitive people have felt that Fotheringhay has never recovered from the shocking deed done there three and a half centuries ago, and I can well believe that on a wet day, with the chestnut trees dripping and the gaunt stone cottages blackened with rain, a note of deepest melancholy would be struck. But on that bright evening, with gnats dancing in the late sunlight, the chestnuts and the hawthorn in bloom, the river singing slowly on its way, I thought Fotheringhay was perfect.

A few elderly people who appreciate peace, and can afford to pay for it, were staying in the hotel, and among them was a retired clergyman who had studied the antiquities of Northamptonshire. He told me that nothing is left of the Castle but a high mound at the end of the village, on the river bank, and we walked out to see it after dinner.

'Only one story of the execution has come down to the present inhabitants of Fotheringhay,' he said, 'which you might think strange, for less important and less terrible events are remembered in some villages. There is a reason for this. When the Castle was pulled down in the seventeenth century, the old families departed and the life of Fotheringhay declined. Even the farm labourers were a new race of incomers, so, you see, Fotheringhay has parted completely from its past.'

We came to the site of the Castle, which is now part of a farm. A huge mound covered with grass and hawthorn trees perhaps marks the place of the central keep.

'I have often heard the story,' said my companion, 'that when James I came to the throne, he put a curse on Fotheringhay and pulled down the scene of his mother's death; but that is not true. Fotheringhay Castle was standing, probably uninhabited, throughout James's reign, but was pulled down about 1626, the year after his death, by an owner who would not spend money on its restoration.'

Hawthorn trees, red and white, now bloom on the site of the banqueting hall where the execution took place; enormous quantities of milk thistles grow everywhere, and these, which are said to grow round all Mary's prisons, gave Agnes Strickland, the historian, the odd idea that the Queen and her attendants went from prison to prison sowing the seeds of the emblem of Scotland. The only remaining masonry is a huge block of rubble which has fallen down and rolled near the river. An archæological society has surrounded it with iron railings decorated with a Scot's thistle.

We sat on the mound smoking our pipes to keep the gnats at bay, and talking of the execution. For nearly six months Mary Stuart looked out on the view which one sees today from the top of this mound, the river winding its way through flat meadows; a peaceful scene, but one which Mary observed from October to February during the dreariest time of the year, a time when rain blots out the distance and grey clouds mass in the wide sky.

I knew of no account of a death more vivid and more affecting than the report of the execution which Sir Robert Wingfield wrote to Elizabeth's Secretary, Lord Burleigh. Elizabeth must have read this calm and observant account of the horrible scene, and no doubt it played its part in her futile and undignified attempt to disclaim responsibility.

The Queen of Scots met her fate with courage and faith. She spent the evening before her death tying up gifts for her servants in little purses; in writing letters of farewell; in having a camisole of thin tartan made without a neck, so that when she was disrobed at the block she would not appear unclothed before so many spectators.

But the most poignant moment was one of which little has been written; indeed, I have read accounts of her death in which it is never even mentioned. The Pope, foreseeing, or having been told, that she might be refused the ministration of a Catholic priest, sent her a consecrated wafer and, with it, dispensation never before given to a member of the laity; the right to administer the Eucharist to herself.

The moment when, with only a few hours to live, she went apart and gave herself the Sacrament, is surely the most beautiful and also the most tragic of her sad life. In the morning, when she stood on the draped scaffold clothed in a scarlet petticoat and her tartan bodice, the handkerchief which her weeping women bound about her eyes contained inside it a Corpus Christi cloth, probably the cloth in which the wafer had been wrapped.

If there is a place in England where it is not difficult to hate Elizabeth and her ministers, it is the mound of Fotheringhay. Even if it be granted that Mary's presence was a danger to

Throne and Church, the rude, unfeeling manners and the levity of those who conducted her
mock trial, and the brutality of those who
struck off her head and allowed her body to
lie in a room at Fotheringhay for six months
before it was buried at Peterborough, are a
foul blot on humanity.

We walked back to the village and entered the
fine church where two Plantagenet Dukes lie
near the altar, Edward, Duke of York, who
commanded the right wing at Agincourt and
died in the battle, and Richard, Duke of York,
the father of King Edward IV, who was slain
at Wakefield. The windvane of this church is
a falcon within a fetter-lock, an ancient and
unusual sign, the badge of the House of York.
A fetterlock in falconry was a circle of metal
with a perch inside it so that the bird appears
to be standing within a small hoop. When the
Yorkists gained the throne it is said that the
bird was shown free and the lock open. The
only fetter-lock I can think of in common use
today is the d-shaped metal clasp used with a
padlock for securing a canvas kit-bag.

'Important things have happened at
Fotheringhay,' I said, pointing to the Yorkist
tombs, 'but everything before and after
Mary's execution seems to have been
forgotten.'

'That is perfectly true,' replied the clergyman. 'Fotheringhay means only one thing: the
execution of the Queen of Scots. Yet the place
played an important part in the rearing of the
House of York. Did you know that Richard
Crookback was born in the Castle? And one of
the few people who seemed to love the place
was Katherine of Aragon, on whom it was
settled by Henry VIII. She spent great sums
of money on it.'

As we walked from the church, I noticed a
hand-written poster on a wall. It was headed:

PROCEEDINGS ADOPTED
ON PROCLAMATION OF
A STATE OF WAR

The Church bells will not be rung or chimed
during the whole period of a state of War
for any ordinary or special services. The
only bell to be used for such occasions will
be the small five-minute bell.

In the event of an enemy air raid threatening
the village, the ALARM will be sounded by
two, or more, of the church bells being rung
continuously for two, or more, minutes.

When the alarm has been sounded

DON'T

Wander about the roads in the village.

Hinder by trying to help the ARP personnel
in the performance of their duties.

Collect in groups in the fields.

Leave your gas-mask behind.

Walk into a gas-contaminated area, or get
down-wind of a gas bomb, or go and look at
the crater.

Step purposely on to any splash on the ground
that may be gas.

Rush to the spot at the sound of a bomb
dropping to see what the damage is, or to
see what it looks like.

Be surprised at anything that may happen.

Here the notice ended, and I stood back in
admiration. It was the first notice of the kind
I had seen in an English village. Fotheringhay,
I reflected, had no faith in Appeasment, and
this village of a hundred and forty odd people
might be right! But I hoped not. How impossible
– how fantastic beyond words – the notice
was in that quiet, lovely place.

'I have forgotten to ask you something,' I
said to the clergyman. 'You told me that a
story of the execution of Mary Stuart still lives
in Fotheringhay. What is it?'

He paused before a fine stone farmhouse
which used to be The New Inn. The central

archway, which opened into a galleried court-yard, still remains, and above the arch are two fine Gothic windows.

'The story is,' said my companion, 'that the executioner, who arrived at Fotheringhay three days before the execution, clothed in black from head to foot, slept in the little room above the arch of the inn. That's the only story which has come down, and when you think of it, it's highly probable that the presence of that sinister person in a little English town would leave an impression that has survived even a change of population.'

The farmer willingly took us over the old house and into the executioner's room in the archway. The house is now a mass of Georgian timber and plaster on a Gothic shell, but it is possible to trace, in the farm buildings, the old galleries that once ran round the inn courtyard.

In the morning I went to look at the church again, and met there a fellow-guest from the hotel, a professor of history. I remarked that the news from Danzig was not too good that morning.

'I know nothing about it,' replied the historian. 'I gave up reading the papers last September and feel better for it in every way.'

'But surely you glance at the headlines?'

'No, I refuse to do that. I like to base my opinions on facts, and there are not sufficient facts available these days on which anyone could base an opinion, therefore I feel I miss nothing. Is it going to rain again, do you think?'

We talked about the weather, as everyone does in England, and about Mary, Queen of Scots, as everyone does at Fotheringhay.

I suggested that it was not easy to understand the callous cruelty of the Elizabethans who murdered Mary, Queen of Scots.

'Now there I don't agree with you,' he said. 'I might have done so in 1914, but not today.

You, as a reader of newspapers, must be aware of the decline in moral values which has taken place in our time. The world has swung back into the immoral atmosphere of, shall we say, Tudor times? The reign of Hitler has taught me a lot about the reign of Elizabeth. It has made the men and the actions of that time entirely credible and understandable. Our world has just emerged from a long and unusual period of law and order, and, as always in times of danger, politicians have become unscrupulous, just as they were in Tudor times.'

He paused to light his pipe and went on: 'Danger produces fear, and fear produces unscrupulousness. Danger and uncertainty are two of the constant factors in human affairs. If you doubt that we are back in the mentality of the Tudor Age, study the social background. The Money Power was paramount, and the State was chained to it as it is today. The Elizabethan State, enriched by church lands, was financing commerce just as we are today. Money, and fear of Catholic Spain were two great factors in Elizabethan politics. Money and the fear of Nazi Germany are the great factors in England today.

'The execution of Mary Stuart was merely a swift and successful political move carried out by men very like modern politicians. Indeed, before I gave up reading the papers, I seem to remember that similar death sentences have been executed from precisely similar motives in modern Europe. It is true that the common people are shocked by them, probably because the common people of Europe are not yet as unscrupulous as their leaders. They are still living in the old-fashioned atmosphere of a more moral world. But their leaders are not. And history proves, if it proves anything at all, that a leader need not necessarily lead forward; he can just as easily lead backward. The only hope for the world, as I see it, is that the people of the world may remain sufficiently old-fashioned to refuse to be led backward. But who can tell?'

Rain began to fall, and we walked back in silence to the hotel.

When I was passing through Oundle I stopped at the Talbot Inn to see the staircase which is claimed to be the main staircase of Fotheringhay Castle. It is a massive oak structure of typical Tudor style, and it stands in the light of a long Tudor window.

'The inn was rebuilt about 1626,' said the proprietor, 'or just at the time that Fotheringhay Castle was being pulled down. It is said that our staircase came from the Great Chamber in which the scaffold was erected. Our fine window is also believed to have come from the banqueting hall.'

If this story is true – and there is no reason to doubt it – the guests at the Talbot go up to bed each night on the stairs by which Mary Stuart descended to her death.

I asked the innkeeper if he knew of any other relics of Fotheringhay. He told me to go to Conington, about twelve miles away, where a chair on which Mary sat on the scaffold is preserved in the church.

I set off across country, travelling due east along the delightful Northamptonshire lanes, meeting nothing but a farm cart here and there. Among English counties Northamptonshire has one peculiarity: its borders are touched by those of nine other counties, a larger number of bordering shires than any other county can claim. This means that you cannot travel far in Northamptonshire, especially in the northern part of it where the county narrows to a few miles, without crossing the boundary. I was soon in Huntingdonshire with the Great North Road in front of me, and crossing that murderous highway I found Conington about a mile on the other side of it.

There was a church standing beside a manor house, Conington Castle, and the moment I entered the church I thought how puzzling it must be to many of its visitors. It contains two entirely improbable tombs: those of David I, King of Scotland, and his son, Prince Henry. What on earth is David I, of Scotland, who died in 1153, doing in an Elizabethan tomb in Huntingdonshire?

The answer is to be sought in the life of a man whose tomb is also in the church, that extraordinary character, Sir Robert Bruce Cotton. He was a book collector and antiquary, and the founder of the famous Cottonian Collection of books and manuscripts now in the British Museum. Cotton, who was born in 1571, was lord of the manor of Conington, and it was the boast of his life that he had the royal blood of Scotland in his veins.

This was true. One of his ancestors had married Bruce's grand-daughter, Mary de Wesenham, who seems to have been generous with the blood royal because, after the death of her first husband, she married another and after him a third. And should you go in search of her you will find her in St Margaret's, Westminster, beside her first husband.

Cotton was prouder of his relationship with her than of anything else. It is said that James I was well aware of this weakness, and used to flatter Cotton by calling him 'cousin' whenever he met him in London. In his love for the royal family of Scotland, Cotton erected the two huge architectural memorials in the church, making them look like tombs, although the persons commemorated were, of course, never buried there.

It was to his antiquarian zeal that we owe the preservation of what is believed to be Mary Stuart's chair, now in Conington Church. The antiquary was a youth of sixteen when Mary was executed at Fotheringhay, and naturally the death of Scotland's Queen affected him deeply all his life. When the castle was demolished in 1626, he bought the whole

'I stopped at the Talbot Inn to see the staircase which is claimed to be the main staircase of Fotheringhay Castle'

of the Great Chamber in which the Queen of Scots had been beheaded and removed the stones to Conington. They are now built into the front of Conington Castle, and are the most interesting relics of Fotheringhay in existence. About eleven stone arches and columns are to be seen on the north and west fronts of the present house, rising from smooth lawns.

The chair no doubt came naturally into Cotton's possession, as so many other things did. It is placed on the south side of the chancel, a high-backed seat of Gothic design decorated with small carved angels holding musical instruments.

I left Conington wishing that some biographer would tackle the life of Robert Cotton. He was the first of the great art collectors, and what wonderful scope he had. The monasteries had just been disbanded and the contents of their libraries were to be found everywhere. I remember reading somewhere that Cotton 'picked up' a copy of Magna Carta in a tailor's shop in London. His house in Westminster, which stood on land now occupied by the House of Lords, was the resort of all the learned men of the day. If his life has a moral, it is that book collectors should never mix themselves up in politics, for poor Cotton collected so many state documents of a grave and incriminating character that his library had to be confiscated, and he himself was thrown into prison.

Upon a long stretch of Ermine Street, about seven miles to the south of Peterborough, I came to the village of Stilton, from which the king of cheeses takes its name. William Camden, who was there in the reign of Elizabeth, noted that the original name used to be Stichilton, but it had already been contracted to Stilton, so mark how Fate was already on the side of the still unborn cheese, smoothing out the name so that Stilton should not go stammering into the world as Stichilton.

If Stilton is the king of English cheeses, Cheddar is the queen and Cheshire is the heir apparent. Other noble members of this family are the dukes of Double Gloucester and Leicester, Little Wilts and Wensleydale, and I have no hesitation in adding to the august company Single Gloucester, which is made from skimmed milk.

The village of Stilton, situated on a suicidal portion of the Great North Road, has nothing to recommend it but the superb grey stone Bell, one of the great post-houses of former days. Travellers who pass through Stilton at less than fifty miles an hour may have noticed the fine copper sign – the finest from London to York – which overhangs the whole width of the pavement outside the Bell and is supported by a stout post.

I encountered an old man inside the Bell who told me that his father well remembered the days when Stilton rang to the sound of hoofs, the jingle of harness, the knock of traces, the tootle of coach-horns and the clatter of teams as they were led over the cobbles. Those were exciting days. The old man had often heard his father describe the flocks of northern cattle and sheep that came in a steady flow through Stilton to pause there long enough for the cattle to be shod, before moving on to the south. One smith at Stilton did practically nothing else but shoe cattle.

'Aye, they was good days,' said the old man, 'but the railways stopped all that. Now they're talking about making one of these bypass roads round Stilton so that nothing at all will happen here, not even accidents,' he added sadly.

The interior of the Bell is not worthy of the exterior. During the past two hundred years the noble proportions of the ancient stone building had been ruined by little bars and cubby-holes of varnished wood, and, though the place has an agreeable air of having been well used and lived in, I should like to see it emerge from the hands of a competent architect. It could be made one of the finest inns on the Great North Road.

It was in the Bell at Stilton that a rich, creamy, maggoty cheese from Leicestershire (not one ounce of which was ever made at Stilton) attracted the attention of stage-coach passengers in the eighteenth century. This superb cheese was occasionally offered to passengers at the Bell while they snatched a hasty meal during the change of horses, and it was natural that discerning visitors should have persuaded the innkeeper to sell a cheese now and then, with the result that the fame of the cheese bought at Stilton was soon carried into all parts of England. But, as I say, although people called it Stilton because they ate it and bought it at Stilton, it was not made there.

Its history is a long and honourable one. It was first made, so it is believed, by Lady Beaumont, the wife of Sir Henry Beaumont, who represented Leicestershire in Parliament from 1679 to 1687. In the following century the recipe became known to the neighbouring Ashbys of Quenby Hall, when their housekeeper, Elizabeth Scarbrow, made it. This Elizabeth married a man called Orton and went to live at Little Dalby in Leicestershire, about four miles from Melton Mowbray, taking her precious secret with her. The cheese was at this time known as Quenby Cheese,

presumably because Elizabeth Orton had learned how to make it when employed at Quenby Hall. Her cheeses became famous in the villages round about, and she evidently guarded her recipe well, for it was whispered that Quenby Cheese could be made only of milk from cows fed on one small meadow called Orton's Close, which, of course, was nonsense, but it helped to discourage imitations.

So carefully was the secret kept that many years after only three other dairy-women were making the cheese, and it is believed that two of them were daughters of Mrs Orton. One of her daughters married a man called Cooper Thornhill, landlord of the Bell at Stilton, and possibly the first cheeses were sent to Stilton as presents from Mrs Orton to her daughter. If so, these gifts were made early in the eighteenth century, because Defoe mentions the cheese in the first edition of his *Tour*, a book that was published in 1724–6. He says: 'We passed Stilton, a Town famous for Cheese, which is called our English Parmesan, and is brought to Table with the Mites or Maggots round it, so thick that they bring a spoon with them for you to eat the Mites with, as you do the Cheese.' This suggests to my mind that Defoe had not eaten Stilton himself, and perhaps mistook the cheese scoop for a spoon.

However, the demand by stage-coach passengers at Stilton for this unique cheese was so great by the beginning of the nineteenth century that all the villages round Little Dalby were hard at work making it, the secret of its manufacture and the superstition about Orton's Close having long since expired.

As I walked up the village street, I noticed that many a little shop advertised its prime Stilton cheeses. I entered a shop kept by Miss Spriggs, who turned out to be the originator of motor-borne Stilton.

'When the stage-coaches stopped,' said Miss Spriggs, 'the sale of Stilton stopped in the village. When I was a girl you couldn't buy a Stilton in Stilton for love or money. I was born at the Bell, and so I've always been interested in Stilton. About twelve years ago, when motor cars were coming through Stilton and the place got busy again, I wondered whether people would still buy Stilton at Stilton, like they used to do in the old days. I tried it out, and it was a great success. Never a day passes now but someone stops at my shop and buys a cheese.'

'Has anyone ever tried to make Stilton at Stilton?' I asked her.

'Never, so far as I know,' she replied. 'I've always understood that there's a weed in the grass here that makes it impossible. As I daresay you know, all good Stilton comes from round Melton way in Leicestershire, as it always has done. It's a difficult cheese to make. I've heard it said that a lot depends on the sense of touch. Some cheese-makers believe that this sense of touch is handed down in families. You see, at one point in the making of Stilton you have to test the curd with the tips of your fingers to see if it's ready for the next stage; and if your sense of touch isn't right, well, you may have spoilt the cheese.'

Miss Spriggs is rightly proud of her success in having brought Stilton back to the Great North Road.

'But you'd be surprised by the jokes they make,' she said, referring to her customers. 'They jump out of their cars and come in here and ask for a tame one, or do I sell dog collars with them? Why, you'd never believe the fun some people seem to get out of buying a Stilton! Well, well, it takes all sorts to make a world . . .'

'That bears out my own experience,' I told her. 'Now what do you, as an expert, think of that small one in the corner, the second from the left?'

'Well,' said Miss Spriggs confidentially, dropping her voice to a whisper, 'if you don't intend to eat it for a bit, if you could put it by, for, say, a couple of months, you'd have a real good Stilton.'

It happened to me at Peterborough. I was sitting in a restaurant which overlooks the market place. The old town hall, lifted on its sixteenth-century columns, stood immediately below me, and I sat there watching people queue up outside it. Each one held in his hand a small cardboard box; inside the box was the State's gift to its children – a gas-mask. Somewhere inside the building the citizens were having their masks tested so that they might face the future with confidence. They were an ordinary-looking crowd. Some were smiling, others were just dull or impassive, and no one could have guessed that they were candidates for survival in a mad world: they looked like people waiting for a bus, not a cataclysm.

The morning paper had described an attack on the Polish custom house at Danzig. Shots had been fired, perhaps the first shots of a war that was surely at last inevitable. The queue moved slowly towards the gas-chambers, men, women and children. What a picture – Civilisation, June 1939.

I knew that my holiday was over. I might have gone on for a day or two, indeed I had intended to go to Lincoln, but the desire to travel had departed and I was well aware that the only thing to do was to go home. However, I had done what I had set out to do: I had enjoyed a last glimpse of pre-war England. I had wandered at will through our country, admiring it and remembering its past, and now I felt, as one is aware of an approaching thunderstorm in summer, the impending darkness of war. How or when it would come, I had no idea, but come it would: of that I was certain. And I was certain too, that when it came, it would bring, for the first time since the Saxon age, widespread death and destruction to a land that is no longer an island.

I went south to London that day, and, as I looked at the green meadows, the little villages and the quiet towns of England, I discovered in my heart anger, horror, fear, pity, and, oddly enough, relief; for there are many things worse than death and destruction, and one of them is the humiliation of attempting to appease the unappeasable. That night in London a man who knows the trend of current affairs better than I leaned across a dinner-table and said: 'My dear fellow, you're a positive jitterbug. I can assure you there won't be any war. It's all a gigantic bluff!' But as I walked home through the quiet summer streets, the sky no longer seemed friendly. It was just a matter of waiting.

CHAPTER SEVEN

*I set off in October 1939 to see something
of war-time England. I find the Baltic Exchange working in a
country house. I see the making of Wellington bombers. I go to
Salisbury Plain, where I ride in a tank. At Weymouth, I investigate
the methods of the Contraband Control; somewhere else I visit
a Flying School, where I am given a lesson in bombing,
and I penetrate the rural hiding-place of the BBC.*

The War came at eleven o'clock on a quiet Sunday morning in September. It was announced by Mr Chamberlain in the tones of an elderly dove whose olive branch had been snatched by rude eagles, and no sooner was his speech over than the sirens wailed in London and everyone said, 'Here they come!'; but they didn't. Then, as the weeks followed one another, there was no singing, no marching soldiers, no splendid brass bands, no appeals to King and Country, but, instead, to that chill goddess Freedom, whose imminent peril meant nothing to people who had always believed themselves to be free. So there was an air of anti-climax over England.

London was the same as ever, except for sandbags by day and a black-out at night, and the shine of autumnal moons turned the city into an enchanted place of turrets and pinnacles. Even Piccadilly Circus was freed at last from the vulgarity of electrically shaken cocktails. And life had changed in the country. Upon a thousand village greens indignant women in London clothes wheeled their perambulators and longed for the roar of the traffic along the Old Kent Road; in stately homes and ancient castles spoilt servitors, perhaps the last of their race, borrowed expressions from the ancestral portraits and viewed with disdain the hordes of clerks and young persons who worked their 'typewriting machines' in the Blue Bedroom and erected their filing cabinets in the Gun Room. Man-

'London was the same as ever, except for sandbags by day'

aging directors dictated their correspondence leaning against grand pianos, while secretaries cast jaundiced eyes towards the autumnal cock pheasant on the lawn. When darkness cast its sinister cloak over war-time England, clerks separated from their wives, and typists from their sweethearts, set off to walk three miles through dank and terrifying lanes to the blacked-out cinema in the nearest town. So hiker and cyclist, until recently so fond of country delights, viewed the rural scene from a new and unexpected angle, and found it not what it had been on Saturday afternoons. There was an air of fantasy about the whole thing: an age had ended in a nightmare, and it would be a long time before the world awakened once again. And the War was only seven weeks old.

In France, the British Expeditionary Force was digging itself in for the winter, hiding its

'The shine of autumnal moons turned the city into an enchanted place'

guns and aeroplanes. There had been a few artillery duels over the Maginot and Siegfried lines, but everyone knew that, while the Maginot Line was impregnable, the Siegfried Line was made of poor concrete and was liable to floods. Poland had been conquered, but everyone knew that the Polish Army, though brave, still wore spurs. The *Athenia* had been sunk; the *Royal Oak* had been torpedoed in Scapa Flow; the Germans had just begun to bomb the Firth of Forth, and the RAF was stunning Germany with pamphlets. Mr Chamberlain assured us more than once that the 'overwhelming resources' of the British Empire made victory a foregone conclusion.

At this fateful moment in history, more precisely upon 17 October, I took my gas-mask in its virgin cardboard box and a small, rather dramatic first-aid outfit which I had bought years before to take to Turkey and had then left behind, and set out to make a journey through England. I was conscious that in the twinkling of an eye all had changed. Gone was the careless, easy-to-see England that had been technically at peace for so long. It was another England I should see, an England technically at war. If I had required proof that all was different I had only to consult my pockets, which bulged with petrol coupons issued by the Board of Trade and with credentials and letters of introduction kindly furnished by the Ministry of Information, the Admiralty, the War Office and the Ministry of Supply.

It was a new experience for me to go out on a circumscribed tour of this kind, for I had always been in the habit of starting off at a moment's notice and going I knew not where, wandering on as the mood took me, loitering here and hastening there with no one to please but myself. But in war-time even the least suspicious nation – and England is of all nations the most easy-going and the least apprehensive – believes that a man with a map is a spy, as of course, he sometimes is. So I found myself obliged to keep up with a programme, or itinerary, prepared for me in Whitehall.

It was one of those mellow, damp autumn mornings when even a London pavement tells you that in the country treetops have turned the colour of egg-plums and white mists are moving from valleys. It seemed to me incredible, as I surveyed an unbombed London, that we had been at war for seven weeks. There was absolutely nothing to show for it except fewer private cars, an almost complete absence of small children and, of course, the balloon barrage. My road was for most of the way the same road I had taken only five months previously, when I had travelled into Kent.

I came to the same fine view over Kent, and was soon running into Westerham, where Wolfe still waved his sword against the sky. Turning to the west, I made for Surrey, and for a remote village in that county where (so it was whispered to me in Whitehall) I should find the Baltic Exchange, or that portion of it most useful to a nation at war: the buyers of wheat.

I stayed the night in a small hotel in Surrey whose bar attracted all the local tradesmen and worthies until you could hardly see the buxom barmaid, known to everyone as Violet, behind the smoke-screen. I gathered that 'that theer Ribbentrop' was much hated in this bar, more so I think even than 'old Hitler' himself.

Sitting in a corner silently, as became a stranger, I thought that of all English institutions the English inn is perhaps the most satisfactory. Parliament may be criticised. Democracy may not be what it is supposed to be. The Freedom of the Press may be suspected, even by the most innocent, to be qualified in some measure by the opinions and interests of a proprietor and his advertisers, but the English inn is really and truly what it claims to be: a common meeting-place for all types and classes, where any man may say exactly what he likes without being clubbed by political opponents and dragged off to jail. Eccentricity and oddity, which have always delighted the English, come into their own when the inn opens its doors in the evening, and the queer characters, the local jesters, the men with the fads and fancies who give English life its salt and flavour, are always present, although their fame is strictly local and the outsider rarely considers them as funny or as witty as their own villagers or townsmen do. Above all, perhaps, humour, the best of humour, has its home in the English inn. It deflates the pretentious, it corrects the erroneous, and it deflects the dangerous. The qualities of laughter are nowhere more noticeable than in the true

Parliament of England, which goes by the name of the Green Dragon or the King's Arms.

As I listened with pleasure to the discussions round the bar, I thought of the black-out beyond the door, symbolic of the black-out of freedom and of free speech that seeks to conquer the world, and as I looked at the ordinary common Englishmen with their tankards and glasses, small tradesmen, farmers, and the like, I thought how surprised they would be if I rose up and told them that, as they stood there arguing in loud, fearless voices about national and local affairs, they represented nearly everything we are fighting to preserve in England.

Many of them were old soldiers, and I heard the words Ypres and Cambrai spoken by men who had fought in the last War. For the first time for twenty years their reminiscences were respectful and earnestly listened to by the

'Turning to the west, I made for Surrey, and for a remote village in that county'

younger generation. Their sons were now in France. Under the influence of a pint or two they talked the kind of talk one heard so often in the early 'twenties – of Ypres, Festubert and Neuve Chapelle, of 'Jerry', of rations and of sudden death and horror. It was like putting back the clock twenty years. Those warriors, men of my generation, seemed to have aged considerably, and I wondered whether I looked as old as they did. There was one old man, a mild little draperish man, who brought up horrible memories for the edification of two glum companions. They smoked steadily and said 'Ah,' or 'Go on,' at the right moments.

'You remember old James Wilkins, him whose father had Upper Court Farm years back?'

'Ah,' said his companions.

'Well, 'e was another of them what got blown up.'

He lifted his tankard and gazed at the stony faces of his companions over the rim.

'Go on,' they said.

''E joined my push with Tony Edwards, who used to keep the White Hart. It was Tony Edwards who told me what happened. They was out one night in a shell-hole waiting to nip over and pinch a Jerry prisoner. You 'ad to do that now and then – and they gave you an extra rum ration before you started.'

'Go on,' said the listeners.

'Well, while they was lyin' there, Jerry started shellin', and one of the shells dropped short and hit James Wilkins. They couldn't find a blessed particle. An awful thing, wasn't it? Yet, do you know, his widow always thought he'd come back some day and come walking in through the door. Funny how women get these ideas, ain't it? Then there was Frank Wilson from Dorking. No one ever knew what 'appened to 'im . . .'

And off he went again on his gloomy reminiscences, deriving some sombre pleasure from it, as gentle people occasionally find pleasure in ghastly stories of the operating theatre.

The group round the bar was debating with vigour and with considerable heat whether we ought to have gone to the rescue of Czechoslovakia. Someone asked Violet to switch on the wireless because it was 'just on news time'. She turned a switch and a hearty voice began singing: 'We'll hang out the washing on the Siegfried Line, have you any dirty washing, mother dear' – then came the news, with details of the latest air raid on the Firth of Forth.

In the morning I motored off to a neighbouring factory that is making Wellington bombers. I came to a mass of buildings which had been hastily camouflaged and sand-bagged. Police were marshalling hundreds of cars belonging to callers in the shadow of trees and walls. Passing through a swing door, I entered a hall, where I was seized upon as a possible spy, made to sign the usual buff form and to declare my intentions and credentials. I was then shown into a waiting-room full of men in an advanced stage of waiting, each one of whom held on his knees, or grasped beneath his arm, one of those limp leather portfolios that suggest homing Frenchmen with square black beards clinging to the backs of tramcars.

In a few moments I was rescued by the man I had come to see, who took me rapidly through a number of workshops. We came at last to a bridge high up near the roof of an assembly shop. Beneath us, ten abreast, to the extremity of the shed, stood bombers which cost £22,000 each, without guns. Below us, they were complete, with wings, turrets and engines, ready to take the air. But, as the lines receded to the extremity of the shed, the bombers became less complete and more elementary, until at the very end they were helpless, earthbound chrysalids of duralumin. As I watched, I noted that the long lines ten abreast were almost imperceptibly moving forward towards us beneath the bridge. The ten planes immediately below would be wheeled out on their fat balloon tyres through an archway into the open field, and the ten behind would take their place; and so on down the line to the end of the shed.

I felt as some minute form of life, such as an ant, might feel as it watched the birth of dragon-flies. As the bare, tailless chrysalids advanced they took on shape and gradually became aerial, sprouting first one wing, then another, then came the tail with a dinosauric horn at the end of it, finally, with engines roaring, the aerial machines groped their way into the sunlight under the sky which belongs to them, ready and fitted to lay their eggs of death.

Standing beside me on the bridge was a designer of bombing aeroplanes, a plump and kindly man who, I have no doubt, is a great

lover of youth and devoted to animals. How odd it is that out of a mind which can love a child or a kitten can proceed such frightful instruments of destruction. Perhaps, I thought, some of his most devastating ideas came to him while playing goodnight games on the nursery floor. His words flew past my ears as I gazed down at his hatchery.

'Two engines developing one thousand, eight hundred horse-power . . . retracting undercarriage, top speed two hundred and sixty-five miles an hour . . . range about three thousand, two hundred and forty miles . . . three guns . . . crew of five . . . bomb-carrying capacity . . .'

'But tell me,' I asked, 'how is it possible for a man to invent a thing like a bomber? How do you begin?'

'Well, of course, no one really invents a bomber,' he said. 'All we do is to build up on what already exists, improve it, apply new theories and so on. All aircraft design is the accumulation and the application of experience.'

'And in all great countries of the world there are men who, like yourself, have devoted their lives to the problem of decanting a ton of high explosive in the most efficient way from a machine moving in the air?'

'That is so.'

I should like to have asked if he thought he had any chance of going to heaven, but I came to the conclusion that I did not know him well enough. Anyhow, in war-time such effete, ethical ideas must be banished from one's mind.

I was taken round the factory, where night-shift follows day-shift round the clock, where machines never stop, where every process is designed to accelerate the inch by inch progress of a bomber from chrysalis to winged body, along the vast parade ground of the assembly shop.

I saw girls in blue or brown boiler suits, their feet, in absurd little feminine shoes, tapping on the pedals of electric machines.

I saw hundreds of men busy with thousands of shining, geometrically shaped fragments of metal. I saw girls' hands sewing fabric on great wings and painting the linen in broad patches of brown and green so that when the bombers are at rest they may seem part of the autumn woods and fields. And I realised that bombers in the making suggest nothing more exciting to the onlooker than that thousands of people are feverishly trying to put together a gigantic Meccano set. The pieces of duralumin, silver-white and as light as aluminium, but as strong as milled steel, come out of presses and jigs punctured with countless rivet holes, and pass onward to be joined together. Something like sixteen thousand separate parts, all firmly bolted, form the skeleton of the fuselage.

But what amazed me, a stage farther on, was the intricate system of nerves, veins and arteries running through the body in arm-thick bunches of red, white, yellow and green electric cable. The organs of the machine, the heart, eyes, lungs and liver, so to speak, to which these veins converge, are instruments which appal by their number and complexity as they offer their shining dials and vibrating pointers to the eye of the pilot.

As I sat in the pilot's seat, I envied the courage of the unknown young man who would some day guide that as yet incomplete engine of death through the high heavens. He would sit where I was sitting, while one thousand and eight hundred horses galloped with him through the skies; and high above sleeping villages and little towns and far churches he would go, always watching the pointers and the dials, and perhaps thinking about a girl in Streatham.

His companions would move steathily with bent heads in the gleaming aluminium darkness of the moving body; the machine-gunner in his protruding glass dome, the bomber lying full length in the nose of the machine, with his eye to the bomb-sights, watching the distant landscape rushing past beneath him.

I was recalled to reality by the voice of a works manager telling me that the machine carried more bombs than any German machine of equivalent size. I climbed out and went to have a look at the bombing rack. This is a miracle of design and workmanship. The bombs are carried in an undercarriage that lifts up into the body of the machine, and is enclosed by two hinged and curved portions of the fuselage. When the moment comes for the dropping of the bombs, the whole undercarriage of the machine opens, the gates of death swing back on their hinges to reveal row after row of what look like young torpedoes.

The departure of these bombers is worth recording. They are wheeled out to a testing field. Pilots put them through their paces. They make the huge things skid and slip about the sky as if they were skittish circus planes. Then they come down, tested and correct, and there is always a line of tested bombers ready to be handed over to the Royal Air Force. A young man in blue, who looks as if he has just left school, throws away his cigarette and approaches the new monster.

'All correct?' he asks.

'Oke,' somebody replies.

'Right-o,' he says.

Then the young man climbs into the bomber, and in a second or so the fair head and face of the infant are observed gazing down through the glass dome. A hand waves in a pert 'S'long!' of the palm and fingers, the great propellers go round to an ear-cracking roar of engines and becomes invisible. The green and brown monster moves. It turns. It begins to race along the ground with a deep roar of engines. Its fat black tyres leave the earth. It is flying!

And so an infant in a blue uniform disappears into the sky with £22,000 worth of the taxpayers' money, and the power of one thousand eight hundred horses.

After a hasty luncheon at the bomber factory, I left in order to race through Hampshire in an attempt to reach Salisbury before the black-out. I had made a resolution never to move one yard after dark, but to stay wherever I happened to be when black-out time arrived; and this I regard as the first rule of war-time travelling.

The only traffic I encountered in open country were lorries and military transport. Near the towns, however, a few private cars were to be seen. Upon that four-mile stretch of straight road between Ovington Down and Winchester there was not a single car, just the long road with its central strip of white stretching into the distance. For the first time for years it was possible to enjoy motoring as those who remember the first Morris Oxfords enjoyed it long ago.

OPPOSITE '*Trees, woods and coppices were
stained in shades of red and gold*'

ABOVE '*I saw the thin spire of Salisbury
rising above a lake of blue smoke*'

The country looked beautiful in the quiet sunlight of late autumn. Trees, woods and coppices were stained in shades of red and gold like a nineteenth-century aquatint. The leaves were rapidly thinning. Every meadow near a wood was scattered with bright yellow leaves, and each time the slightest wind blew there would be a movement among the trees as more leaves fell to earth. Long before the black-out, indeed some time before the sun had set, I saw the thin spire of Salisbury rising above a lake of blue smoke, and so I came down gladly into busy streets.

The hotel was nearly empty and, leaving my bag there, I went out at once into the twilight. There was a tramp of feet in the Cloisters, and I saw approaching, walking two by two, choristers returning from Evensong. They wore black cloaks, four-pointed black caps of the pattern Cranmer wore, and round each neck was a little starched ruff, like a pie-frill. As these impressive songsters walked, clasping their books, a cloak would be kicked out here and there, and I saw that beneath the trappings of the Reformation were ordinary little boys in grey flannel suits, with bare knees and woollen stockings.

In the huge dark space of the cathedral, where a whisper of organ music moved, there were four women in late middle age kneeling in prayer. I sat there, too, in the darkness from which we should soon be turned into the deeper darkness of the streets, thinking that as long as the War lasted I should remember the four praying women of Salisbury. They had strips of cheap fur round the collars of their coats, and two of the four hats had been bought for gay occasions and now, bent forward in the darkening church, their finery tilted and lowered towards the Deity, they looked repentant and pitiful. In France, the sons and the husbands of those women were standing-to in the hour before dark; in Poland the ruins of Warsaw still smoked: and ahead of us lay God only knew how many years of pain and sorrow and prayer and black-out. The verger became busy with the doors, and we knew that we must go.

The darkness in the streets of Salisbury could almost be felt. I walked groping with my hands for the sides of the houses. Approaching walkers shone hand-torches on the pavement to give warning of their presence, or to see the kerb when they crossed the road. In the main streets the red, green and yellow traffic lights looked preposterously gay and brilliant in the utter blackness as they winked and changed, and on all the chief pavements there was a surge of invisible men and women, soldiers and young women in khaki, whose boots and voices alone proclaimed their existence.

Memories of long ago – indeed, so long ago that they seem like the memories of someone else – assailed me as I saw the wide spaces of the Plain in the early morning, the tawny stretches of stubble, wind-bent, lying to the edge of the sky, the rabbits scurrying round their burrows, the clouds wheeling above the landscape. Military lorries charged about, full of young men wearing that strange garment known so dramatically by the name of 'battle-dress', a term never coined surely by the unemotional British soldier, but by a cinema-going tailor. Now and then the bang of a trench mortar sounded from a far hill; machine-guns stammered for a second on distant ranges; and the whole Plain was alive, as it was in 1914–18, training the youth of England to defend its birthright.

I saw tanks, bren-gun carriers and all kinds of queer motor vehicles, some of them specially designed for war, others civilian touring cars in a uniform of camouflage, but every one of them a clear declaration that the moral sense is unable to keep pace with the inventiveness of mankind. What would the pioneers of motoring have said at the beginning of the century, those grotesque, fur-clad, goggled figures who steered their coal-fed cars along the roads of England at fifteen miles an hour, had they been told that their toys would one day breed a tank, that they were leading the new cavalry charge? Who would have believed when I was a boy that the laughable arrangement of struts and strings known as a flying machine – seen generally in a field surrounded by an amused crowd of cyclists and horsemen – would within thirty years conquer the air and give birth to the Wellington bomber?

It was different on the Plain in the last War, as I remember it. Sitting beside me now in the car was a child with a captain's stars on his shoulders, who had been detailed to show me round, and to him I confided some of my memories of the Plain: the long columns of marching men, the jingling GS wagons with their horses, and the cavalry at squadron drill in the early morning. The child looked at me with the expression of one who sees before him a veteran of Agincourt.

We came to a high, windy hill, where we paused a moment to watch men firing trench mortars. They were NCOs on a course, about a hundred of them, 'a mixed grill', as the colonel described them, and they were in charge of staff instructors, a breed of men more solemn and determined than any other. When they know how to do a thing, it must be done that way and no other way. Placing the tip of the left boot half an inch this way or that way makes all the difference, to them, between orthodoxy and heresy, and no Pope of Rome was ever harder on a heretic. I was glad to see that this breed has not altered, so far as I could judge, since the last War, for it is one of the best breeds in England.

The staff instructors loved their mortar. They ran with it to the cover of a dip of ground and then split up. One party sent over a smoke screen while the other pumped trench-mortar bombs on an imaginary battery two hundred yards ahead. It was well done, and we could follow the bomb through the sky right over the arc, then we lost it until a burst of flame and dust far off on an unfortunate rabbit warren told us where it had fallen.

'A lovely spray of shrapnel!' said the colonel.

'A beautiful little weapon!' said the major.

'Wish we had six to a battalion!' said the captain.

An officer asked permission to take a photograph of the team in action. The chief Staff Instructor saw the camera.

'Are you going to take a photo, sir?' he asked.

'Yes.'

'Hi! Number One!' sang out the Staff Instructor in a voice of thunder. 'Unsling that rifle!'

He ran up and saluted.

'All correct now, sir,' he said to the photographer, then, in an aside to me, 'Can't be too particular, sir. Hitler might see it!'

We returned to the car to find the beautiful member of the FANY, its driver, gazing over the great spaces of the Plain, lost in whatever dreams come to members of this oddly misnamed nursing yeomanry during the long absences of their cargoes. The young captain timidly, in the face of such beauty, asserted his presence, and the girl, with a delightful pretence at obedient repentance, sprang out of her reverie to the door; and we were soon on our way across the Plain.

We came to a place where tanks fire their guns, and I asked to be allowed to travel in one during target practice. The tank chosen for me was a big new cruiser tank, and they told me that you could sit inside in perfect safety while a machine-gun was sprayed on you.

I climbed the armour plates and let myself down feet foremost through a steel manhole. I found myself in an armoured strait-waistcoat. Although I knew there was not much room in a tank, I was surprised to discover how closely a modern tank is built round the crew. There was literally not an inch of spare room. We were imprisoned in steel. On the level of my feet, as I stood in the commander's turret, was the gunner's head. He sat gazing through the telescopic gunsight, his head pressed into a brow-pad, his left hand on the hydraulic turret control, his right hand on the gun triggers. Next to me, on a lower level, stood a man who popped a shell into a gleaming gun-breach, which instantly closed; and the gun was ready to be fired. He slipped a loaded belt into a machine-gun.

When gun-turret and tank were facing in the same direction, I caught a glimpse of our friend, the driver, but at other times, when we swung round, he disappeared.

The loader closed the turret and we were in semi-darkness. He took up a hand telephone. The gunner and driver slipped on ear-phones – imagine three men almost side by side having to telephone to each other! – and then the man with the telephone shouted: 'Advance!'

Our steel prison was filled with a deepening roar, and the tank began to move with a smooth, snaky motion, something between a small boat at sea and a fair-ground switchback. Looking through the commander's plate-glass slit, I saw that we were advancing into a pond. We sank into the water and ploughed our way up on the other side.

We were now roaring along at about fifteen or twenty miles an hour. The target was on a distant hillside. The gunner held it in his telescopic gun-sight by revolving the turret, and, no matter how the tank dipped and rose, or swayed from side to side, his whole mind was bent on the task of keeping the guns on the target and the target in the hairline of his sights.

'Fire!' shouted the man with the telephone.

The gunner pressed the trigger, there was an ear-splitting crack, the shell case shot into a canvas bag, the tank filled with a smell of cordite that was instantly blown out by fans, and far off on the hillside the brown earth spat up in front of the target.

We were now running past the target. The gun-turret kept swinging round to the rear, and three times came the crack; and three shells plastered the target, dead on. The tank suddenly swerved, dipped its nose into a pit and, turning in its own length, began to race back at full speed. I should think we were travelling at thirty miles an hour.

The guns nosed up, moving independently of the body of the tank, and as we came in view of the target again the gunner opened up with his machine-gun and a steady stream of bullets spattered up all round it.

We performed other evolutions. We roared full speed into a dip of ground and lay hidden, like some prehistoric monster waiting for its prey. Then our guns crept up on the target, and we just had time to see a direct hit before we roared off and away.

LEFT '*I let myself down feet foremost through a steel manhole*'

BELOW '*He sat gazing through the telescopic gunsight*'

OPPOSITE '*We roared full speed into a dip of ground*'

While all this was going on, what impressed me was the superb team-work necessary between the members of the crew if a tank is to preserve itself in action. One slack or inefficient member and that tank is in fearful peril, with all the lives inside it.

The tank is a partially blind and almost totally deaf monster, impregnable against some forms of attack, easily vulnerable to others. And as I saw these men at action stations I compared them, for courage and inter-dependence one upon the other, with the crew of a bomber or a submarine.

As we drew to a standstill, three laughing young men in jaunty black berets climbed out and leaped to the ground.

'Rotten shooting, Jack,' said the loader.

'Not so bad,' said Jack. 'I think we should have made it.'

The driver strolled round and lit a cigarette.

'Did you hit anything?' he asked innocently.

'No, but you did,' they replied. 'I suppose you had to take us through that pond twice just to show what a blinkin' awful driver you are.'

And as they stood chipping one another, I thought to myself: 'Here we have Athos, Porthos and Aramis.'

I was up and out of Salisbury before the mists were off the fields. My next call was upon the Navy at Weymouth.

The instant war was declared, contraband bases were established round the coast where all ships must submit to examination in order that any cargo destined for the enemy may be inspected and, if necessary, seized. This is the legal way of blockading a country by stop and search; there are other methods, as practised by German submarines. Our three contraband bases are at Kirkwall, in the Orkneys, and Ramsgate, and Weymouth, which, between them, bottle up the North Sea.

Kirkwall and Ramsgate are compulsory contraband bases. That is to say, cargo-boats bound for Germany or neighbouring neutral countries are stopped at sea by British warships and are taken into these two ports for examination, whether they like it or not. Weymouth, on the other hand, is a voluntary base. Ships put in there for examination of their own accord. There is no compulsion about it. But many prefer to do this because it saves time, and the Navy sends them on their way with a few friendly tips about mine-fields, and other matters which mariners discuss in time of war.

I travelled south through Blandford and Dorchester, and was soon looking at that grand bay whose sands in happier years I have seen dotted with children. There was now hardly a soul to be seen. But Weymouth Bay was full of ships, ships of every type and nation; ships big and small, rich and poor, old and young, all anchored, waiting the pleasure of His Majesty's Navy.

The headquarters of the Control are in an old hotel near the waterside, which has probably not known such activity since stage-coaches arrived there in the last century. A naval guard was posted on the steps, and in the rooms upstairs naval officers sat at tables, writing, typing, telephoning, opening telegrams, and consulting the charts which covered the walls. Glancing through the window, I saw, moored to a jetty, a smart motor-launch and two Lowestoft drifters painted grey, ready at a signal to cast off and visit the 'League of Nations' in the bay.

Half the officers were Royal Navy and half were RNVR. All of them wore war ribbons. I could see at once – and this is the secret of the Contraband Control – that this organisation is a fine collaboration between the Navy and the Mercantile Marine.

'We should be helpless without officers with experience of the merchant service,' said a naval commander. 'They know all about ships' papers and cargoes, and there's nothing you can tell them about the kind of thing a tramp skipper or a purser is trying to put across! They've developed a wonderful nose for contraband. It's a pleasure to see them on a strong scent.'

'And some of the scents are pretty strong, I can tell you,' put in a lieutenant, glancing up from his papers. 'Come out with us before breakfast and board tramps that have been fourteen days in the Atlantic . . .'

'You all served in the last War, I see.'

'Yes, we're all dug-outs. I was stockbroking before the War. One of our officers was chicken-farming. Another was in the Bank of England. Another had a most peculiar calling, if we can believe him. He grew willows for cricket bats! And here we are back in uniform!'

'And what does it feel like?'

'At first it was a bit strange, but we've snapped back into it. And anyhow we're too busy to analyse our emotions. I suppose you noticed the bay as you came in? Well, that's a nice little packet to unwrap and pack up again and send on its way with our blessing!'

The procedure is simple and effective. As soon as a ship anchors, two officers of the Control, known as a boarding party, go out to her, apologising to the captain for being such a nuisance, and return to shore with the ship's manifest, or list of cargo.

This is teleprinted to the Ministry of Economic Warfare in London from a specially fitted room in the hotel. Sometimes a reply comes almost at once, instructing the Control to release the ship. If the cargo, or a part of it, is suspect, a search party of naval ratings goes abroad and descends into the holds, and once again the teleprinter reports to London. If everything is above board, the ship is released; if not, orders are given to seize the cargo and take the ship to a specified port for its unloading.

When this happens, an armed guard is sent aboard: officers with revolvers at their waists and sailors with rifles and fixed bayonets.

'As soon as a ship anchors, two officers of the Contraband Control go out to her'

Politely but firmly the British Navy instructs the captain to make for Liverpool, Hull, Bristol, or wherever his particular cargo is to be landed.

'Don't the skippers get rather angry?' I asked.

'Strangely enough, only British skippers. The neutral captains all seem anxious to help. They know that we're doing a difficult job as quickly as we can, and with no danger to the safety of their ships or the lives of their crews.

'It is admittedly inconvenient for a ship, particularly if she carries passengers, to be held up sometimes for a week or ten days while London negotiates with the Embassy of a foreign Power to make absolutely certain that a suspected cargo is not going to Germany; but they take it in good part. No, neither passengers nor crews are allowed to land. The ship must lie at anchor and wait until we release her or escort her elsewhere.'

'The passengers must get restive.'

'Sometimes they do. They get very tired of playing deck tennis at anchor. In one case, when we had to hold up a liner for a long time, we transferred the passengers to another ship of the same line whose release came earlier, and sent them on their way.'

In the room of the Commanding Officer hangs a list of all the ships examined in Weymouth since the outbreak of war. It contains the name and nationality of the ship, the cargo it carried, what action was taken, and 'remarks'.

Some of the 'remarks' are interesting, such as 'sighted conning-tower of submarine', or 'report striking submerged object'. I also liked the implied drama in the following: 'Ship's name changed three times. Encountered submarine. Passenger wants to land.'

Among the nationalities examined are Greeks, Norwegians, Rumanians, Jugo-Slavs, Portuguese, Danish, Italian, Dutch, American and, of course, all British ships plying to neutral ports.

I left the Contraband Control full of admiration for the way it does its difficult job. It is a carry-over from the last War, otherwise such an organisation could never have sprung fully experienced into action. In the first seven weeks of war the Control has seized 400,000 tons of merchandise from the enemy, and in doing so not one life has been lost and not one ship destroyed.

I had overstayed my time in Weymouth, and had to race up to Gloucestershire as quickly as I could. I hurried through Sherborne, Shepton Mallet and Bath, arriving in Gloucester in the first moments of the black-out.

During that long run through a lovely portion of England, I thought that once you leave towns and cities it is difficult to believe that we are at war. The villagers of England had not taken much interest in gas-proof rooms, gummed paper for windows, or ARP. The shops were full of every kind of food, and only the presence of obvious townspeople, women and children, in remote parts of the country, indicated the enormous social upheaval that was going on.

In the public-house between Frome and Bath where I paused a moment for a sandwich, the tap room was full of the usual country characters, all talking about the War and listening to the BBC news bulletin. Until the War the names of BBC announcers had never been divulged, but as soon as War was declared, these gentlemen owned the best-known names in England. At first the phrase 'and this is Frank Phillips reading it,' was as startling and extraordinary as if *The Times* leaders had been signed.

The countrymen in this tavern took the War light-heartedly, and thought that our chaps, let alone the French, would soon give old Hitler a bit of stick. One man had a boy in the gunners in France, but he wasn't allowed to say much in his letters home. His father didn't know where he was. But it was like that in the last War, wasn't it? Then the talk turned to 'they evacuees' from the city. Mrs Higgins had been given a couple of children who had never apparently had a bath in their lives, and so ragged and out at heels were they, that they had been reclothed by their foster-mother. There was some ill feeling, too, that strange women from the cities were in the habit of coming into the tap room in the evening and drinking half a pint, or even gin, like a man. Such a thing had never happened before in the village, and no one liked it.

I became aware of a strange breach between town and village. A youngish man related with obvious gusto and pleasure the fact that certain townsfolk billeted in a neighbouring parish were worse than beasts in their habits. In other days town had always affected to look down on the countryman as a crude bumpkin,

'The talk turned to "they evacuees" from the city'

'*The air-raid wardens had eventually
fitted everyone with gas masks*'

and in the presence of those slick townsmen
many a villager had at some time or other felt
himself clumsy and rude, but now at last the
great illusion had been shown up and the
town-dweller revealed in his true, insanitary
colours. Would you believe it?

Few, if any, of these villagers had heard an
air-raid siren blown in earnest, and the lack of
shelters proved what they thought of the
danger from air attack. The air-raid wardens
had eventually fitted everyone with gas masks
and warned them not to let the children play
with them. Such things were clearly the idio-
syncracy of a paternal Government and would
never be wanted. What was really important
were the decisions of the local War Agricultural Committee, with its ploughing-up campaign and its threat to take over Farmer
Brown's farm because he was making a mess
of it, as he always had done.

The War was far away from rural England.

I found a room at the New Inn at Gloucester.
It was always old fashioned, with its gallery
and central courtyard, but that evening as
darkness fell it sank right back into the early
Middle Ages. It became, in the black-out, a
labyrinth of rambling, gloomy, ill-lit passages,
an autumn mist floating about in the darkness
and hanging in the faint glow of blue ARP
lamps. I groped my way from my bedroom to
the gallery, descended the outside stair and
crossed the inn yard to the dining-room. There
was a heavy black curtain to pull. Here was a
scene of warmth and good cheer, all the
brighter for the horrible chill mist that lay

over Gloucester. Waitresses were bustling about with a good dinner: kidney soup, boiled turbot, roast duck and apple sauce, fruit salad and gorgonzola cheese.

After dinner I went out with the idea of finding my way to the Cathedral, for I had remembered the exquisite beauty of Salisbury Cathedral in the black-out. But there was no moon over Gloucester that night. The streets were black as ink, and I found it almost impossible to cross the road. The pavements were crowded with young people walking up and down, surging, singing, cat-calling and whistling.

The girls walked together in two or threes and the young men in groups, jostling each other, giggling, and generally attempting, without realising it, to obey the laws of selection. This Stygian parade extended only for the length of the main street, but soon after ten o'clock the young people vanished and a welcome silence settled down on Gloucester.

I have no idea whether black-out is always as sociable there, or whether I happened to strike a night when the combined youth of the city had decided to go out and become acquainted, to snub each other, to strike matches in each other's faces, and to wrestle in shop doors with shrill cries of 'Oh, isn't he awfool!' or 'I'm stronger'n what you are!' Whatever the reason, Gloucester had turned the black-out into a sombre Saturnalia.

I never saw the Cathedral, for I was unable to find my way there in the dark. I was glad to grope my way back to the more than mediæval darkness and sanctuary of the New Inn.

I hastened in the morning to a place some distance from Gloucester which is still on the secret list. My letter of introduction, an unimpressive document, was redeemed by the striking phrase that it must be 'burned with fire' the moment it had been surrendered.

I came at length to a harmless-looking lane

and a noticeboard which read: 'Emergency powers: This highway is stopped.' In a few yards or so my path was barred by an Air Force sentry with a rifle and fixed bayonet. I produced my credentials, but he was such a good sentry that, still thinking I might be a spy, he took me to a corporal, who took me to a sergeant, who took me to two more sergeants, who took me to the orderly room.

Eventually – it was rather like having an interview at the Vatican – I progressed to grander and grander regions, until I found myself in the presence of the adjutant, and next door, actually next door, to the Commandant of the Royal Air Force Flying Training School.

It was one of those days when I was looking less like my passport photograph than usual. Therefore, as the various officers gazed suspiciously at me, I had plenty of time to look through the windows and admire the lay-out of what is actually a town of flight. These Training Schools were started before the War as part of our rearmament scheme, and it is fortunate that many of them were completed by the time war was declared. Here is a nursery that is enabling us to gain control of the air. I was astonished by the size of the place. It looked rather like a young son of Port Sunlight and Bournville.

The Commandant was a man of middle-age and therefore, by the standards of his pupils, almost senile. He had flown in the last War and, as a chestful of ribbons proved, had seen a lot of trouble one way and another.

He read my letter of introduction slowly and with care, and then, with a smile, asked for my passport and identity card. I was waiting to see if he would really 'burn with fire' the letter from the Air Ministry, or whether it was merely a matter of form. To my delight, he solemnly produced a box of matches, lit one, and holding the letter in the flame, watched it curl up and blacken. The remains floated into his wastepaper basket.

He turned to me with a pleasant expression.

'And what would you like to see?'

He reminded me of a vigorous schoolmaster preparing to show a parent round his school. I asked how the young men of this War compared with ourselves – the 'young men' of the last one.

'Oh, I think they're a better lot than we are,' he replied heartlessly. 'I like 'em. I'm proud of them, too, but I don't let them see it. We're getting a grand type of fellow. He's full of spirit, initiative and guts. He's well educated; in fact, he's got to be. I'd like to tell you what splendid men the Dominions and Colonies are breeding. They take to the air like birds. They're born pilots.'

And he told me that a man must be something of a born pilot these days, otherwise he could never stay the course. Having passed a selection board, which ruthlessly weeds out doubtful cases, the pilot-to-be has to pass a stiff medical examination before he is posted to an elementary flying school, where he learns the ABC of flight, engines and guns.

He then takes a course at an RAF depôt and is taught to march and drill. He also works at as much theory as if he were studying for a university degree. Then he receives £50 from the Air Ministry to buy a pilot's uniform and kit, and, proudly dressed, he goes to one of the Flying Training Schools to add wings to his tunic. This is a gruelling four months' course of practical and theoretical work. In the last war many a pilot had to complete his training over the enemy lines, but this time our pilots go out masters of their job.

In the few hours I spent wandering round the Flying School, I was struck by the extreme youth of everyone I encountered. I saw about twenty class-rooms, in most of which sat a grimly intent group of young men in blue, watching a lecturer at a blackboard. In the next and the next were the same young faces, lifted to the lecturer or bent over note-books. I have never before entered a class-room which did not welcome the arrival of even the most uninteresting intruder, but these young

pilots were too engrossed in their work to notice that they were being watched.

What a curriculum it is: engines, armaments, administration, signals, air navigation, airmanship, airframes, maintenance, and mathematics. Those are the 'junior' lectures in this university of flight. The 'seniors' specialise in air photography and reconnaissance.

Walking round from lecture room to armament store, and from store to hangar, I had the impression of young men in various stages of training, some proudly 'winged', others as yet unfledged, all performing different tasks with remarkable absorption.

I could have stayed a long time in the darkrooms, watching them develop those bird's-eye glimpses of distant landscapes which, to the unaccustomed eye, make a countryside look as if it has been ironed flat. But I was rushed off to the flying-ground, where a group of pilots was advancing towards a line of training machines, each man strolling forward heavily garmented, a parachute dangling behind like a cushion that had become attached to his seat.

'You can quickly tell the fellow who's cut out to be a fighter and the man who should be a bomber,' said an instructor. 'For a fighter you want a quick, practical-joking kind of bloke, who will take risks without making an ass of himself; but a bomber must be a calmer kind of chap. I should say that for a fighter you want spirit, and for a bomber you want nerve. A bomber must hold on his course quite calmly when the shells are getting nearer . . .'

The young men, laughing, climbed into the line of machines. In a minute or so they were several hundred feet overhead.

War's attraction for youth, I thought, is that years of slogging and dreary routine and subservience to age are instantly abolished, and a man finds his feet among his contemporaries in the full spring-time of life. It is rather as though a doctor, a barrister or an accountant could reach eminence in his profession in twelve months.

Knowing nothing about flying, I was fascinated by an invention which is I believe a commonplace in all flying schools, the Link Trainer.

I went into a room occupied by a young officer who sat at a desk with ear-phones on his head, studying a kind of planchette which slowly traced lines on a chart. The room buzzed electrically.

Every now and then the officer glanced towards a weird truncated aeroplane in the centre of the floor, which turned slowly and swayed as if in flight, although it was firmly attached to a gigantic bellows. Inside this machine, concealed from view and sitting in darkness, a young pilot was learning to fly blind. He received all his instructions by phone from the officer, and he altered course, elevation and so forth accordingly.

'He's flying at two hundred feet and at a hundred and thirty-five miles an hour,' said the officer. 'And he's made a good flight,' he continued, pointing to a series of firm lines on the map.

He whispered an order into his mouth-piece. The 'almost aeroplane' changed course and made a kind of curtsey.

'Oh hell!' said the officer.

'What's happened?' I asked.

'He's crashed!'

He whispered again, and the lid of the cockpit was pushed up to reveal a pink, embarrassed face.

'I'm awfully sorry, sir,' said the face.

'I should think so,' replied the officer. 'You're dead.'

So perfectly does this earth-bound aeroplane reproduce the act of flying, that a man can be taught in this way to pilot a real machine and, although he may never have

'I was fascinated by the Link Trainer which is I believe a commonplace in all flying schools'

been in the air, he could go from the Link Trainer to a real machine and take it up in fog or by night; but of course that is only part of the story.

Another ingenious invention is the Camera Obscura Hut, which tells an instructor whether a man in a bomber several thousand feet above him has, in theory, bombed the hut. The place is dark save for a circle of light reflected upon a table through a lens in the roof. A spot in the centre of the table represents the hut.

When an aeroplane is flying overhead you can watch its shadow slowly cross the table, as it is reflected by the lens. As it nears the centre a tiny white flash is seen, which is really the firing of a magnesium bulb in the aeroplane. This represents the bomb, or rather the exact moment at which the bomber pressed the bomb-release.

The instant the flash is seen, it is plotted on the table. It is a simple matter to allow for the time taken for the bomb to drop according to the height of the plane, and the angle at which it falls, according to the speed and the wind, and this shows you how near, or how far, the bomber was from his target.

But the Air Force has another wonderful toy. This teaches the bomber how to drop a bomb.

We entered a building like a deep bear-pit. On a wooden floor above the pit a complicated piece of machinery was erected which I was unable to explain in any detail. In principle, it was a photographic projector pointing downward, so that the lens flung the image of an aerial landscape on the concrete floor of the pit below.

By extraordinarily clever mechanism, this huge photograph is made to revolve and to reproduce the effect of a distant countryside moving beneath the body of an aircraft in flight.

An ingenious arrangement regulates the speed at which the landscape moves, and it can be altered to correspond with the speed of a flying plane. Equally ingenious is the system of enlarging, or making smaller, the picture, according to the height of the imaginary aircraft from the ground.

You can set the picture for, say, a speed of two hundred miles an hour and a height of a thousand feet (or any other given set of speeds and heights), and when you look down you see the buildings, the roads, the belts of woodland, and the towns, exactly as they would appear to a man travelling in an aeroplane at the determined speed and height.

The instructor switched off the lights and switched on the lantern. Setting the machinery in motion for a speed of one hundred and thirty miles an hour, and a height of one thousand, five hundred feet, he led the way down a flight of steps into the pit beneath.

Projecting from the wall of the pit and jutting out over the floor, and perhaps twenty feet or so above it, was the platform of a bomber. It was complete in every detail: instruments, bomb-sights and bomb release. The pupil lies full length on this platform, just as a bomber does when he is approaching his target, and the instructor, standing behind, gives him a mark and takes his navigation orders.

'Would you like to have a shot at it?' asked the instructor.

I climbed up to the bomb platform and lay down. There were various instruments in front of me, none of which I understood. However, the bomb-sights were not difficult to grasp after a few moments' practice. You look through them as through binoculars, keeping the object you are going to destroy in view all the time. The bomb-release was the simplest of all: it was just like a press-button on a self-working lift.

'Are you all right?' asked the instructor.

'I'm not feeling very efficient,' I said, 'but otherwise I'm all right.'

'Good. Now we're flying at one hundred and thirty miles an hour at a height of one thousand, five hundred feet, so that you've got a good view of the earth. I want you to bomb this . . .'

And the long shadow of a pointer suddenly streaked across the moving countryside below me and came to rest on a house which bore an astonishing resemblance to my own.

'I don't like that target,' I said. 'Can't you find me something that looks a bit more suspicious?'

By this time the harmless-looking house had slid into safety beneath me.

'Well, what about that railway station?'

The pointer touched a network of rails which had just come on the outer rim of the picture, and was advancing beneath me at the speed of a slow-motion film. I willingly agreed to bomb the station, and I lay there watching it, keeping my bomb-sights on it; but then the station suddenly swung off to the left and I was unable to find it again.

The instructor told me that the wind velocity was so-and-so, and the target was off our course, so that unless I gave him directional orders we should never get above it. By the time I had said 'left' when I meant 'right', the station also had slid below me into safety. Bombing is not as easy as I thought it would be.

He gave me a third target – another railway junction – and this time I was determined to make good. As the rails came towards me, I pressed myself firmly on the platform and squinted along the sights. I sang out 'left' (and he swung the machine into line with the target, but a trifle too much), and I sang out 'right!' (and now we were dead on), and at the precise moment when I saw the station below – there were two trains and one in a siding – I pressed the button of the bomb-release!

Down through one thousand five hundred feet of air fell a small cross in electric light. Actually, the pressing of the release had reflected this light immediately on the picture, but, as the picture continued to move for several seconds, it looked as though the 'bomb' were actually dropping through the air.

These seconds represented the time taken by a bomb to fall from the moment it leaves the bomb-rack to the moment it hits the ground. Then, abruptly, the whole landscape became still, and looking down, I saw the cross shining in the place where I would have made a hit if it had been a bomb. I had missed the station and hit a farmhouse about a quarter of a mile away! I was horrified.

Before I left the school, I spoke to several of the infants there. I asked them why the RAF attracted them. They found this rather difficult to formulate, but I pressed them hard.

'Well,' replied one, who was unborn at the time of the Armistice, 'it's exciting and it's quick. I've always wanted to fly.'

Another, who must have been an infant in a perambulator when the Kaiser slipped into Holland, said: 'I want to be a pilot because – well, it's like the knights of old, isn't it? You come out of the clouds, pick your enemy, and do your stuff and dash off again.'

That, I thought, was getting nearer to the heart of it. The RAF has revived the romance of single combat. For the first time since the age of chivalry armed men charge together in mortal combat and fight their tournaments in the boundless lists of the sky.

The black-out came upon me in a country town, where I had difficulty in finding anywhere to stay because the town was occupied by musicians, vocalists, educationalists, professors and others who had been called to the microphones of 'Hush Hush Hall'.

When the story of the War is written, the removal of the BBC into the country will take a high place in the fantasy. The location of the new broadcasting studios was a State secret. At the moment of writing, although it may be permissible to whisper the name of the place, it is necessary, if you wish to write to the BBC, to address the letter to a box number at the local Post Office; so the fiction is maintained that the BBC is secretly hidden away, no one knows where.

The town accepted its distinction with enthusiasm. It was great fun to watch the crowds of people bearing cellos, drums, and other bulky articles, which every London express deposited upon the station platform. Men and women familiar until then as voices became visible personalities, and autograph albums were soon sold out. In addition to the daily visitors, there was a large resident staff of administrators, secretaries, musicians, choirs, electricians, and mechanics, all of whom were installed in hotels or billeted in houses. Those without cars were given bi-cycles in order that they might reach Hush Hush Hall.

I received a call in the morning from a director of programmes whom I had often met in London. Instead of the faultless town clothes in which I remembered him, he now wore a riding-coat, breeches and boots. I asked if he rode on horseback to the micro-phone, but no, he said, he still had his car, but he lived some distance away in a thatched cottage approached by a sea of mud, and so found his present attire more suitable.

I gathered that Hush Hush Hall had to be seen to be believed, and that the exiles from Langham Place were enjoying themselves in the country. Few of them ever wanted to see Broadcasting House again.

Having procured a pass, I was taken off to see the hall. It lay beside a country road some way out of the town. We passed cyclists, male and female, busily pedalling in its direction. We passed a small motor omnibus containing an orchestra.

'We run a bus to and from the hall every hour. It's absolutely essential, especially after black-out.'

We came to a pair of wrought-iron gates. Standing outside them, looking extremely out of place, was one of the commissionaires from Broadcasting House. He halted us, examined my pass, and although my friend goes in and out every day and is well known to everybody, he insisted, like a good martinet, on viewing his pass as well. We were then at liberty to enter the sweeping drive, which soon brought us in sight of a remarkably ugly country house.

It is a queer, eccentric-looking house. Not quite English and not quite anything else. It was built, I was told, during the last century by an exiled nobleman who amid English meadows dreamed of his eventual restoration of the dignities of his ancestors.

The hall itself is occupied by the adminis-trative members of the staff and stables and coach-houses had been turned into studios. All the concerts and talks – everything, in fact, but the news bulletins, which still come from London, and the theatre organ, which was apparently too large to move – is broadcast from the stables of Hush Hush Hall.

We explored the house, a gloomy place full of dark panelled rooms decorated everywhere by the coronet and escutcheons of the previous owner. The bathroom shower terminated in a coronet and every door-plate bore the same uneasy symbol.

Glancing through the windows, I saw a number of men and women approaching the house on bicycles, and among them I recognised Mr Stanford Robinson, the conductor. Several of the girls were members of the resident choir.

Leaving this strange Anthony Hope mansion, I approached the range of red-brick stables, lofts and outbuildings, where I found the greatest surprise of all. Here, where grooms once whistled as they cleaned saddles, where coachmen washed down the emblazoned carriages, where horses stamped in box and stall, are microphones which record the voices and music which we hear every day.

The engineers have made a wonderful job of it, and the studios are almost as efficient as those in Broadcasting House. The big studio where the orchestral concerts are broadcast is a long coach-house with a high, girdered roof, but the soundproof walls and doors and the blaze of electric light have disguised its former purpose.

At intervals of an hour the motor omnibus drives up from the town, and out of it step vocalists and instrumentalists and other performers who are due to broadcast; those who have just given a broadcast take their places in the coach, and the BBC bus goes back along the country road to the town.

The nightmare of programme director, announcer, and conductor is that some distinguished performer may be discovered, at the moment of his broadcast, miles away in the blacked-out town.

I asked someone to explain a notice-board which bore the words 'To the Bear Pits', thinking that perhaps some facetious member of the BBC had put it up, in reference maybe to the war-time studios. I was told that the previous occupant had satisifed an aristocratic eccentricity by keeping wild bears!

Pressing my way through dank bushes and trailing briars, I came to a slight rise of ground on which were built cages for wild animals. As I was inspecting them, a creature wilder and more ferocious than any bear flung itself from the gloom of a cage and leapt in fury against the bars. He was a dog, but of what fabulous breed I do not know, a creature as big as a Great Dane and as shaggy as an Airedale. As I looked at him, I seemed to recognise the Hound of the Baskervilles.

His cage was a mass of beef-bones chewed white. He was, I think, the most savage-looking dog I have ever seen, and I wondered why, of all the previous owner's wild animals, he alone should have survived, an unhappy legacy for the BBC. Perhaps nobody was brave enough to take him away.

But no, he is the BBC's own watch-dog. He was procured on the outbreak of war to prowl the grounds, and he is let loose every night after dark; so let me warn you never to attempt to enter Hush Hush Hall over the fence! If a Beethoven Symphony should ever be interrupted by a series of blood-curdling barks, you will know that the Hound of the Baskervilles has earned his keep and caught a spy.

CHAPTER EIGHT

*I travel to the armament towns of the Midlands, where I see tanks in
the making, also shells and AA guns. I go to Chester, which looks
superb in the black-out, and visit the Postal Censor at Liverpool.*

I have known Stratford-on-Avon all my life, but never have I seen it looking more beautiful than it did that night. There was a high, cold moon, and a few banks of drifting dark cloud in the sky; the streets were empty and the moonlight silvered roof-tiles and cut slantways across the zebra-striped, black-and-white buildings, almost as if a producer had skilfully stationed a limelight there for the purpose.

All the pseudo-Elizabethan buildings looked genuine, and I might have been walking in the Stratford of Shakespeare's day. I went down to the Avon, where I saw a pale river moving in the night, a river on which the face of Ophelia might have shone for a moment before the current bore her onward to the place where the spire of Holy Trinity rose above the woods. And in those woods surely Titania was that night assembling her small elves.

I suppose the day is not far distant when we shall long to see street lamps and lighted windows at night, but in these first few weeks of war the beauty of the black-out in certain old towns like Stratford, given starlight or a moon, is something never to be forgotten. The darkness obliterates everything that is vulgar; it makes everything harmonise. The roofline becomes important; the most commonplace objects become almost operatic; and in fancy every approaching footfall or dark figure shares in the air of mystery.

Stratford has been practically unchanged by the War. Shakespeare's birthplace has been sand-bagged on the outside, but, so far as I could discover, all the relics and folios remain there. The famous hotel, whose visitors' book is a *Who's Who* of America, was taken over by the Government in the first moments of war, when it was believed London had only a few hours to live, and the occupants were given about twenty-four hours to get out. Since then nothing has been heard from the Government, and the hotel remains closed, just as it was requisitioned, with the chairs and tables piled up in the lounge, as you can see through the

windows. It would be pleasant to think of Treasury officials operating from a room called 'Much Ado about Nothing', or members of the Inland Revenue sending out their forms from one named 'As You Like It', for all the bedrooms in this hotel bear the title of a Shakespearean play.

Accommodation being scarce in Stratford, owing to the closed hotels, I stayed at a small and comfortable inn which was almost empty. The only other occupant of the drawing-room after dinner was a pleasant, fair-haired lady of middle-age, who told me with a sigh that she had saved up her petrol coupons to visit Stratford upon a house-hunting expedition. I gathered that she had sold her house to an evacuated school because her retainers threatened to leave in a body if evacuees should appear. The newspaper outcry against well-to-do people who have cold-shouldered evacuees has been, in my opinion, monstrously unfair. It is, generally speaking, the servants' hall that has cold-shouldered the evacuees and by threats of resignation has blackmailed the employer into imploring billeting officials to take their unfortunate mothers and children elsewhere.

The only house that had rewarded this poor lady in her search was one marred by a prehistoric kitchen into which, she said, she would not dream of putting her servants.

'Although they have been with me for years,' she explained, 'they would give one look at that kitchen and go.'

'Before the War is over, madam,' I said, 'it is possible that there will be no servants; therefore, if you like the house, I should take it.'

'Do you really think that will happen?' she asked, and I left this servant of servants mournfully glancing through the advertisements in *Country Life*.

All the warmth and life of this inn had been gathered into its bar, where before a blazing coal fire stood a grand collection of local men. They were bidding farewell to the 'Captain', as they called the barmaid who was, I gathered from the jokes, leaving to be married. She was plump, cheerful and tremendously capable. Every glass and bottle obeyed her hasty movements. As she pulled down the beer-handles she gave back chaff for chaff, and everybody agreed that her prospective husband was a lucky man.

Among the company was a thin, hatchet-faced little man, who might well have been one of the lesser characters in the *Dream*, a little man in a suit of thick black cloth. He was the local jester. His reputation was such that every word he uttered brought forth roars of laughter. The broad Warwickshire tongue can be most difficult to pick up if you are not accustomed to it, and I tried in vain to understand his stories, wondering why they were so funny. It appeared that he had just returned from a horse sale at Stow-in-the-Wold, but had bought nothing. As he related this, the whole bar broke into shouts of mirth, in which the little man joined. England is full of such men, comedians to their friends and acquaintances, but a puzzle to strangers who, ignorant of their story and reputation, marvel at their popularity.

I came one afternoon to a city famous in the industrial history of Britain. Like most of our cities, it was suffering from a distressing attack of mumps; unsightly sandbag swellings were bulging everywhere, and some of the worst statues in the country had been expensively protected against 'blast'.

I found a way into my hotel between a right-angle rampart of sandbags, but, once inside, there was an extravagant blaze of electric light. My old friend, the lift man, who had lost an arm at Villers Brettoneaux, greeted me with: 'Well, I never thought we'd live to see another one, did you? You can't make head or tail of it, can you? The only thing that's the same is Jerry, still the same old dirty dog with his mines and his submarines and his "Gott strafe England".'

'Good heavens, you mustn't say things like that,' I told him. 'You must remember that we have no quarrel with the German people!'

'That's what the politicians say, but what I should like to know is who's to blame for Hitler if it isn't the German people?'

He shot open the lift doors to let me out.

'There's many who say they don't know what this war's about,' he whispered with the air of a minor oracle. 'But take it from me, they'll be shouting, "God bless you, Tommy Atkins!" before very long! Just you wait and see . . .'

He banged the doors upon himself and shot upward, standing angrily to attention, like a prophet caught up to heaven.

The black-out in this city was indescribably black. The darkness was something thicker and blacker than anything I had experienced in the country, where darkness is natural on moonless nights. The tall buildings, which I sensed but could not see, intensified the blackness. They were the sides of an immense pit in which I groped helplessly. How the omnibuses managed to keep to the road, or to any time schedule, I do not know. They were perceived by the sound of their engines, then, as they crawled past, I saw a faint blueness in the black-out, and a driver bent tensely forward in a glow-worm light, trying to keep his eye on the kerb.

By shining the light of an electric torch downward, I managed to find my way along the main street of the almost deserted city – although it was only six o'clock in the evening – and in several adventurous and unforgettable movements I even managed to cross the road.

I came to a small stretch of green luminosity, rather like a badly lit aquarium. It was a cinema, and it was open. I groped my way into the phosphorescence and stood in the foyer. A man came up to me.

'Where's your gas mask?' he asked.

'In the hotel,' I replied.

'Sorry, you can't come in without it.'

'Are you expecting a gas attack?' I asked.

'The police are strict,' he said curtly.

So I stumbled into the black-out again, where I heard what an inhabitant of this city can say to a public telephone box when he takes it in his stride. As a door was opened and closed I saw a faint light. I thought it was a restaurant. I pushed the door open and found myself in a church. It was empty save for an old woman who was vaguely busy with a broom. I sat alone in a pew in this church, looking at the unlit altar. I may have sat there for twenty minutes. At length the old woman came to me and touched me on the shoulder.

'I very nearly locked you in,' she whispered.

So out again into the black-out and the uncertain, wandering ghosts of the main streets. For one unhappy moment I feared that I was lost, but I got my bearings, and was soon blinking triumphantly in the harsh light of the hotel.

After dinner, I went to bed. Red hand-pumps stood at intervals along the corridors, and beside each pump was a coil of hose, a spade, a pick, and a long-handled rake for incendiary bombs.

I undressed in a dim light, adding to my collection the wording of a notice which is to be read in most hotel bedrooms nowadays. This one said:

> In the event of an air raid, staff have been detailed to advise guests as to the facilities available for their protection.

I thought this was a masterpiece. No one could invent a notice like that: it had to spring straight from the managerial heart. The word 'advise' calls up a picture of a *maître d'hôtel* bending forward from the waist with a menu of shelters. Amid the crash of falling masonry and the roar of escaping water and gas, one can imagine him saying: 'Possibly the basement shelter is not dry enough for your taste, sir. Might I recommend Number 426, a fine, dry, and, if I might say so, full-bodied shelter . . .'

To the English eye, there is something extraordinary about the sight of armed police. In ordinary times our police are able to do all that is necessary with a warning, a rebuke, a summons or a frog-march. To see them, as I have seen them outside war factories, with the black butts of revolvers protruding from their holsters, is to be surprised and somehow jarred. They do not fit into the English scene. Still, despite sinister leather holsters, they fail to look like Hitler's jack-booters: they are the same dry, humorous, friendly men who in kinder and happier days warn, rebuke, summon or frog-march us.

Presenting my letters of introduction at a tank factory, I was shown into a waiting-room whose sole adornment was a poster warning the workpeople to beware of spies and to guard their tongues. This, too, is a strange warning in England, where men exchange the most preposterous confidences, and impart the most surprising information, as a matter of course.

When it had been suggested that I ought to see a tank factory, I wrote to the Ministry of Supply asking for some information about the origin and development of the tank. I received in reply a skittish letter from a general referring me to the prophet Nahum, chapter two, verse four, where I read the following: 'The chariots shall rage in the streets, they shall jostle one against another in the broad ways: they shall seem like torches, they shall run like the lightnings.'

I replied that I was unconvinced by his quotation, and referred the general to Ezekiel, chapter four, verse three, where the prophet is directed to 'take unto thee an iron pan and set it for a wall of iron between thee and the city'. I think Ezekiel's 'iron pan' was more of a tank – in the sense that it was probably a moving assault tower – than Nahum's chariots, which were, after all, merely horse-drawn.

If we may define a tank as an instrument of

*'They are the same
dry, humorous, friendly men'*

war capable of movement, in which soldiers fight under cover, we can trace its origin to many ancient devices of war, not excluding perhaps the elephants of Hannibal. But the tank is more exactly defined as an armoured motor vehicle which is not dependent on road surfaces, and, as such, its origin is nothing more exciting than the American agricultural caterpillar tractor.

No one person can claim authorship of the tank: it is an engineering anthology created to counter machine-gun fire. As early as October 1914, General E. D. Swindon, of the Royal Engineers, put up an idea for an armoured machine which could plough through barbed wire, and it was this idea, sponsored by Mr Churchill against much opposition, that helped to inspire the first tank.

This machine was made in great secrecy at Lincoln, in 1915, and was called 'Little Willie'. By this time dozens of engineers were at work on its design, but, despite everything, 'Little Willie' could not keep to his tracks. He was therefore scrapped in favour of an improved tank called 'Mother'. Her trials at Hatfield Park were successful.

To the astonishment of all beholders, she crossed ditches, a stream and a golf course. Her gunnery trials were held at Burton Park, near Lincoln, in such secrecy that people who lived near were ordred by the police to pull down their blinds whenever 'Mother' shambled into view.

This was the pattern for the tanks that took the Germans by surprise on the Somme, and indeed was the 'mother' of all tanks.

I assure you that I had plenty of time to reflect on such matters as I sat waiting in the tank factory. At last, convinced that I was genuine, they led me into an astonishing place, where I could see nothing at first but hundreds of individuals standing at machines which dripped with what appeared to be milk.

The noise was not exciting, nor was it necessary to raise my voice except in certain broad acres of the factory. There was no rushing about. All those hundreds of men were as stationary as cobblers at their lasts.

It was an almost austere combination of man and machine. Everything was dressed by the right in long rows. Bending over their machines, the men might have been pupils in some gigantic technical school. I stopped here and there to watch the lubricating milk flowing over a drill or come spurting upon a machine that was slowly, and with terrifying exactitude, shaving from a great chunk of steel

a tiny ringlet of bright metal that curled up and fell noiselessly to the floor. And somehow – somewhere – in all this was the beginning of a tank!

As I walked on into this factory, the jigsaw began to join up. I saw that under the immense, blacked-out roof of glass, a roof like that of Euston Station, metal was going in at one end as thousands of variously shaped parts, some big, some small, and emerging at the other end as – tanks!

I had not expected it to be like that. I had expected to see huge bolted plates swinging through the air on overhead cranes. I had expected to see men sweating with great hammers; riveters with red-holt bolts. That tanks

'Bending over their machines,
the men might have been pupils in
some gigantic technical school'

are made by hundreds of quiet men, in an atmosphere not unlike that of a model dairy, was difficult to believe.

By mounting to a high place, I could see that though the men all round me were working at sprockets and little wheels, a hundred yards or so off, at the end of the shop, huge green and brown tanks were roaring out towards the testing ground in bursts of exhaust smoke.

'Do you ever think of the fellows who will take over these tanks in France?' I asked one of the men. He was a gentle little man in spectacles. He looked up from the machine he was controlling.

'Oh, yes, I do – often,' he replied. 'My boy is there in the Tank Corps.'

I examined hulls, which is the name for the body of a tank, bogie wheels, tracks, which is the name for the caterpillar belts, turrets, engines and gear-boxes; then I passed on to the assembly point where all these parts were put together.

A small boy was standing on a wheeled electric riveter. He took up a cold rivet in a pair of tongs and held it a second in an electric current, where the rivet took light.

First it turned red, then bright vermilion, and, at the moment of its greatest brightness, the lad suddenly moved his tongs with an artistic flourish – rather like a waiter lighting a cigarette – and gave the glowing point to a man who, in a second, had thrust and hammered it into armour-plate.

The act had the precise monotony of a mechanical toy. You could count the rivets per minute and reckon how many go to the hour. The finest thing about it was the boy's proud flourish of the tongs. Even a machine cannot completely suppress an artist.

One of the hardships suffered by factory workers in this war is lack of daylight. Many factories are lit by roof-glass; the more modern the factory the more numerous are the top lights and windows. In order to blackout these buildings, it has been necessary to blacken the glass and sacrifice all daylight, so that work is performed day and night in artificial light.

At this time of year the day shifts arrive at work before the black-out has lifted, and they return home in the evening after it has been resumed, so that many of them rarely see the light of day unless they make a point of looking for it during a luncheon interval.

I spent a day motoring through the dreary, red-brick, industrial Midlands, a region always hideous and deformed, and now made even more horrible by the means taken to protect it, in the form of municipally erected shelters, sand-bags, home-made dug-outs and trenches. To come upon such signs as 'To the Trenches', 'First Aid Post', and 'Air Raid Shelter', with which all towns are plentifully provided, was to rub one's eyes in astonishment, for this intrusion of war's makeshift untidiness into civilian life was still new enough to be grotesque.

Tall chimneys belching smoke, factories making guns and shells, long rows of red-brick villas, blackened parks and open spaces cut about with sandbagged trenches – this is the new battleground. The enemy's bombs may as easily fall upon the Black Country as the front line. Indeed, one may well ask where is the front line of this war?

In the course of my journey, I paused at a factory which is turning out shrapnel shells. The whole process was carried out under one enormous roof. Chunks of metal came in at one end and emerged at the other as highly finished shells, ready to go off to an ordnance factory to be filled with death.

While I was going round the factory, I asked several of the men whether they could tell me the origin of shrapnel. And not one of them knew it. This is the history of it.

OVERLEAF *'Tall chimneys belching smoke'*

The shapnel shell was the invention of a clever young gunner officer, Henry Shrapnel, who was born at Midnay Manor, near Bradford-on-Avon, in Wiltshire, in the year 1761. At the age of twenty-three, he came to the conclusion that the old-fashioned cannon ball, even when heated red-hot as our ancestors liked to use it in naval actions, was capable of improvement, and he began to spend his private fortune in experiments. By the time he was in his forties his hollow shells filled with shot and fired by a time-fuse were so obviously an improvement on the old cannon ball that even the Board of Ordnance was bound to admit the fact and to adopt the shell in the service.

Shrapnel's shell was the 'secret weapon' of the British armies throughout the Peninsular War and the Waterloo campaign. Its effect was devastating, and Wellington, together with his generals, was not backward in paying their tributes to the inventor. They put on record that this shell had helped to win the battles of Vimiera and Talavera; and Sir John Wood, who commanded the artillery at Waterloo, wrote to Shrapnel from Waterloo Village on 21 June, 1815 to say that without his shells it is doubtful whether any effort of the British armies could have dislodged the enemy from La Haye Sainte. 'Hence,' he concluded, 'on this simple circumstance hinges entirely the turn of the battle.' Foreign armies did not use shrapnel until 1834.

It goes almost without saying that Shrapnel was never adequately recompensed for the money he had spent in perfecting the shell, and he was obliged to give up the ancestral manor. And I believe if you go to Midnay Manor, you will see on top of the lodge gates a pile of round iron balls, which few passers-by notice. These are the first shrapnel 'shells' ever made.

Leaving this factory, I travelled through a district occupied almost entirely by armament works. Some of them have been specially built to make armaments and others are peacetime factories which have been turned over to war-work.

My next call was at a factory which is turning out hundreds of shells a day for the 3.7 Anti-Aircraft gun. This factory was one of the cheeriest I had visited. Managers, works managers, foremen and men seemed to be having a thoroughly jolly time together, calling one another by their Christian names and yelling jokes into each other's ears at the tops of their voices, above the hideous scream of tortured metal.

The 3.7 AA gun can pump bursts of death into the sky at the rate of fifteen shells a minute. The shells are high-explosive shrapnel shells which burst in the air, creating a wide 'cone of dispersion'. This factory does not make the tall copper shell-case, of the kind which was so often picked up on Flanders Fields and used at home as umbrella stands, but only the explosive shell itself.

I was taken first to the furnaces, where demons with long rakes were hopping about withdrawing little tangerine-coloured ingots of metal from the very mouth of hell. They picked them out as delicately as Mrs Brown picks up a lump of sugar in the tongs, and, with something of the same polite grace with which she consigns it to the tea-cup, they placed each livid lump under a piercing press.

The gigantic hammer came down with the inevitability of Fate, neatly pressing the ingots as a grocer pats a pound of butter into shape. Did I count four a minute or five, or was it six? Never mind. In one operation the press had elongated them and pierced them with a cavity.

They then came along a travelling band, while a man in the attitude of a Greek priest administering a blessing with an aspergillum, swiftly touching each moving shell with a spoon as he tipped in a pinch of graphite to lubricate it. Along they came in an endless chain, moving in their own hot breath, to be water-cooled and tested for trueness. They were now definitely shells, the objects you would not be surprised to pick up on any battlefield or see in any hall.

I watched as they were rough-turned, and so changed from dull cylinders of metal into shining silver, by a machine which cut them with a point of tungsten carbide. I noticed that the machines were German, and the one I happened to be looking at was worked by an ex-soldier. The proportion of old soldiers in this factory was unusually high.

'Two men who had last seen each other in France during the last War met at this machine a few weeks ago!' said a foreman.

'And what did they do?' I asked foolishly.

'Adjourned to the local!' was the reply.

The most spectacular moment in the creation of the shell is the process known as shot-blasting. This takes place in soundproof cabinets. Each cabinet has a little square of glass through which you can look and see what is happening inside.

Nobody warned me what to expect and, glancing through, I saw probably the most grotesque sight in war-time industry: deaf mutes dressed in protective armour, moving slowly and clumsily because of their cumbrous garments as they directed the nozzles of the machinery to the shell cavities.

It looked as if this factory had managed to capture and imprison a new race of man, inhabitants from Mars, or perhaps from the nether regions themselves. Leather helmets with air tubes attached covered their heads. Their hands were gigantically gloved. Their shapeless bodies bore small resemblance to the human figure.

'When we first started this process,' I was told, 'the noise was so terrific and incessant that no one could work the machines. So we advertised for men who had never had any sense of hearing. Since that time we have managed to silence the blast-proofing – comparatively speaking – and there's no need to employ deaf men, but we continue to use them.'

At the end of the long shed I was shown thousands of AA shells. They were ready to go away to be fitted with the cases, and then to go on to an explosive factory to have the charge put into them.

Each shell was a superb piece of workmanship. The cavities had been varnished with a brownish lacquer. I was asked to run my finger round the inside. It was as if each shell had been french polished, and this, I was told, is absolutely necessary in order to avoid the slightest friction when the explosives go in . . .

Off I went across the ugly landscape, where tall chimneys smoked and the forges glowed.

Gun-barrels of incandescent steel swing through the darkened foundry. They come noiselessly, save for the hum of an overhead crane which picks them from the kiln as easily as you would pick a pencil from the floor.

With the terrifying intelligence of machinery, the heavy bars are pushed this way and that, retreating and advancing beneath the giant hammer of an hydraulic press, an object as high as a house. They lie there motionless at first, until the great hammer comes down and squeezes them as if they were bars of vermilion butter. Then the hammer curtly rejects them, and they go away, no longer white-hot, but dull and metallic in appearance; and another bar, as orange-red and as covered with jumping salamanders as the first, swings through the air.

Even if your back is turned, you can tell when a gun-barrel goes past by the hot air on your back. And the men, like pygmies in silhouette, stand with long rakes and probes of iron as they dodge about in the glow of white-hot steel.

I stood watching this process in one of the factories which is producing the new 3.7 Anti-Aircraft gun, the most amazing weapon of its kind ever produced in this country. Twenty years ago we should have said that such a gun was impossible. To a non-technical observer

*'At the end of the long shed
I was shown thousands of AA shells'*

like myself nothing is more fascinating than the start of these complicated processes. I like to see the raw chunks of metal, from which these miracles of engineering and invention are made, setting out on their swift career.

I know that a few stages further on I shall become fogged and be unable to distinguish the material from the machine. But here in the foundry one can see and understand something simple and uncomplicated; for even today a gun begins, as it did in the days of the Armada, as a bar of metal with a hole down the centre of it.

The works manager told me how many times a barrel is reheated and hardened, and how often, at certain stages of its manufacture, pieces are cut off to be examined by chemists and to be tested. He then led the way into an unbelievable factory, said to be the largest works under one roof-span in Europe.

He smiled when I expressed surprise at the size of it, and said that in spite of the roof-span you could put it in a corner of Krupps

and not notice it; but to my eyes it seemed colossal.

Here I saw gun-barrels receiving their first rough boring. The cylinders of steel, which are twenty feet long, are placed horizontally in machines fitted with two drills, which bore a hole from each end. They bore at the speed of twelve inches an hour. When the drills are about to meet in the barrel one is stopped and the other is allowed to pierce the last thin film of steel. He told me that the average error in this first boring is only 0.10 inch.

This is only the first of many similar processes, each one of which makes the bore larger and more accurate, until, at last, an electric light is placed at one end of the barrel and the testers, gazing through the other end, see a tunnel of what looks like mirror-glass.

But the barrel is only one of the three thousand parts that go to make a 3.7 gun. As

*'The barrel is only one of the three thousand
parts that go to make a 3.7 gun'*

we walked past batteries of machines, I saw
jackets, breech-rings, breech-blocks, and every
other part of the gun being made. There were
machines which were busy on objects as large
as recoil cylinders and others making the kind
of screws you might put into a clock.

One might describe this factory as an
orderly chaos of machinery which does incredible refinements to rough castings, turning
brown steel into silver glass, each machine
watched by a technical-looking fellow in blue
overalls.

Some of the largest machines, holding their
particular portion of the gun in a vice-like
grip, worked slowly to a drip of lubricating
liquid, and the only sign that they were working was a thin slither of steel that curled up
like a piece of apple rind and fell among the
steel shavings below.

The secret of our industrial war effort is the
application of mass production to the manufacture of high precision engineering. Everywhere in our factories today you see the same
thing: highly skilled men operating almost
miraculous machines and turning out prod-
ucts at incredible speed, each one a perfect
scientific instrument.

In places where men work with their muscles, they drink beer; but in our factories
today, where all the muscular work is done by
pressing a button on an electric switchboard,
you come across hundreds of milk-bottles and
cartons. In shell factories and gun factories
and other armament works all over the country, I have seen the same collection of white
bottles standing among the machinery.

I asked again if those who made the guns
ever thought of the men who would some day
fire them.

One man said that a good workman always
saw his job through, but nowadays he was
more careful than ever not to 'cover anything
up', because the slightest error in high preci-

sion work might let down the fellow at the front.

'All this beautiful work – and you must say it's beautiful – to cause destruction!' said one operator. 'It's all wrong. But if a bully won't stop bullying, you can't stop him by writing him a letter about it, can you? At least, I've never met a bully you could stop without a punch on the nose.'

His machine claimed his attention, and I walked on for a quarter of a mile into a shop where the guns were taking shape.

The guns stood with their barrels pointing to the roof, men climbing about them, adjusting this and that. They are so delicately balanced on the centre of the trunnions that a child could elevate them. In the same way the traversing gear works so smoothly that the huge pieces of machinery can be moved almost with a touch.

As I turned the handle and saw the long barrel bow, I thought that the instinct of self-preservation is an amazing thing. What has brought this astonishing gun into existence but the same will to live that makes you jump at the sound of a motor horn? Aeroplanes will kill you if you don't shoot them down! Therefore, we protect ourselves with this terrible, intelligent gun.

Not long ago we tried to bring down aeroplanes with field guns mounted on lorries. Then came the 'Archies', which sometimes put up a good show without inspiring much confidence in the eyes of observers. And, in the years between, inventors have been busily solving the problem – a most difficult one – of hitting a fast-moving plane.

First you have to locate it; secondly you have to know its height, speed and course; and thirdly, you must not fire at it but at the point in space which it will occupy by the time the shell arives there. Although the time taken by a shell from the moment it leaves the gun to the moment it reaches a distant point in the air may be only a few seconds, an aeroplane may have travelled a mile in that time.

Other factors in aerial gunnery are the force of the wind, the curve of the trajectory, and, at certain times, the variation in barometric pressure thousands of feet above the earth. There are, indeed, so many factors to reckon with that no man, except by an amazing fluke, could set his gun, time his fuse, and bring down an aeroplane without the aid of instruments.

As an aeroplane is detected by the senses of sound and sight, the gun must have mechanical ears and eyes capable of swifter and more accurate reactions than those possible to human ears and eyes. The 3.7 height-finder, and the Predictor used with the gun, are these ears and eyes.

As soon as a plane comes in to view, the height-finder estimates its height. The Predictor then communicates to dials on the gun not only the bearing and the elevation, but also the correct fuse setting, so that the shell shall burst on the target. It estimates even the wind velocity and the barometric pressure. Thus, in a matter of seconds, those super-human ears and eyes have made a calculation which enables a trained gun crew to fire at a raiding plane.

There was a morning frost on the fields as I sped north into Shropshire. Rooks like bits of burned paper were fluttering over the dying woods and settling upon the newly turned furrows. There was a piercingly cold wind blowing from the Denbighshire highlands.

Chester was crowded, prosperous and cheerful. The shops in the Rows were crammed with everything the human heart and stomach can desire. Whenever I find myself in Chester, I go to a shop which sells the best Cheshire cheese you can buy, and there I select a pink monster. The proprietor told me that a cheese boom was in progress,

'There was a morning frost on the fields'

for all the strangers in the town, chiefly officers and their wives, liked to buy a cheese and post it home. I said jokingly that perhaps Cheshire cheese would be rationed, as I believe it was in the last War, but he glanced round at a shop full of great cheeses and said there didn't seem to be much sign of it.

Even fish, which is scarce in most places, seemed plentiful in Chester. A fishmonger told me that the supply varied from day to day. There had been a complete absence of cheap fish from the first week of the War, and this – together with the black-out – had killed the fried-fish trade as dead as a door-nail.

If the black-out in Stratford was romantic, what can I say of Chester as I saw it that night lit by the moon? It was the city of a dream. The only lights were feeble blue gleams beneath the Rows, and in the light of the moon the black-and-white shops leaned against the stars. Even Woolworths, joining in the romantic masquerade, formed part of the exquisite pattern.

When I retired to rest, I found that the hotel management had propped the following notice on the mantel-piece.

> In the event of an Air-Raid Warning you are asked to kindly make sure your electric lights and fires are extinguished, and all windows and doors closed.
>
> After this is done, you are asked to kindly proceed by way of the main staircase to the entrance hall, where you will be met by the Hotel Air-Raid Wardens, who will conduct you to the Air-Raid Shelter in the Cellar.
>
> Do not forget to take your Gas Mask with you.

We are surely, even when we split our infinitives, the most polite nation on the face of this earth. Where but in England would you expect your life to be saved with such courtesy? Of course the timidity of inexperience is to be traced in this and other such notices up and down the country, and I have no doubt that when a few bombs have fallen,

and old ladies have fought the air-raid wardens in order to return and retrieve a hairbrush or a carriage-clock, and when old men have refused to leave their beds, these warnings may become a trifle more peremptory.

I hope someone is collecting such notices. They reflect in a remarkable way the impact of the uncomfortable upon minds trained to regard comfort as the first rule of life. You have only to have stayed in an hotel at a time when a fellow-guest has had the bad taste to die to know what panic such an act of God can create in the managerial breast. You can but pity the hotel managers of England who are now obliged by law and logic to anticipate and provide for a holocaust of guests.

The Postal Censorship in the last War was admitted to be wonderful. An entirely new science was developed: the science of examining foreign mails in the interests of war. When war began in 1914 the post was censored by one Army officer and a few typists; by the time it ended the Chief Censor controlled a staff of six thousand. In this War some one thousand and three hundred censors are already at work on foreign mails, and their number is likely to increase.

The Department is installed in a huge, hideous concrete skyscraper in Liverpool, which was the headquarters of the biggest football pool in the country until the outbreak of war. The building is as difficult to penetrate as any armament factory, and once you are inside it is impossible to find your way about without a guide.

The Chief Censor received me in an office of the former football pool magnate. Much of the ornate walnut furniture had been banished to a corridor as hardly in keeping with the stern atmosphere of war.

'Postal censorship,' said the Censor, 'is a War measure which is only justifiable so far as it bears directly on the prosecution of the War. What does not concern the War does not concern the censorship.'

'Forgive me if I seem childish,' I said, 'but I should like to hear something about spies.'

The Censor played with a paper-knife for a moment, and I wondered whether I had asked an embarrassing question.

'Why should you appear childish?' he said with a smile. 'In war-time spies are everywhere.'

I am sorry that I cannot print much of our subsequent conversation, but I can say that it was an education in the cunning and ingenuity of man. Dodges that no writer of fiction has ever thought of are commonly employed by spies when they write to each other through the post.

Every kind of code it is possible to invent is on record in the Censorship archives; and it is difficult to believe that any new methods of communication will turn up in this War. But you never can tell.

One spy in England during the last War, a woman, used to write freely to a friend in a neutral country about a horrid, noisy woman called Pauline, and about a clever boy who was always passing his school examinations with credit. After some weeks a censor, who specialised in this lady's correspondence, tumbled to the fact that Pauline only appeared on the day of a Zeppelin raid, and that the clever boy's prizes at school coincided with U-boat sinkings. Germany was referred to as 'Uncle P', who was always seriously ill when things were going badly for the Fatherland.

It was only a question of time before this lady was removed to a place of safety.

Some spies specialise in invisible inks, known technically as 'sympathetic inks', because they will reveal themselves only under sympathetic chemical action. As such inks are not easy to obtain, spies during the last War were issued with ties and socks specially prepared so that when soaked in water they would produce the necessary solution. When King George V visited the Postal Censorship during the last War, he signed the visitor's book in 'sympathetic ink', which was made for him on the spot from the tie of a German spy.

His Majesty watched with interest as the tie was submerged in a tumbler of water. Slowly the water changed colour, turning to a rich sparkling yellow. King George, who had imposed prohibition in Buckingham Palace for the duration of the War, turned to his equerry and said: 'Don't you wish that was what it looks like?' And then, taking up the pen, dipped it in the solution and signed his name.

One of the Censors took me first to the place where all outward and inward foreign mails are stacked before inspection. Mail-bags of many colours, and from every country, were suspended in wooden racks.

The outward mails are of two kinds: letters and parcels from Great Britain to addresses in neutral countries, and mailbags consigned to Germany, but seized on the way by the Contraband Control.

Inward mails are the usual foreign mails to this country from all parts of the world. This means that every communication to and from a neutral country must pass through the filter of postal censorship before it finds its way to the address on the envelope.

Upstairs, under one gigantic girdered roof, sit the one thousand, three hundred censors. The male censors occupy one section of the room, and the women the other. They sit at long tables and look like students in an over-sized public library.

At the end of each table, printed on a card, are the list of languages spoken at that table. People who speak the ordinary European languages are as common as blackberries in September. Persian, Urdu, Hindustani, Yiddish, Hebrew are also ordinary accomplishments.

But there are rarer specialists. Some tables can produce men who have made Chinese dialects a life study, and others there have written learned works, known only perhaps to the Foreign Office, on the language spoken by tribes on the Afghanistan frontier.

The male censors deal with trade communications, the women censors the private letters; and this, I should have thought, is the most interesting task of all. Apparently it is not.

'The business of reading other people's letters has a charm that soon wears off,' said a woman censor. 'At first it is thrilling. You suspect a spy in every envelope, then you realise that the majority of human beings are not spies. However, you soon develop a kind of second sense which tells you when a letter is fishy. But the day's work consists, not in detecting enemy agents, but in saving thoughtless people from giving away information that might be of use to the enemy or to his propaganda machine, and in picking out little bits of information from foreign sources which might be of use to ourselves.'

'No doubt you read some fairly amusing letters?'

'We do indeed, but, officially, no censor ever remembers what he, or she, has read.'

'Cupid must have his wings clipped pretty closely in your department.'

'Oh yes, and Cupid is exceedingly busy in war-time. It's hard luck on people who happen to have fallen in love with the enemy! For instance, a father wrote to us and begged us to stop letters from a young German with whom his daughter is in love. We did so in the normal way of business, but the other day we relented and – we let her have one! But we had to tell her that she couldn't send a reply!'

A special branch of postal censorship is the detection of invisible inks and other methods of communication. This is done in a laboratory staffed by chemists who became familiar with the work in the last War.

One of them handed me a blank sheet of paper. Even when I held it to the light, I could see nothing on it. He told me to hold it for a moment in a machine like a magic lantern, which emitted a blue light. Instantly the paper became covered with phosphorescent writing. In a bold German hand I read the credentials of a spy. This was a relic of the last War.

'Have any spies turned up in your laboratory yet?' I asked.

'There are some questions you must not ask!' I was told. 'If they haven't turned up yet, we've no doubt they'll soon arrive.'

CHAPTER NINE

I go to an explosives factory and, travelling in the North, visit a German officers' prison camp, where I see the first Nazis captured in the War. I come to a shipyard where an unborn fleet is on the stocks. I travel down the East Coast and meet fishermen.

There are portions of England which look as the North Country must have looked during the opening years of the Industrial Revolution. Factories are still invading the fields, and two worlds stand side by side, one symbolised by haystacks, the other by chimney-stacks.

In this queer country agricultural labourers and mechanics bicycle home together. On one side of the road they grow crops; on the other side guns are made. The towns and villages are also an odd reflection of the old world and the new. In some, the pretty village church and a few cottages are still intact in the heart of a hasty and incoherent jumble of buildings put up in recent times. A grand old village inn, called, perhaps, the Bay Horse or the Falcon, does its best to counteract the alien triviality of the local cinema.

In these regions of the North the agricultural eighteenth century has nowhere quite faded out, and its influence lingers even in the factories, for on Saturday afternoon you may meet boys from the gas-mask works fishing for pike, and the man with the gun, or the man with a terrier round the haystacks, is probably from the time-fuse factory or the big armament works whose chimneys can be seen on the other side of the hill.

In this strange and not unattractive region I approached an explosives factory. Many of the workers arrive by special trains and step out on the factory's own railway station, which has an up and a down line platform. It is indeed a town of TNT.

No visitors were encouraged in this factory, even in peacetime, and now in war-time you are halted by armed policemen, long before you get there. They take you behind a wire fence and ask for your identity card and your letters of introduction.

They told me to drive along Central Avenue and report at the main police station. The gates were swung wide, and I entered the strangest place you can imagine. Spread over what so recently was open country are miles devoted to deadly explosives. But the odd thing about the place is that it looks like a garden city. It is not unlike an American city, laid out with its public parks and recreation grounds and a few factories, but, for some reason, with no dwelling-houses.

The art of building an explosive factory is to spread out the buildings over a large area in order to lessen the risk of disaster. If the place is to blow up, it must explode in sections.

So I motored for a mile or so along straight roads and over concrete bridges, and on each side of me, and dotted at regularly spaced intervals in the distance, were huge mounds covered with beautiful green turf. Beneath each mound, deep in the earth, were dumps of TNT, cordite, and other materials.

All the avenues are bordered with turf, and it would not surprise me, for this is a grotesque world, to return there in the spring and find daffodils and primroses growing above the cordite dumps. But for the miles of iron-fencing and barbed wire, and the words in red letters DANGER AREA, this factory is just the place you would take the children to play on a Saturday afternoon.

Finding the main police-station, I was again examined and asked to sign books, and I was then given in return a red card, proving that I had passed my examination with credit. Grudgingly the police opened some more gates, and I soon found myself led through administrative offices as large and as lavish as a new town hall to the room of the Superintendent.

In the course of conversation, I asked how he would define an explosive. Without a moment's hesitation, he replied:

'An explosive is concentrated energy in a small space which, given certain conditions, will release itself.'

I fancy that even a lawyer could not tighten up that description.

We set off together in a car to explore the factory.

We motored to one of the danger zones, where he was going to show me how the shells, which I had seen elsewhere in the making, are filled with 'concentrated energy'. Some people may imagine that shells leave a factory ready for the guns, but shell-making and shell-filling are two separate trades. When they leave the factory the shells are as harmless as umbrella stands. It is only when they leave the explosive factory that they become lethal.

As we approached the danger area, an attendant asked us to turn out our pockets. He confiscated matches, pipes, cigarette lighters, cigarettes, tobacco; and I saw on a notice-board that snuff also is among the forbidden articles. They told me that nothing likely to cause friction is allowed past the barrier, and snuff is a gritty substance which is feared almost as much as matches.

We entered a dressing-room, the entrance to this particular danger zone. A barrier runs

'Shell-making and shell-filling are two separate trades'

down the centre of it. One side is 'dirty', the other is 'clean'. No workers and no visitors are allowed to cross the barrier in the shoes or boots they are wearing.

Visitors must stand on one leg while the attendant fits them with rubber overshoes, and, having fitted one foot in mid-air, he carefully guides it to the 'clean' side. So, standing with one foot in the 'clean' and one in the 'dirty', the second rubber shoe is fitted; and you step across the barrier. Workers in the factory have to strip to their underclothes in this room and put on special safety clothing.

We walked out on paths made of gritless asphalt. This substance is as smooth as marble. If, by any unthinkable chance, a man got in wearing hobnailed boots, he would strike no sparks; but this has never happened, nor is it likely to happen.

Shells are not filled in one large factory, but in concrete sheds dotted at skilful intervals, one or two to the acre.

'I am not allowed to take you any farther,' said the Superintendent.

There were twelve men inside, clothed in thick whitish garments. They wore round white caps with a number stencilled on them. Their trousers were of white felt. Their shoes were marked with broad arrows.

They were standing at a table, handing shells to each other at the speed of a slow-motion film. As the shells reached one man, he slowly dipped a long spoon into a tin and, as slowly, poured whatever was in the spoon into the shell. No one man looked up to see who was watching him. Every man's eyes were on the shells. They looked to me like a number of reluctant convicts attending a cookery class.

'What are they doing?' I asked.

'I'm sorry,' said the Superintendent, 'I mustn't tell you. But you can see they are filling shells. . .'

We walked past a number of bays like bastions in an old-fashioned fort. They were made of steel and concrete, and were several yards in thickness, and were designed to be good places to take shelter if anything happened.

We encountered four men wheeling a trolley loaded with shells. They wore the same kind of white shapeless garments as the shell-fillers. They were bending tenderly over the trolley and pushing it more slowly than I have ever seen men push a trolley, even when they are feeling tired. The dangerous cargo came along inch by inch, and we stood aside respectfully to let it pass. I should hate to work in this factory. It is always expecting the worst to happen.

Continuing our journey, we came to a shed in which more slow, white-garmented men were filling the shell-cases of anti-aircraft shells. Slaves who had been building the Pyramids without a mid-day break might have moved with just those lagging steps when the taskmaster's back was turned.

'Why do they all move at that mournful pace?' I asked.

'They must do so. There must be no haste and no quick movements in explosive sheds. Skylarking and joking are against the regulations and would bring instant dismissal.'

I watched them moving like sleep-walkers as they pushed long bundles of brown vermicelli wrapped in silver paper into the tall brass cases.

'Sticks of cordite,' said the Superintendent.

Then each shell-case was attached to the shell; and the projectile – about four feet in length – was ready to go out to the anti-aircraft batteries.

We went into acrid-smelling rooms where snail-like men were presiding over stills and vats full of chemicals. We went into a huge factory where shells are washed before they go to the filling sheds. Here I saw machinery for the first time, and extraordinary machinery it was. An endless chain was in slow movement round the fctory, carrying shells from tank to tank. First, it dipped them in caustic soda, then in water, then in sulphuric acid, and finally into two separate tanks of water. As the shells approached the tanks, the chain described a graceful bend downward so that the plant looked like some imprisoned sea serpent that was in constant undulation.

'Each shell-case must be absolutely free from dirt, grease and grit,' said the Superintendent. 'One speck of grit may cause trouble.'

'Are shells never filled by machinery?' I enquired.

He answered this question by taking me into a neighbouring building. Here was probably the most modern shell-filling plant in the world. It was not in operation just then, so that we could walk round and examine it.

The explosives are automatically fed from a hopper into the shell-cases. Each operation is conducted in a blast-proof shelter made of curved walls of two-feet-thick steel and concrete. The operator stands in safety behind this wall. When the explosives are getting low in the hopper, a bell rings and an electric light warns the operator to go along the gallery above and replenish the supply.

An even more dangerous-looking machine fills about eighteen shells in one action. As far as I could see, the success of this operation depends upon the shells coming up to meet the feed with an accuracy that can be measured in fractions of an inch.

I disliked the look of this place, and was glad to get away towards the only cheerful sound I had heard in the factory. It was the sound of women singing. I thought the Superintendent frowned as he heard it, but I may be wrong.

We entered a shed in which stood thousands, perhaps millions, of shells of various calibre, from factories all over the country. As we entered, the singing ceased, and I saw about fifty girls and women standing on each side of a trestle table, examining the shells.

It was a strange sight. Some of the women wore the regulation safety clothing. I noticed that these garments, which gave men the appearance of convicts, caused women to look as if they were wearing pyjamas several sizes too large for them.

I should like to have talked to them and to have found out what they thought of work in an explosive factory, but conversation is not encouraged in this vast gunpowder barrel. Even the men rarely talk among themselves.

As I drove away, I felt my spirits rise as I left those eight miles of 'concentrated energy' behind me.

I remembered the shell-makers in the factories I had seen; the men raking out the red ingots from the forges, the men at the stamping presses, the turners, the testers, the shot-blasters, and all the others.

Then came the singing women in their 'pyjamas'; the 'convicts' with their lagging steps and bowed shoulders; the slow men ladling out death in a spoon; others with their bundles of brown vermicelli, the stalks wrapped, like gardenias, in silver paper.

And so we come at last to the equally nice ordinary men who will some day bring about those conditions which release 'concentrated energy': the men who place the shell in the gun. Up it goes into the air, either missing its mark or else – high up there in the sky a plane spins out of control and comes tumbling down, over and over, like a bird shot through the head in mid-air: and, as it strikes the earth, something which was once a young man lies slumped and broken at the wheel.

That is what shells are for.

I expressed a wish to see some captured German submarine officers. I wanted to find out how we are treating them, what kind of men they are, what they do with themselves, and if they are grateful to us for having literally fished them out of the jaws of death.

The officer commanding the district gave me an introduction to the Commandant of the prison camp, and I set off to motor fifty miles into a wilderness – a beautiful wilderness, whose solitude deepened as I went on.

The German prisoners captured during the first ten weeks of war did not include one Army officer, NCO or private. They were all either U-boat officers and men rescued at sea, or crews of raiding aircraft shot down over our coasts or in our territorial waters.

Men are sent to one camp, officers to another. As in the last War, large country houses have been taken over to accommodate the officers, and the first one to be occupied – the Donington Hall of this War – was the place to which I was journeying. I cannot tell you its name, but it is known to all the villages round about as the 'U-boat Hotel'.

It is the heart of a district familiar to the more adventurous kind of hiker and cyclist, and I went on for many a mile without meeting a soul. It was a land of stone walls and streams. Ahead of me I saw hills dusted with the year's first snow.

I felt that I must be getting near my destination at last, and this became a certainty as, turning the corner of a lane, I was obliged to pull into the side in order to make way for a remarkable procession led by a mounted policeman.

He rode in this remote solitude as if he were patrolling Whitehall. Behind him marched several old soldiers wearing the ribbons of the last War, rifles and fixed bayonets at the slope.

Marching four abreast came about twenty young men, laughing and joking in German as they strode between a line of guards. Most of them were bare-headed, and all wore strangely assorted clothing. I was to learn that some of it belonged to British naval officers who had rescued them from the sea. Many wore the leather trousers which German submarine officers wear on duty, and these garments had been supplemented by civilian coats and waistcoats. The procession ended with more armed guards and a British officer.

In the orderly room to which I was conducted by a sentry, the Colonel in command of the 'U-boat Hotel' was telephoning to a dentist in a distant town, arranging for the teeth of six Germans to be stopped.

'If I am allowed to have heard that conversation,' I said, 'might I say that six seems a high proportion to require dental treatment?'

'Many of the U-boats were in position two months before war broke out,' replied the colonel, 'and I suppose even a U-boat officer puts off going to the dentist as long as possible. Anyhow, the fact remains that their teeth are in a bad way. I shall send them to the dentist with an armed guard in a motor-lorry.'

The Colonel had been through the last War, and was on the reserve list when called up to organise the 'U-boat Hotel'. He is the ideal man for the job: a bachelor who likes living in the depths of the country, a humorous, humane disciplinarian, who is resolved to make his captives as comfortable as regulations allow. He has under him five officers and one hundred and fifty men of the National Defence Corps, all old soldiers, several of whom were, by some ironic twist of destiny, once British prisoners of war in Germany.

The officers and guards live in the estate cottages, the barns and stables, while the Germans live in the more spectacular surroundings of the Hall itself.

Before we went to the Hall, we had a look at the quarters in which the guards were living. A canteen is being fitted up in an old coach-house. Coke stoves are being installed in barns and stables where the men sleep. These old soldiers appeared delighted to be back in khaki. I thought that perhaps their wives would not be too pleased to see how gaily they have taken to the old life! As we walked past their beds and looked at the kits neatly set out on the blankets, I noticed that above every bed had been placed a picture of the King or the Queen.

A veteran was sitting near the stove solemnly adding to the art gallery. He had a pile of old *Sketches* and *Tatlers* and a pair of scissors. I watched him at work, gloomily passing over film stars and dancers, but whenever he came across a picture of the King or the Queen he made a pause of sombre satisfaction and dug the scissors into the page. It will be a loyal and regal barn when he has finished with it.

We now approached the Hall itself, a huge and gloomy Edwardian country house in a style that might be termed Shipowner's Tudor. It was empty when war broke out, and has been unoccupied, I think, for two or three years. It is the kind of house in which few people except orphans, committees, or lunatics can afford to live nowadays.

It has been surrounded by a double system of barbed-wire entanglments. Armed guards patrol the place day and night, and are assisted in their vigilance by high look-out platforms all round the barbed wire. A circle of powerful electric lights illuminated the Hall and its grounds after nightfall, causing it to be the only unblacked-out place in England.

The Germans sleep in dormitories, formerly the best bedrooms, and as more prisoners arrive, more rooms are opened up. They sleep on comfortable iron bedsteads and box mattresses, and have an adequate supply of warm blankets.

Men who are rescued from the sea rarely have any possessions, therefore the officers have had to be provided with razors, soap, shaving-brushes and other articles, which are to be seen neatly arranged above each bed. Their possessions will grow, no doubt, as their captivity lengthens and as parcels are received from Germany. At the moment they have no money, but arrangements for an Anglo-German prisoners of war finance scheme is going through with the help of the Dutch Government, which is acting as go-between. When this scheme is complete, money will go to Germany for our prisoners, and money will come over here for Germans. Lack of money, of course, means no cigarettes, but the British officers have supplied cigarettes at their own expense.

The huge panelled dining-room on the ground floor, in which the shipowner once entertained his guests, is the German common room. It is furnished simply with a few chairs and a ping-pong table. The only decoration is a photograph of Hitler shooting out his arm in salute.

'Every prisoner is a hundred per cent Nazi,' said the Colonel. 'At first, when addressed by an officer, they would come to attention and give the Nazi salute with a "Heil Hitler". But we have stopped that, and they don't attempt to do it now.'

'What do they do all day?'

'They play cards and ping-pong. A local Bishop has sent us a lot of German books. I hope, as time goes on, to be able to organise other amusements for them, so that they won't get too bored.'

A serving-hatch from the dining-hall communicates with a large, modern kitchen. Four German naval ratings, who had been submarine cooks, have been detailed to look after their officers.

They receive ordinary military rations – exactly the same foods as that in the British officers' mess – and this the German cooks are allowed to prepare as they like, or rather as their officers like.

While we were looking at the bathrooms upstairs, we heard the tramp of approaching feet and saw the Germans returning from their morning exercise. The sentries sloped arms. The gates in the barbed wire were hastily unlocked, and the young men passed inside.

'See that young fellow, the third in the last file,' said the Commandant. 'He's a submarine lieutenant – a mere boy – and he sobbed his heart out the first night because he is now of no further use to the Fatherland.'

We went downstairs into the dining-room, where the Germans were now gathered. They sprang to attention until the Commandant told them to relax. A sentry stood at the door with rifle and fixed bayonet. The young men gathered round the Commandant and talked freely to him in excellent English, and I could see that they liked him. I think these young fellows also repected the long row of ribbons on his chest.

It was surprising to realise that such average-looking young fellows – just the kind of young men one might have met at any Anglo-German party in London before the War – were the men who have launched torpedoes against our ships and have attempted to make a mess of the Forth Bridge. But 'the enemy', when he is not actually trying to kill you, is always a surprising sight.

I have known a number of Nazis and have been impressed and irritated by them on many occasions, and I have always found that, on the essential doctrines of their faith, it is impossible to argue. For a non-Nazi to talk politics to a Nazi provokes precisely the same kind of mental deadlock as that between an atheist and a Catholic. I had no need to look twice at the German officers to see that they carry their faith into captivity. They had been fished out of the sea, or picked up from the land, positively bursting with love and homage for their almost divine Leader, and

nothing could convince them that Germany could fail to win the War.

Had they not been our prisoners, I should have asked them some leading questions and have drawn them into argument; instead, I asked them only the usual things about the food and the beds. They were all anxious to receive letters and parcels from home. They also wanted money so that they could buy comforts. One asked eagerly if, when their money arrives, they would be allowed to get in a stock of wine for Christmas.

One young fellow, the commander of a submarine, has become a father since the War began. He was out on his station weeks before the declaration of war, ready to attack merchant ships. Of course he received no news of his wife, and he worried all the time, wondering whether 'it' was a boy or a girl. Then one

'It was surprising to realise that such average-looking young fellows were the men who have launched torpedoes against our ships'

day a depth-charge sent his ship spinning down to death. In the hideous chaos of machinery and the pitch darkness – for the emergency lighting went out – he heard the hiss of the entering sea, and thought that now he would never know if it was a girl or a boy. But he was in the sea! He was picked up and soon he found himself in the lonely Hall. And still he did not know.

He wrote to his wife, but no letter came in reply. Then one day the door opened and in walked a German submarine officer, who had been picked up a few days before in the ocean – and he was able to put his mind at rest. 'I saw your wife at Wilhelmshaven,' he said, 'and – it's a boy!'

After lunching with the British officers in their mess, I noticed with interest that they were all reading *The Escaping Club*, by A. J. Evans, an admirable account of British prisoners in Germany during the last War. I was told that the Commandant had suggested it was their duty to study the psychology of war captivity.

'It is impossible for men captured in war not to dream of escape,' I was told. 'No matter how awful the horrors from which they've escaped, and how sure the knowledge that they are safe, the boredom, the lack of news, the very fact of being held against their wills in enemy country, makes any risk, and even a return to danger, seem worthwhile. . .'

And here is an instructive story which some of our war sentimentalists might take to heart. A compassionate lady who lives in the neighbourhood wrote recently to the Commandant saying that she would like to lighten the captivity of the German officers by providing them with books and cigarettes. She ended by saying that she felt they should be told that the British people had no quarrel with the German people, but only with their form of government.

Permission was obtained for this letter to be read to the prisoners. They listened appreciatively to it and murmured their gratitude, but, when the interpreter came to the last sentence, there was a burst of laughter, and one officer, speaking for the rest, said:

'We do not wish to accept any favours from people who hold such foolish ideas!'

There spoke the true Nazi.

'Yet,' said one of the camp officers, 'politicians have the nerve to talk about 'having no quarrel with the German people.' What are these soldiers but the German people in uniform? What strikes us all about these young Germans is their astonishing bumptiousness. They are the most arrogant fellows you can imagine. They clearly regard us as a definitely inferior race. Some of them believe that England has already been invaded and that it's only a matter of weeks or days before the German Army comes along and rescues them.

'I heard of one airman who, when he was captured, kept on asking in the most insolent way to be directed to the nearest post of the German Army. Another one, so I've heard, was decently treated by a family on the coast when he came ashore in a rubber boat. As the military were taking him away, he turned and asked the civilians for their name and address, adding: "I may be able to do you a good turn when we invade your country."'

I asked him if the prisoners knew where they were.

'No, they haven't an idea,' was the reply. 'They think they're in Scotland.'

My next call was at a famous naval shipyard, where more than seventeen thousand men are now employed. The air was hideous with the sound of hammering and the ear-splitting machine-gun spurts of riveters.

I looked down on a stark forest of poles set in the brown mud of a river estuary. Each cluster of poles was the nest of a ship. In some, the ship was visible as a rusty hulk; in others she was almost ready for her guns; in still more she was an embryo of bolted keel-plates on which men stamped about with hob-nailed boots.

The seagulls called mournfully as they flew in white flocks, driven inland by storms at sea. They perched perkily on the tops of the poles as if anxious to see how the ships were getting on; they alighted on the keels of unborn warships, and stood in white rows on the piles of armour-plate.

The works manager pointed towards the dark etching of masts.

'I've got one there,' he said, 'and two there, and in that shed one, and in the second shed three, and over yonder – you can't see it from here – I've got another one, and near that

bunch of tower cranes I've got four, and am making ready for a fifth!'

He was like a backyard poultry fancier counting his chickens, but his chickens were cruisers, destroyers, aircraft carriers and submarines, the ships of the unborn fleet.

'What a programme!' I said in astonishment.

'Yes, but it's nothing really,' he replied. 'Think of all the other shipyards, every one of them as busy as this. It looks to me as if the Admiralty is not preparing for a three years' war, but a twenty-three years' war! Honestly it does. Look here . . .'

And he proceeded to tell me a few things about naval rearmament.

As we walked round the slipways, we saw destroyers, submarines, and aircraft carriers. We also saw something which would be deleted by the Censor, so there is no point in mentioning it. In dock we saw merchant cruisers being fitted out with guns in order that they may attack U-boat pirates.

And I might tell you that this is not as simple as it sounds, for the task of turning a peaceful ship into a merchant cruiser is complicated and full of snags. I saw one vessel with her whole stern cut open down to the water-line. Men swarmed about her, strengthening her to stand the strain of guns.

I had always believed that a warship was known by a number until she was christened by the Lords of Admiralty, or whoever it is who finds the splendid and romantic names for warships. But this is not so. All the workers in this shipyard called the new Fleet by name. They would point up to a brown cliff of armour-plate and say: 'That's *Illustrious*. She'll be away soon!' Or, indicating a mass of rusty plates, hardly waist-high, 'There's *Industrious*, only laid down last week.'

'The air was hideous with the machine-gun spurts of riveters'

There is nothing more hush-hush in Britain today than such nurseries of the Navy. No one is encouraged to talk about what goes on there. In theory, the workmen are supposed to forget what they have been doing all day as they pass out of the gates at night. And when the time comes, the great ships go their way in secrecy. The bottle of champagne is no longer cracked against their prows. No distinguished person presides over their going. Like grey ghosts, they slip out on the full tide to join their companions at sea.

We entered miles of darkened sheds in which, because of blacked-out roofs, men work all day by electric light as if they were on night shift. It was strange to see that battleships are cut out as a woman cuts out a blouse to a paper pattern. Prints come down from the draughtsmen, and armour-plate is cut to pattern as if it were satin.

Someone comes along with a piece of chalk, or a paint-brush, and numbers them; and off they go, great chunks of hardened steel bordered with rivet holes, to be dumped near the appropriate slipway.

While men are building the keel and bolting the hull, other men in neighbouring shops are busy with gigantic turbines and gun-turrets. The 'heavy shop' in a battleship factory is about the most impressive thing you can see in modern industry. Can you imagine what several quadruple 14-inch mountings look like in course of construction? They are vast enough when you see them on a ship, and stand beneath the muzzles of the four great guns, but in the shop where they are made they look preposterous. You wonder how on earth they ever got in and, still more, how on earth they will ever get out.

Lying sixty feet deep in the earth, the gun-turrets are made by men who descend into them as if into a bridge caisson. You look over the edge and see them working by electric light at the bottom of the pit. The steel castles also loom up to the roof. Men swarm up ladders to work on them.

Upon the armour-plate of a gun-mounting that will soon take its place in a new battle-ship, some shipyard joker had written in chalk: 'Run, Adolf, run!' Upon another, some-one else, not to be outdone, had writen, ''Arf a mo', Hitler!' and had supplemented it with a sketch of the Führer.

That kind of humour is shattering. I won-dered what the Germans would have made of it. Perhaps in some German factory at this moment unborn submarines may bear illumi-nating graffiti, but I think they would prob-ably take a more violent form, something like the old 'Gott strafe England'.

One thing that was noticeable about the last War, and is already evident in this, is that, as a nation, we see the funny side of our adversaries. The Kaiser and 'Little Willie' were once popular humorous characters; and so, by some strange twist of our character, are Adolf and his satellites.

We entered a range of machine shops where the 3.7 mobile guns and also the fixed Anti-Aircraft guns, were being made. The Navy likes the 4-inch AA gun because of its 'high ceiling', as they call its ability to rake the heavens. We then saw a terrible weapon, the multiple pom-pom, which is eight guns in one. It pumps out death as a fire-hose pumps water.

Among the guns and gun-mountings, I came across an instrument of so strange and sinister an appearance that I dropped my voice to a whisper and asked what it was. I told the works manager that if it were one of those things for sweeping up magnetic mines, or even something more secret, he could tell me in confidence and I would not mention it.

'That!' he said. 'Funny you should have spotted it. That's the only 'left-over' from peace time in the whole shop. It's a machine for making Lux!' He patted the Lux machine affectionately.

'We'd rather make *them* than guns!' he said.

Yet when the shipyard was idle during the years of disarmament, half the shops in the town closed. Skilled men lived on the verge of starvation, or migrated to starve somewhere else. Others cast aside the experience of years and, rather than live on unemployment pay, took to all sorts of jobs. And now this war has opened all the shops again, and has sent money coursing through the veins of the town.

'The only difficulty we have,' said the works manager, 'is to get the right men back. We've dug them out from all kinds of places. See that man on the lathe? He's got shipbuilding blood in his veins. A wonderful workman. We found him working in a newsagent's shop.'

For another mile or so we trudged from shop to shop. It was as tiring as a conducted tour round the British Museum. At last we emerged again beside the river estuary, where skeleton masts rose out of the river mud.

'That's one you haven't seen,' said the works manager, pointing to a slipway. I could see only five or six men walking in the mud, preparing the track for the keel-plates while others were strengthening the uprights.

'But there's nothing there yet,' I replied.

The works manager pointed to a mound of rusty armour-plate.

'Oh, isn't there?' He smiled. 'She'll be off in about ten months!'

And 'she' was still only a draughtsman's dream, a mass of blue prints and a few thou-sand tons of unassembled steel. Already he saw 'her' as a grey ship proudly carrying her guns and slipping off into the darkness of the seas.

Such are the men who make the Fleet behind the Fleet; the ships which are growing up every day and night to take their place in that brave company whose task it has been for centuries to see that no enemy makes war on British soil.

I turned homeward down the East Coast and put in to a port that was famous in peace time for its North Sea trawler fleet. As I entered the town, a number of schoolgirls were standing before the contents bill of the evening newspaper, which read: 'Air Battle over East Coast Town.'

'Oh, I wonder if it's ours!' cried the girls, as if it were something to be proud of.

'No, it ain't ours,' said the news-vendor, whereupon the girls pouted in disappointment.

'It isn't ours!' they cried. 'He says it isn't ours. Come on, Mabel, don't waste a penny: it isn't ours!'

And they walked away.

The black-out in this town was total darkness. And when night fell I discerned a new alertness in the air, for the East Coast feels very different from the West. Although the whole of England is on guard, the people on the East Coast are acutely aware that they are, so to speak, in the firing line. They have seen battles in the air; the ports of the East Coast are full of fishermen who have been machine-gunned at sea, and just across the way is Germany. The East Coast feels that when the raids begin in earnest they are the nearest and the most convenient target.

The hotel near the docks in which I stayed was well provided with fire-pumps, hand-pumps, spades, buckets, sandbags, and incendiary-bomb scoops. They were put out in the corridors by chambermaids as soon as darkness fell. They had also systematised the shelter problem, as I read on my bedroom wall:

> In the event of an Air-Raid Warning the occupant of Room 61 should proceed to Shelter No. 1 situated in cellar across side road from hotel.

There is a strong flavour of the last War in many of these strange instructions. I detect in that word 'proceed' the authorship of an old soldier. Troops in the last War never 'went' anywhere: they always 'proceeded'. And I expect it will be the same in this one.

Shortly before dawn, I went down to the harbour mouth to see the fishing fleet come in.

While you and I are asleep in our darkened houses, the fishermen of England are sweeping a blacked-out sea. Some of us hear the wind whistling at gale force over the chimneys, and think of the men who pull up trawl-nets, menaced by mine, submarine and aircraft. Theirs is the truest form of courage: they go off in cold blood into the war zone, and calmly earn their living as they used to do in peace-time.

Now and again, as we listen to the BBC Home Service, we hear the neat voice of an announcer say that the Admiralty regrets to report the sinking of a trawler with the loss of eight hands; or we hear that a drifter stuck a mine; or that an enemy plane appeared suddenly from the clouds and machine-gunned the crews of a fishing fleet. But the trawlers and the drifters still go over the top each time they put to sea, with no fuss and no drama, and no medals at the end of it.

If anything in this strange war-time world has been won by sheer bravery, it is the fish that miraculously appear on the fishmonger's slab, at a cost sometimes even lower than in peace time. It is as if you and I had the courage to take our typewriters and our telephones into No Man's Land each night.

It was not yet daylight as I stood at the harbour mouth, neither was it entirely dark. An icy wind blew in from the North Sea. Water lapped the quaysides; and beyond the bar an angry sea rose and fell, and sometimes long walls of spray would be whipped slant-wise over the breakwater.

There was a small crowd waiting in the growing light, men with coat collars turned up, market officials, harbour men, and perhaps relatives and friends of the crews; for every going out and coming in is now an adventure; and landsmen wait eagerly for news of the returning fleet.

So narrow is the entrance to the harbour, that those standing on land can shout up to the crews as they steam past.

'Here they come!'

Looking seaward, I saw a line of trawlers in file, with smoke-plumes at their chimney-stacks, come rolling out of the grey sea.

They had been away, so a man shouted in my ear, for ten days, 'somewhere up north', and the wild weather had stained them and the seas had broken over them. As they passed one by one into calm water, I looked up and saw in each trawler a placid skipper muffled to the eyes behind the glass of the wheel-house, a pipe in his mouth and his hands on the wheel.

'See anything, Bert?' a voice shouted as one went past.

'If anything in this strange
war-time world has been won by sheer bravery,
it is the fish that miraculously appear
on the fishmonger's slab'

The skipper opened a window and removed his pipe for a moment: 'Seven mines, and not a rifle among us!' was the reply. 'Ask Andy what he saw!'

The next one came in.

'Where's Andy, and what did he see?'

'Andy? Oh, they tried to machine gun him!'

'Anybody hurt?'

'No!'

One by one the grimy little heroes pass inside, the muffled crews in their sea-boots clumping about the decks and hauling on ropes. Then a breath of excitement passes through the chilly band of watchers.

'Here's old Andy! Hi, Andy, what happened to you?'

An angry face like a chunk of Aberdeen granite is thrust out of the wheel-house.

'A've naething tae report!'

'Did they machine-gun you?'

'Ye're verra inquisitive, I'm thinking.'

And Andy indignantly removes his head, but, as he goes past, we notice that the dingy has been drilled with a number of small holes.

It is now daylight, and the trawlers nose their way beside the quays. Because of the black-out they can no longer unload the catch in the early hours of morning, as they used to do when the fish market was a blaze of light.

Soon, however, baskets of fish and ice swing through the air. The gulls come screaming in white clouds. The floor is a perilous slide of ice and scales. No one refers to the War. After the first burst of interest as the ships came in, the subject is dropped and no one thinks about anything but the number of fish caught and the price they will fetch at auction.

The merchants survey the few hundred yards of cod, codling, plaice, soles, skate, hake and dog-fish.

'Aye, it's pathetic when you know what this market can look like in peace-time!' says a merchant.

But it should be explained that if our fish supplies sometimes fall below normal, this is not due to any fear of mines or U-boats, but to the fact that nearly all the largest trawlers are now mine-sweeping and many of the richest fishing grounds are closed to fishermen. Our skippers are utterly fearless. Indeed, unless the Navy keeps its eye on them, they will take the most fantastic risks in order to come back with full holds.

As time goes on more and more fishing grounds are opened up by the Navy, and the

fisherman, who now lives in a constricted world, gets a little more space in which to cast his net.

I approached a fisherman, who was standing in duffel coat and hobb stockings, and I asked him what fishing is like in war-time.

'I never think of it,' he said. 'If I'm to die out theer,' and he pointed to the sea, 'well, I shall die out theer. If I'm to die in me bed, then I shall die theer.'

In those words he expressed the philosophy of his calling.

'I don't say but that some of the young lads got a bit windy,' he said. 'Sometimes it's like having a lot of girls aboard, seein' things that aren't theer, imaginin' mines and submarines when theer's nothing theer at all. But they mostly gets used to it and settles down.'

'And have you seen any mines?'

'Everyone sees mines. They comes drifting past you, but so long as it's daylight you can dodge 'em.'

One of the great dangers of fishing in war-time is the submerged mine that becomes caught in the trawl-net. When that happens 'it's all up to you'.

My informant had never been machine-gunned, but his trawler had that very trip been subjected to the scrutiny of a German aeroplane, which dived out of low cloud and circled the ship almost over the smoke-stack, 'so that you could feel the rush of air as he went past and were almost deafened by his engines.'

'When do you go off again,' I asked.

'On tonight's tide,' he said.

If you had told him he was a hero, he would have returned the compliment with withering contempt. That's book talk, that is!

He was born and bred a fisherman, and he'll fish until something stops him. Whether it's a storm at sea or a German mine doesn't much matter, for the result is the same; and, anyhow, such things are written in the stars.

Such is the armour of philosophy which all men in dangerous occupations assume at need. It was the philosophy of the front line in the last war. If your name was on a shell, well, you were 'for it'; if not, you were one of the lucky ones.

No industry in this country has been so disorganised by war as that of fishing, yet the complaints about lack of money and hard conditions could almost be counted on the fingers of one hand.

The port I was visiting is fortunate in the possession of large numbers of trawlers not quite up to Admiralty standards, which means that fishing still goes on there. A neighbouring port, famous for its fine modern fleet, is almost silent, for the ships have been taken over by the Navy. This has caused considerable hardship and unemployment, because the Navy does not always commandeer crew with ship. I saw the process of converting a fishing-boat into an armed mine-sweeper, and was surprised by the amount of reconstruction involved. The whole ship has to be strengthened to take the guns. The fish-holds are gutted and turned into sleeping quarters for the crew. Places where boxes of iced fish formerly reposed are full of ammunition, and a neat wireless cabin is tucked away, also below deck.

Commenting on the skill necessary for such a task, I was told that the workmen at present on the job were men who had converted trawlers in the last War. They had taken jobs during the depression wherever they could get them, and one odd result of the War has been the discovery of skilled ships' fitters in sweet and tobacco shops. Such men have been called back to work and have gladly responded.

If you wish to hear about the war at sea, go to one of the public-houses patronised by the trawler skippers. Every time the fleet comes in, the skippers go home, have a wash and shave, put on their best suits, with collars and ties, and walk down to the King's Arms.

They sit in a cloud of tobacco smoke, tankards of ale at their elbows, and discuss financial and other aspects of their latest outing. Nearly everything they say would be deleted by the Censor, for the North Sea in war-time is as full of secrets as a net is sometimes full of fish.

What impressed me about such men is that war to them is merely a risky kind of game, with rules which you break at your peril. If you do break them and get away with it, there are bursts of loud laughter in the King's Arms when 'the boys' get together; if not, your health is drunk in a momentary silence, and someone remembers that you always were a rash and careless old basket.

There are certain men so wedded to their craft that by no effort of the mind could they be imagined in any other. They say of a born fisherman that if you threw him into a canal, he would come up with a trawl round his neck. Such men could never be kept from sea by fear of death.

So next time you buy fish, remember that some brave man, who would never admit it, risked his life to catch it.

CHAPTER TEN

My journey ends with some reflection
on travel in England during the Great Inertia.
Then comes 1940, Dunkirk and Reality.

There are certain places in England where a boot-jack becomes part of the bedroom furniture. Oakham, in the county of Rutland, is one of them. I had a bedroom in the Crown which might have been slept in by Jorrocks. The hotel reflected the ease, the elegance and the wealth of a happier and, in retrospect, ideal England. Silver candlesticks gleamed everywhere. Hanging upon the walls of rooms and passages, were aquatints of horsemen and hounds, of men in pink astride attenuated hunters, of dismounted men lying in ditches, of cub-hunters saluting the perfect morn. There was a sitting-room curtained and chintzed entirely from top to bottom in a fabric which depicted hounds in full cry and coaches rattling along the turnpike roads.

Many of the men of Oakham had, so I gathered, gone off to the War, and in the atmosphere of the bar, with its prints and relics of a past age, anyone might have been forgiven the impression that the war to which they had gone was Napoleon's, not Hitler's. The saddler was offering for sale two excellent revolvers, one an automatic and the other a Webley. I looked at them, thinking that it might be a good idea to get a firearms certificate and buy one of them. Then I dismissed the idea as rather fantastic. There was pheasant for dinner.

In the sombre Georgian bedroom was a notice, signed by V. A. Barnacle, saying that 'in no circumstances may the curtains be interfered with between sunset and sunrise'. As I slipped into the four-poster bed (there was a hot-water bottle in it) I wondered what the Georgians would have made of this age. The world since Waterloo has been nothing to boast about. It has gone from bad to worse. We have piled up money, machines and discontent, and now the whole conception of Western civilisation is in the melting-pot for

'I had a bedroom in the Crown'

the second time in less than a quarter of a century.

Not one gleam of candle-light must escape from Oakham into the night, for the death-ships may come from Germany, raiding through the sky just as Teuton pirates came raiding through East Anglia in the last days of Rome. When I opened my eyes in the morning, a chambermaid was interfering with the curtains.

'It's a fine frosty morning, sir,' she said.

I journeyed south to present my last letter of introduction to the principal of an agricultural college. I came to an ugly Edwardian mansion which had once been the home of an industrial baron. The pupils sleep in the house and pursue their activities on the home farm. Among the pupils are girls of the Women's Land Army. As we were walking round, a shapeless female figure in voluminous garments passed across the weeping landscape. Her feet in gum-boots made great kisses as she withdrew them from the glutinous earth.

'She used to be a fashion artist,' said the Principal.

Another figure in corduroy breeches clumped past with a spade across her shoulder.

'She was a typist,' said the Principal. 'No, I'm wrong, a ladies' hairdresser.'

A herd of wet cows came slowly down the lane, presided over by a girl with fair fluffy hair. She hovered on the flanks, grasping a small hazel switch with which, now and again, she administered a timid tap.

'She,' commented the Principal, 'used to be a children's nurse.'

So I watched a fraction of the Women's Land Army pass on its duties. Forty-five women and girls from every kind of city job had recently started a month's course in farming. At the end of the month they would be fitted out by the Government with garments suitable for the Tropics, and then turned out into the wintry countryside.

Many more women have volunteered for farm work than farmers can at the moment employ; but if the Ministry of Agriculture's scheme for the cultivation of an additional million and a half acres comes to pass, I am told there will hardly be a land girl out of work by the time the next harvest is gathered.

Land girls, like women in general, are of two kinds: true and false. The false are those who, having appreciated rural scenery during periods of prolonged drought, believe that they would like to go back to the land. They rapidly discover that farming is among the hardest jobs on earth, and that Nature is by no means what she seemed during a holiday in September. With something of a shock, such workers discover that the Dame has moods of revolting callousness in which she evidently hates man and beast; and such agriculturalists are probably wise to retire speedily from the fray.

'Mind you,' said the Principal, 'women are deceptive. Some of the toughest to look at turn out to be the softest, and some of the sweet little ones, with girlish laughs and big blue eyes, will wallop into the pig-sties and then ask, as a great favour, if they can put in over-time in the cow-sheds.

'I remember a girl in the last course who came to me one morning and said: "You know that *darling* little calf that was born last Tuesday?" That was how she used to speak! Everything was *darling* this or *darling* that. But, my hat, could that girl work? And she had the patience of Job. He's a lucky farmer who gets her on his farm, I can tell you.

'Then there was another strange one on the last course. She had been an actress. She came up to me when she'd been here for a couple of days, and she said: "I'm worried about the cows this morning. They've got catarrh. I don't like the way they're coughing. It's all this cold water we give them. It can't be good in such quantities."

'Well, you'd say, wouldn't you, that anyone

'Silver candlesticks gleamed everywhere'

'As I slipped into the four-poster bed
I wondered what the Georgians would
have made of this age'

who talked like that ought to go back on the stage? But not a bit of it. She got down to work and soon took a really intelligent interest in things. And how that girl changed! She turned up with long red nails, but when she left they were cut short, and they weren't very clean either!

'Although she lived in a state of constant surprise, nothing dismayed her. She would work up to her knees in mud and muck and come out ready for more. You never can tell with women! With fellows, you can spot a dud almost at sight, but some of the softest and sloppiest girls are really as tough as they make 'em. Funny, isn't it?'

'What kind of girls have you got on the new course, and where do they come from?' I asked.

He handed me a list of occupations. Here are some of them: book-keeper, factory hand, typist, domestic help, shop assistant, milliner, hairdresser, children's nurse, clerk, confectioner, fashion artist, dance instructress, actress, archæologist and dressmaker.

Such are the varied backgrounds of the maidens whom the most conservative of callings is asked to assimilate in time of war. As farming might be described as a constant fight with Nature based on centuries of prejudice, the farmer is a man who does not take willingly to new-fangled ideas; and what could be more new-fangled than a manicurist at milking-time?

We went to see the girls at work.

They are given a sound introduction to the various branches of general husbandry. They are taught something about crops and the rotation of crops, about arable land, about the growing of food-stuffs and fruit. They take turns to run a model dairy, a range of pigsties, stables, and a small chicken farm. In a field I found a class learning to drive mechanical tractors and to set ploughs.

I thought the girls were extremely workmanlike and, apart from a pardonable bashfulness, for it must be something of a shock to come straight from a Remington to a tractor, they were admirable candidates for the land.

'They take turns to run a model dairy'

I asked one girl, who was grasping the wheel of a tractor, what she was doing before she joined the Land Army.

'I was a secretary in London,' she said.

I asked her why she had chosen the Land Army.

'Because I feel that land work is real work,' she replied. 'I don't fancy being drilled or wearing khaki, although I know that lots of girls like being in uniform. Then I'm interested in animals and I love the country, even in wet weather and in winter. I don't care how hard the work is, how early I have to get up in the morning, or how cold it is; and it's jolly cold now at six in the morning! All I want to do is to learn enough to be of some use on the land.'

The girls are not coddled. They have to rise in the dark and go down to the stables and the cow-sheds. Their day begins before dawn and ends with darkness. They do all the rough work under the supervision of instructors.

They drive cows out to the fields in the morning, and bring them back in the evening for milking. I watched girls, who ten days before had been working in the city, prepare to milk the cows. Some preliminary instruction was given on the mechanical milker, and then the girls, washed and in white overalls, were allowed to approach the genuine animal.

First they groomed the cows, and then, taking their milking stools and pails, got down to work. It was amusing to see with what an air of professional brusquerie, yet of temerity, some of the maidens smacked the cows over to the right side of the stalls, and I admired the courage of one girl, who was obviously not fond of these animals at such close quarters, for hers was true courage.

A distinguished lady visitor was being shown round at this moment. She approached one of the girls, who was engaged in grooming a cow, and asked: 'What were you doing before you joined the Land Army, my dear?'

The girl gazed round a corner of the cow and answered: 'I was in Bradley's.'

'Oh, really!' said the lady with interest. 'What department?'

The girl dropped the cow's tail.

'Lingerie,' she replied.

So silence settled over the sheds, broken only by the metallic ping of milk hitting the pails. Secretary, fashion artist, dressmaker, domestic help and shop assistant, sat with heads professionally bent towards the beasts, sometimes flinching from a moving hoof, now and then in trouble with a kicked pail. But the sight amazed me. I should never have believed that not one of those girls had ever milked a cow ten days before.

Suddenly the silence was broken by a chat-ter of voices, and I looked up to see fifty schoolboys, aged about ten to fourteen, gazing into the cow-shed with faces on which amazement, verging on horror, was plainly written. They were evacuated schoolboys from the Paddington district, who had been invited to look over the farm.

Everyone knows that milk is neatly crated in bottles and appears on the doorstep in the early morning. To see its origin in this dim, musty shed, among swishing tails and blowing nostrils, was, I think, something of a shock to most of the lads. I approached one and asked him if he had ever before seen a cow milked.

'Coo lumme, yus!' he replied. 'And I've seen their teeth pulled out.'

'Where on earth did you see that?' I asked.

'Bombay,' he replied; and I left him hurriedly for a less sophisticated specimen.

The Principal of the college, who is keen on interesting town children in country matters, loves to have evacuated girls and boys on the farm, and, after they have seen it, he lines them up and asks if they have any questions. When he does so, hands instantly shoot up. These are some of the questions asked by the London boys:

How many eggs can a hen lay in a day?

How old is a pig before he is killed?

How much hay does a cow eat a day?

Is any preservative added to milk before it is sold?

One boy came up to me and said: 'I've been drinking milk straight from a cow! It's warm and fizzy!'

I lined them up and asked those who wanted to go back to London to put up their hands. Not one hand was lifted.

The schoolmaster told me that almost a normal day's schooling is now going on, and the people in the town where the children are billeted could not be kinder to them. That bore out my impression, gained all over the country, of the genuine kindness with which people in general, and country people in particular, have treated children from the town.

We have heard too much of the other side. The grousing of town-sick, grumbling mothers has been given too much publicity. This is not only mischievous, but it is not a fair or true reflection of the situation. Were it true, it would be a terrible reflection on the charity and kindliness of the nation.

If in years to come anyone should ask me what it was like to travel through England during the first weeks of Hitler's War, I should say that the outstanding emotion was one of incredulity. A generation brought up during the Rise, Decline and Fall of the League of Nations, and taught by politicians and writers that war was evil, painful and out-of-date, a generation firmly pacifist in mentality and believing in its heart of hearts that years of crisis were only 'newspaper talk', was suddenly faced by the incredible. The last vestige of romance had long since been stripped from war. Only the Royal Air Force and the Navy were capable of stirring the imagination. The Army, which has never been truly popular in England, was less attractive than ever in its lorries and battle-dress, and only when the 'boys' went overseas did something of the warm spirit of 1914–18 come back to England, as wives and mothers packed up parcels to send to 'the front'.

The incredulity was deepened because, the incredible having happened, it had not happened in accordance with prophecy. The great air raids on cities, which had been prophesied for years as the inevitable prelude to the next War, had not taken place. Millions of people, at the instigation of the authorities, had made a room gas-proof with brown paper and tape; yet the promised gas attack had not occurred. Millions had deformed their gardens with air-raid shelters, yet there had been no air-raid. Nothing seemed to be going according to plan. It was, of course, fortunate; but how bewildering it was!

There was a feeling throughout the country that this queer, unexpected waiting time was due enirely to Hitler's realisation that now at last he had taken on someone of his own weight. That Poland had been savagely attacked and vanquished, and that no Pole could call it 'a phoney war', did not affect the English point of view because, as everyone knew, such horrible things often happened in foreign countries. Poland was just another example of 'hitting a fellow smaller than yourself'. But England and France were another story. No wonder Hitler was thinking twice before he started anything in a big way on the Western Front. *We* should do the starting! And the fact that he had not yet gassed us or raided us proved that he was not anxious for us to get busy. That was the kind of talk one heard.

While everyone spoke of the lunacy of war, no one doubted the inevitability of the War. I heard men at the benches of armament factories, works managers and directors of armament firms, speak of war as madness, yet all agreed that England had no choice but to go to war in order to 'give Hitler the licking he's been asking for'. I met no one who feared that we might lose the War; indeed, I detected in many parts of the country a dangerous tendency to underestimate the enemy. Many bets had been taken in factories all over the country that the War would be over before Christmas 1939.

There was a strange absence of grousing. No one would have believed that so vast a social upheaval as the removal of hundreds of thousands of women and children from their homes into other homes could have occurred with less trouble. People were extraordinarily generous and patient. The only trouble was caused by town-sick mothers who loathed the country, by the introduction of verminous children into clean households, and by well-to-do people whose servants walked out on them when the evacuees walked in.

But the question asked everywhere was: What is going to happen, and when is the War

'*Millions had deformed their gardens with air-raid shelters, yet there had been no air-raid*'

going to begin? The inaction bred a bewilderment which one enemy air raid would have dispelled overnight.

It would probably be true to say that England went to war in the spirit, not of a fiery crusade, but rather in the mood of a National Rat Week. There was no flag-wagging, no bands, no appeals to patriotism, no pictures of the King and Queen; no one knew the names of any generals or admirals, and the attempt on the part of the Press to give 'Tiger' Gort heroic status fell completely flat. The cold, objective attitude of the Government, and that of the Prime Minister, who rattled his umbrella ominously once or twice, did not exactly help the country to get excited about the War. There was nothing full-blooded about it. And, indeed, how could there be when the mental attitude for a quarter of a century in Parliament, the Press and on platforms had been one of disarmament and pacificism? It would have been difficult if the expected air raids had happened, for then the country would have been plunged at once into suffering and anger.

But the tepid attitude of the Government was such that it almost seemed to be apologising for the War. While calling upon the country to plunge into the war effort, it at the same time deplored the necessity for doing so, which was extremely confusing. A good old swingback to 1914, with appeals to King and Country, with brass bands and Hitler burned in effigy, would have worked wonders with the spirit of the country, but no one knew how to do it, or was willing to do it, deeming it perhaps undignified, or maybe fearing that an attempt to whip up a war spirit might have been a flop. But, of course, it would not have been a flop. One or two people in the Ministry of Information became alarmed by the apathy, and there was some talk of working up a hate campaign; but it is typical of the thought of the time, and of the attitude of the rulers to the mysterious populace, that it was not called a hate campaign, but an 'anger' campaign! It

was never launched; and the horrible stories from Czechoslovakia and Poland were never permitted to work the country into a white heat of fury as the Belgian atrocities had done in the War of 1914–18.

What England wanted in the first months of the War was a full-blooded leader who would have given blow for blow, and have expressed the contempt and indignation that existed in England for tyrants and aggressors. It seemed to be the first hour of English history that had not produced its man.

To anyone familiar with the placid English scene the outward transformation was almost amusing. It was entirely fantastic to see in English towns and villages trenches and sandbags that recalled the Ypres Salient. A policeman in a steel helmet, standing outside a village police station, was a sight for the comic muse, while windows criss-crossed with brown gummed paper as a protection against blast, and open spaces and parks invaded by trenches, and front gardens by air-raid shelters, gave to town and country an untidy, squalid air of waiting for the unthinkable.

Only in and around cities and towns was the war atmosphere noticeable. It was easy to pass out of this into rural areas where the War might never have been in progress, and where ARP was still a bit of a joke. As shops everywhere were full and food was plentiful, the inhabitants of villages were thinking less about the War and its problems than about the shortcomings of city dwellers who had been introduced into their homes.

Shopkeepers everywhere were alarmed by the prospects of declining trade and by Government interference. Some of them had expected another 'business as usual' War, and they did not realise, and no one informed them, that a totalitarian war is fought by a nation in uniform and overalls. It does not matter how much peacetime commerce dies as long as war industries live; indeed, the more peacetime shops that close the better the State likes it. 'But where is the money to come

OPPOSITE '*It was entirely fantastic to see in English towns and villages sandbags that recalled the Ypres Salient*'

'*Open spaces and parks invaded by trenches*'

'*Windows criss-crossed with brown gummed paper as a protection against blast*'

from if we can't pay our income tax?' inquired many simple-minded citizens. Others, wiser in their generation, asked: 'What is money?' and 'Did lack of money ever stop a war?'

'ARP was still a bit of a joke'

The black-out was one of the ruling facts of life. It stopped the traveller in his tracks. It drove millions of people into their own homes. It killed the life of great cities at tea-time and filled them with an eerie silence and a mystery. No one could have believed before the War that all the great cities of England, even London itself, could have been utterly abandoned to the dark. So frightened was it at first that even burglars stayed at home.

So upon a winter's day I returned from my journey through war-time England, vaguely disturbed by the apathy of a nation that lacked a leader, a nation that was not even half at war, a nation sound as a bell, loyal and determined, war-like but not military, a nation waiting, almost pathetically, for something – anything – to happen.

'Upon a winter's day I returned from my journey through war-time England, a nation waiting for something to happen'

Almost twelve months to the day from the time I set out to travel through peacetime England, Holland was conquered; Belgium fell; Italy entered the War on Germany's side; France collapsed and the British Army was brought home from Dunkirk. Upon 11 August 1940 four hundred German aircraft attacked the British coast, and the Battle of Britain had begun.

We heard the crash of bombs by day and by night. The summer sky was streaked with high white lines and spirals; the sound of machine-guns came out of the clouds; and sometimes we head the scream of a shot 'plane diving to its end. When darkness fell we saw the summer night red with burning fires as we stood, rifle or shot-gun in hand, guarding our little bit of England.

It was a still night. The moon was hidden by high cloud. I stood on the church tower, watching and listening. Pale fields of oats moved in the night wind, gleaming like water.

When I climbed the belfry ladders a few moments ago to keep the second watch, I came out on the lead-covered tower with its breast-high parapet, and there I saw, outlined against the sky, the heroic shape of my companion.

His forage cap might have been a Norman helmet or a mediæval casque; and I paused in admiration, telling myself with incredulity that it was only old Tom Burns, the cowman from Brambles.

At the sound of my approach, the figure turned, and a rich, loamy voice said:

'They searchlights be praper busy over Gallows' Hill way to-night.'

Then old Tom turned heavily and, insinuating his bulky frame into the trap-door, vanished into the stone tube of darkness, leaving me alone upon the church tower.

And now the clouds part and the moon, shining through, casts green shadows so that I can see the little hamlet lying below among haystacks and fields, the lime-washed cottages with front gardens bright with Canterbury Bells, geraniums and poppies; and I think that a more peaceful bit of old England could not be found than this village of ours. Yet in every cottage sleeps an armed man. If I range the bell now, they would come running out with their rifles, ready to defend their homes. Such a thing has not happened in Britain since the Middle Ages.

It would not surprise me to know that a generation to come will look back upon the trials and anxieties which now beset us as the most dramatic and adventurous incident in the whole of England's history. I think one is peculiarly conscious of this in a country district full of old farm-houses which have been standing for centuries: buildings whose panelling conceals secret rooms, whose wide chimneys lead to 'priests' holes', whose windows have known the tap of a secret code in the night, whose barns and outhouses have stabled many a strange horse and have concealed many a mysterious rider.

As I look down upon the sleeping village, and away over the dark woodlands to such places as Brackett's Farm – a notorious hiding-place for Cavaliers during the Civil War – I think that the awareness of these once sleepy old villages is merely a return of their

'They searchlights be praper busy over Gallows' Hill way tonight'

'The responsibility of defending our own village'

youth. Danger has skipped us for a century or two; and now we are back in Danger, with a gun under the bed and an ear cocked for the sound of a signal.

Nothing I have known in English life has approached the eagerness with which ordinary men have run to arms in order to defend their homes. My own point of view, and, indeed, it is that of all the farmers, the farm labourers and the cowmen who compose our Home Guard, is that should the rest of England fall, our own parish would hold out to the last man. The responsibility of defending our own village has given to that village a gigantic significance in our eyes. To us it seems the main objective of any invader. When I look at the map, I am sometimes amazed to see how small and unimportant it must appear to anyone not in our Platoon. But if all villages throughout England think as we do, what a hedge of opposition they present to anyone who dares to set an invader's foot upon this island.

Standing up there like some Baron's man brooding on these parish matters, it comes to me that one of the most remarkable things about this War is the quiet way England has ceased to be a country or even a county for many of us, and has become a parish. All over our land, villages once proclaimed dead and done for have awakened to arms. People scarcely on speaking terms have come together to organise defence. Cross roads, ditches, hedges and old tumble-down barns have achieved an unsuspected importance after survey by the slightly myopic eyes of those of us who were soldiers twenty odd years ago.

I, who once thought of England as a whole, and was in the habit of going to Cornwall or Cumberland on the spur of the moment, have not left my parish for months. Neither do I wish to do so; my parish has become England. This is a wonderful thing, and I never get tired of thinking about it. Since France collapsed and flung us all back into the early nineteenth century, with 'Boney' on the door-step, life in the country districts of England has become romantic and realistic. Danger has given us a common purpose. It ha given us a meeting-place. It has accomplished for the villages of England what musical young men from Oxford, with bells at their knees, and earnest women in Liberty silk gowns hoped to do a decade ago; it has made England almost 'merrie' again.

It has blown to a flame smouldering local loyalties and traditions. It has roused the English genius for improvisation. It has brought us face to face with the fact that we love our country well enough to die for her.

Another remarkable feature of war-time England is our almost unconscious slide back into the atmosphere of the seventeenth century. Here we are to-day, surrounded by those shining achievements of Science and Invention, aeroplanes, cars, wireless; yet we are really living in an isolation unknown for three hundred years. The excellent roads which we can no longer use, and the smooth voices of those who read the news from Broadcasting House, afford us the illusion that we are living in a modern world; but it is only an illusion. Our post-bags have shrunk to almost seventeenth century proportions; and those friends who still occasionally write to us are concerned, if they have anything to say at all, with simple seventeenth-century matters such as the preservation of fruit, the growth of increased crops, the keeping of hens, of goats, of geese, and, of course, current events in the parish. In spite of our cars, our range of movement is probably less than that of an energetic horseman a century or so ago. So, confined to our parishes by responsibility, lack of petrol, and also, let us hope, by the knowledge that there is no better place to be in war-time, we have without realising it tapped wells of satisfaction which had begun to dry up when the world became restless and irresponsible.

When the social historian reviews modern England, I should not be surprised if he came to the conclusion that, so far as movement and social life go, we to-day are in a more secluded backwater than our ancestors of the Napoleonic period. Reading the histories and memoirs of that time, I had the impression that life in those days of professional armies went on much as usual: prize-fighting continued; the coaches were running; London was not made into a shabby area of self-defence and, if Martello Towers ringed the coast, and Militia and Yeomanry numbered nearly half a million, English life was not interrupted by Napoleon as it has been interrupted by Hitler. But Hitler has struck the same fine sparks from England: for this we owe him gratitude. He may have led us along the primrose path to bankruptcy, but in the process we have touched old simplicities and have known again the feeling that we belong to our country and our country to us.

Still, proud as I am to be parochial, I confess that, as I stand on guard, I relieve the weary hours with memories of those lovely places in England which I shall not see again until the War is over. My mind flies from the Downs of Sussex to the grey stone country of the Cotswolds; from the luscious Midland shires to the cold, walled country of the North. I remember how the waves come rushing up the white face of Flamborough Head; how the tide leaps upon Lindisfarne; how the bore runs between the banks of Severn; and how the slow, sweet Avon sings through Warwick's meadows.

I think of Ely kneeling like a nun above the fenlands; of Durham like a knight in armour, most pious of fortresses, and of the Galilee there, so eastern and mosque-like, as if a Crusader, bringing some trophy from the Holy Land, had planted it on a hill above the Wear. I love to remember Wells and Exeter, Winchester and Salisbury, Hereford, Worcester and Gloucester. I remember the walls of Chester; the Minster bells of York, silent now; the Seven Sisters rising like a hymn; Beverley, and then the Moors; Fountains, a

'*The thatched barns*'

'*The cornfields and the dark woods*'

white ghost on green grass; Rievaulx and Jervaulx; the high castles of the Welsh Marches; and, by way of contrast, Oxford, and Cambridge too; the ripe, red fields of Devon, and the wild splendour of Exmoor.

Then my eye falls to the nearness of my own parish: to the group of ancient cottages, the thatched barns, the cornfields and the dark woods. And I say to myself how good it is to have been given the chance to guard a few square miles in England.

And now my watch is drawing to its end. The light is coming into the sky. The first larks are up. The general chorus of bird song, which will soon drown them, has not yet begun. Colour is slowly welling back to field and copse.

A night has passed with 'nothing to report'. That is strange and lovely, in these days – 'nothing to report'.

I climb down the three perpendicular ladders. At the foot of the belfry, old Tom stirs in his blanket.

'What, five o'clock already? Holy Moses, they pigs must be attended to at once! The old sow was not looking too good last night. A delicate old sow, she be and doant take to this 'ere new swill.'

Well, well, let's fill in the log-book . . . 'nothing to report . . . visibility good . . . searchlights active on the first watch . . .'

He gets out his bicycle and goes off into the fresh morning; and I remember how heroic he looked in the darkness, leaning out against the stars – old Tom, the cowman up at Brambles.

I should like to thank Dave Larkin for his creative inspiration and support; the National Trust for their part in keeping England intact, and in particular Arthur Pratt of Quebec House, Richard Wakeford of Knole, Rita Skinner of Hever Castle and Carole Kenwright of Ightham Mote; Captain David Husband of Chevening Park; Viscount De L'Isle of Penshurst Place; Dr June Chatfield, formerly of The Wakes, Selborne; Major Simon Allen of the Royal Scots Dragoon Guards, Salisbury Plain; the Reverend Michael Higgs of St James the Great Church, Egerton, Kent; Vicky Saker, Primrose Hanson, Desné Marston, Mary West, Robin and Nicky Saker, Mary Pickett and Auntie and Uncle for all their help and the many miles of companionship; my husband Alan; Ann Mansbridge of Methuen for her unstinting support; and, last but not least, Martin and Judith Miller of Chilston Park for letting me 'steal' their copy of *I Saw Two Englands* which set me off on this quest.

Tommy Candler

Acknowledgements and thanks for permission to reproduce the photographs are due to the Imperial War Museum for those on pages 6, 158, 175 and 176; to His Grace the Duke of Marlborough, JP, DL, for Tommy Candler's photograph on page 140; to the Hulton-Deutsch Collection for those on pages 159, 185, 203, 205, 210, 216, 219, 223, 226, 228, 229 and 230; to Popperfoto for those on pages 160, 189, 190, 192–3, 196, 197, 212, 220 and 223; and to the RAF Museum, Hendon, for those on pages 164 (ref. 5846–10) and 179 (ref. PO 17006). The photograph on page 173 was taken by H. V. Morton. All other photographs are by Tommy Candler. The map on page 8 was drawn by Neil Hyslop.